THE INDIAN CIVIL JUDICIARY IN MAKING

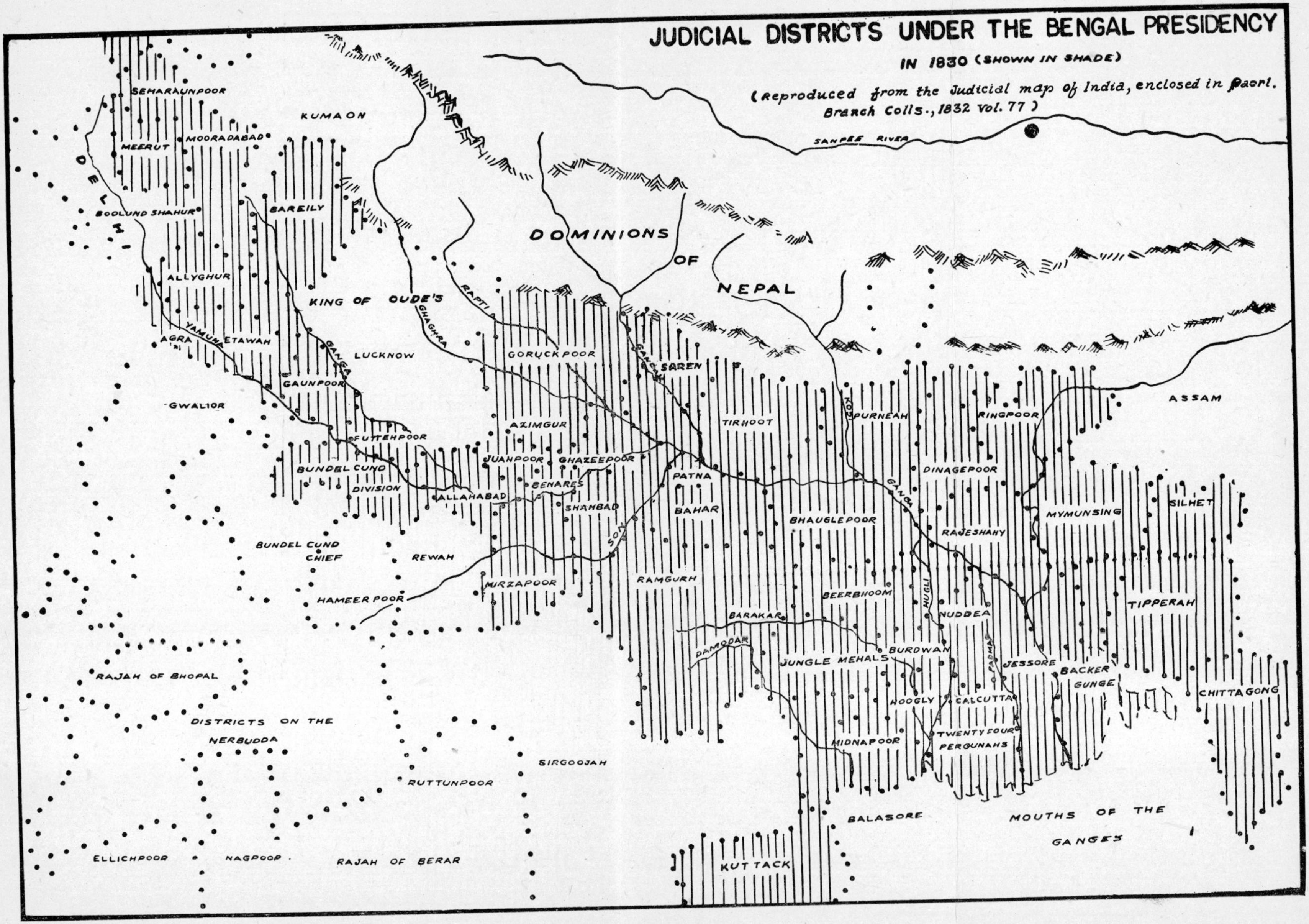

JUDICIAL DISTRICTS UNDER THE BENGAL PRESIDENCY
IN 1830 (SHOWN IN SHADE)
(Reproduced from the Judicial map of India, enclosed in Parl. Branch Colls., 1832 Vol. 77)

THE INDIAN CIVIL JUDICIARY IN MAKING

1800-33

by

Chittaranjan Sinha

MUNSHIRAM MANOHARLAL NEW DELHI

MUNSHIRAM MANOHARLAL
Post Box 5715
54 Rani Jhansi Road, New Delhi-55
Show-room : 4416 Nai Sarak, Delhi-6

First Published May, 1971

PRINTED IN INDIA

PRINTED BY KEWAL SONI AT SONI PRINTERS, CHANNA MARKET, NEW DELHI-5 AND PUBLISHED BY DEVENDRA JAIN FOR MUNSHIRAM MANOHARLAL, NEW DELHI-55

Preface

ANTHONY HAMMOND, THE Advocate General of Bombay Presidency, remarked in 1830 that the result of Cornwallis's endeavours was "to sketch the mere outline of the [Judicial] system, leaving it to experience, reflection and other contingencies, to fill up [the gaps] and to lay the foundation of a permanent judicial establishment".[1]

This is a sentiment with which the present writer agrees entirely. The foundation of a 'permanent' judical establishment in India was completed through a process of consolidation, reform and rejection of Cornwallis's ideas, stretching over a period of thirty years. This process began with Wellesley in 1800, and culminated with Bentinck in 1833. The first move for making a major change in Cornwallis's arrangements was made in the year 1800, when Wellesley began his efforts for separating the Sadr Diwani Adalat from the Supreme Council.[2] It was about the same time that the first impulse towards the modification of Cornwallis's structure was conveyed from London.[3] The process of reform thus begun continued relentlessly for the next thirty years, resulting in the emergence of a greatly transformed judicial structure by 1833. The period 1800-33 forms, therefore, a coherent and vital phase in the judicial history of Bengal and India to which the present work is primarily devoted.

While the developments in the judicial structure under Cornwallis have been most thoroughly treated by A. Aspinall in his

[1] Hammond to Sir John Malcolm, 20th Jan. 1830, Bentinck MSS, Nottingham University Library, Pw Jf. 2653.

[2] [General] Letter from Bengal to court of Directors, 9th July 1800, Vol. 40.

[3] Concerned at the heavy accumulation of arrears the Directors desired the Bengal Govt. to take immediate steps for making the judicial machinery equal to the demand. General Despatch from Court to Bengal, 23rd March 1800, paras, 6-8, Vol. 35.

book, *Cornwallis in Bengal,* (1931), and forms a favourite, as well as, indispensable topic for discussion in nearly all the other works dealing with the history of East India Company's Administration, the only worth mentioning studies bearing on the structural developments in judiciary in the post—Cornwallis period are Dr. B.B. Misra's *The Central Administration of the East India Company, 1773-1834* (1959), A.C. Patra's *The Administration of of Justice under the East India Company in Bengal, Bihar and Orissa* (1962), and Dr. B.S. Baliga's unpublished London University doctoral thesis on *Influence of Home Government on land-revenue and judicial administration of Bengal, 1807-22.*

Dr. Misra's work devotes a long chapter to the administration of Civil justice. It covers a very wide field. One half of the chapter is devoted to the judicial administration before 1793, the other to the scheme of 1793, its working, its drawbacks and all the changes made between 1800 and 1831. The narrative presents a compact picture of judicial administration during the period reviewed but gives scant treatment to the changes made to Cornwallis's system. Dr. Misra's main sources for the post-1800 period are the Judicial letters to and from Bengal, the Home Miscellaneous Series, and a report on the judicial administration of Bengal compiled in 1818. Only one volume of Civil Judicial Consultations has been referred to and the Private Papers and the Parliamentary Reports of the 1830s do not appear to have been used at all. The Bengal Civil Judicial Consultations is the fundamental series for a study of judicial administration and the present writer has made intensive use of it.

A.C. Patra's book treats the development of the judicial system primarily from the point of view of a lawyer. The changes after 1793 have been described only in terms of the Regulations incorporating them and the working of the Company's Courts has been studied only through the reported decisions of the Sadr Diwani Adalat. The policies guiding the evolution of the judicial structure, and the reasons why the structure took the particular form that it did after 1831, have, therefore, been missed. Patra devotes a chapter

* A series of reports of cases decided by the S.D.A. covering the period 1791-1829 was published in four volumes by W.H. McNaghten. J.C. Sutherland published three more volumes which carried the 'reports' up to 1848. These have been one of Patra's main sources.

each to the Sadr Diwani Adalat, the Sadr Nizamat Adalat, the Provincial Courts of Appeal and the Courts of Circuit. But the most vital part of the structure, the mofussil branch, consisting of the District Judges, the Registers and the Indian Judges, has been almost entirely neglected.

Dr. Baliga's thesis concerns primarily the impulses to reform supplied from London and those only up to 1822, which year does not form any landmark in the judicial history of India.

It has been the universal tendency to presume that the controversy between the Supreme Court and the Government of Bengal was terminated for ever by the Act of Settlement of 1781, which restricted the latter's jurisdiction, and that the Court and the Bengal Government functioned in harmony after that. This is not the case. On account of the undefined conditions of the Court's power and jurisdiction it came into conflict with the Government on several occasions even after 1781.

The present work is an attempt to bridge these gaps in the present state of our knowledge of the history of the East India Company's judicial administration.

Although primarily concerned with the evolution of the structure of Civil judiciary in Bengal Presidency in the post-Cornwallis period, a brief Chapter (I) on the earlier developments has been provided as a necessary introduction to the subject, whilst the subsequent Chapters (II to VI) of the book, have each been begun with a discussion of the arrangements made during the administrations of Hastings and Cornwallis. For coherence and continuity, Chapter VII on the Supreme Court and the Bengal Administration, deviates slightly from the general scheme of periodisation followed in the other Chapters. In it the main narrative begins right from 1781, the year of the passing of the Amending Act, which redefined the Court's jurisdiction following the bitter controversy between the Court and the Bengal Government during 1774-80.

I also wish to express my thanks to Sri Devendra Jain of the Editorial Department of Munshiram Manoharlal, New Delhi for accepting the work and publishing it in such a short duration.

Chittranjan Sinha

Gaya College,
Gaya

Abbreviations

S.D.A.	Sadr Diwani Adalat
S.N.A.	Sadr Nizamat Adalat
Civ. Judl. Cons.	Bengal Civil Judicial Consultations
Judl. Despatch	Judicial Despatch to Bengal
Judl. Letter	Judicial Letter received from Bengal
H.M.S.	Home Miscellaneous Series
Parl. Papers	Parliamentary Papers
Parl. Branch Colls. (*P.B. Colls.*)	Parliamentary Branch Collections
Govn. Gen.	Governor-General
J.	Judge
G.G.-in-C.	Governor-General-in-Council
Magt.	Magistrate
C.J.	Chief Justice

Contents

Chapter I

ASPECTS OF JUDICIAL ADMINISTRATION, 1765-1800

WHILST THE BATTLE of Plassey marks the establishment of the Company's political supremacy in Bengal, the grant of *Diwani* to them in 1765 marks their accession to administrative responsibility. The term Diwani needs elucidation.

Under the Moghul polity the Bengal Provincial government was bifurcated broadly into the revenue and military branches, called the Diwani and Nizamat respectively. The former was under the Diwan, the latter under the Provincial Governor, called the Nawab or the Nazim. The Nawab was the chief of the army and the head of the Executive. Being responsible for the maintenance of law and order, he also supervised the administration of Criminal justice. The Diwan was below the Nawab in rank, prestige and authority, but in revenue matters he was directly responsible to the Emperor. His function was to collect revenue and manage the Civil branch of judiciary. Both the Nawab and the Diwan were appointed by the Emperor. The idea behind bifurcating the administrative functions between them was to create a system of checks and balances.

The East India Company stepped into the role of only the Diwan in 1765, but so far as the actual situation was concerned, the constitutional supremacy of the Emperor at Delhi and the traditional superiority of the Nawab over the Diwan had become a myth. The Emperor had no means of compelling the Company if they stopped paying the tribute and the Nawab was merely a figurehead. He had no army under his control and no voice in policy making. He was living as a pensioner of the Company.

In 1765 the Company became the supreme power in Bengal. But they shrank from undertaking any responsibilities, even those which devolved upon them by virtue of their constitutional status as Diwan. Instead, they employed two Indian officers, Mohammad Reza Khan at Murshidabad and Raja Shitab Rai at Patna for discharging the functions of the Diwani on their behalf. The Nawab still remained the head of the administration in theory. His responsibility for the maintenance of law and order and the administration of Criminal justice also continued. Thus arose a very anomalous situation. The Company exercised complete control over the Nawab through their Resident who had the final say in the policy making, but undertook no responsibility for running the administration. The Nawab had to run the administration but had no power to make his authority effective. This was the so-called 'Dual Government' devised by Clive, which resulted in complete chaos in the administration.

The form of judicial administration in Bengal after 1765, under the management of the Nawab and Reza Khan and Shitab Rai was the continuation of the Moghul system. The highest tribunal of Civil justice at the capital, Murshidabad, was that of the Diwan. There were two other Civil Courts besides—those of the Darogo Adalat al-Alea and the Kazi ul Kozat or the Head Kazi.[1] The Civil Court at Patna was presided over by the Shitab Rai, the Naib Diwan and that at Dacca by a deputy of Reza Khan who managed the collection in that area.[2] According to Verelst, a contemporary observer, the Civil judicatures at Burdwan were the Bara Adalat, Amin Dastoori and Chota Adalat.[3] They also seem to have been presided over by officers concerned in the collection of revenue.

The jurisdictions of the Courts described above hardly extended beyond the cities where they functioned. Under the Moghul system the kazis were the traditional Judges in the interior. They were appointed over every Pargana and sometimes over large villages. They administered both Civil and Criminal justice to the Muslims according to the Koranic law. But to Hindus they administered Criminal justice only, because in Civil cases they were governed by their own laws and customs. The Hindus residing in the interior settled their Civil disputes through

[1] Govn. Gen.-in-Council to Court, 3rd Nov. 1772, quoted in 7th Report of Committee of Secrecy, Parl. Branch Colls., 1772-3, Vol. 7, pp. 324-6.

[2] *Ibid.*

[3] Harry Verelst, *Views on the rise . . . etc. of English Govt. of Bengal*, 1773, pp. 219-20.

Panchayats. The Committee of Secrecy, appointed by Parliament in 1770, to investigate the affairs of the East India Company, noticed a report from the Supervisor stationed at Rajshahi which stated that kazis had been administering both Civil and Criminal justice in that area. But on a consideration of all the other evidences, the Committee was led to conclude that in most areas the local Zamindars had been presiding in both the Civil and Criminal Courts of the interior.[1] The revenue cases were decided by the Naib Diwans, who were Indian officers employed in different areas by Reza Khan and Shitab Rai for collecting the revenue.[2] The Panchayats were a popular agency for arbitrating Civil disputes among the Hindus.[3]

Warren Hastings asserted that the judicial authority of the Zamindars had no legal basis. They had assumed that power "for which no provision had been made by the Law of the land."[4]

Hastings's view may be correct. Under the Moghul system the Faujdar used to be the head of the District administration. He must have exercised a control over the kazis. He was responsible for the maintenance of law and order in his territory, and he also exercised a powerful control over the Zamindars. *Ain-I-Akbari* (completed in 1593) provides instruction for his guidance in dealing with refractory Zamindars.[5] But with the decline of the power of the Nawab after 1757 the internal administration of Bengal was completely disrupted. As a result both the Faujdars and the kazis who drew their power from the central authority became weak and helpless. The Zamindars taking advantage of this situation became all-powerful and independent in their areas. In this process they also seized the judicial authority from the kazis and made it the instrument of private gain. In Criminal cases the fines levied on the culprits became a perquisite of the Zamindar and in Civil cases he became entitled to one fourth or one fifth share (called *Chauth*) of whatever was recovered through his agency.

The self-assumed judicial authority of the Zamindars was,

[1] 7th Report of Committee of Secrecy, 1773, Parl. Branch Colls., 1772-3, Vol. 7, pp. 324-6.

[2] *Ibid.*

[3] *Ibid.*

[4] Hasting's Minute, 7th Dec. 1775, quoted in 6th Report of the Select Committee of House of Commons, Parl. Branch Colls., 1782, Vol. 14, Appx. 15.

[5] H. S. Jarret, *Ain-i-Akbari*, Vol. II, pp. 40-41.

however, acknowledged as a necessary evil. Hastings himself stated : "The Zamindars . . . assuming (sic) that power for which no provision is made by the law of the land, but which, in whatever manner it is exercised, is preferable to a total anarchy . . . In effect, the greatest oppressions of the inhabitants owe their origin to this necessary evil."[1]

Another significant feature of the pre-1772 period was the interference of Company's servants and their Indian agents with the judicial administration. The Secret Committee was told that ever since the establishment of the political supremacy of the English in Bengal, the Banias* of English gentlemen had become unrestrained tyrants in the interior. They not only entirely governed the Courts of justice wherever they resided but often sat in them as Judges.[2]

The Company made its first attempt to improve the judicial administration of the country in 1769, by the appointment of covenanted servants, designated Supervisors, in various areas. These officers had two functions. First, they were to see that the Company received the full revenue collected on their behalf by the Diwans (Reza Khan and Shitab Rai) and secondly, they were instructed to keep an eye on the working of the judicial Courts with a view to preventing oppression and injustice. But the Supervisors had no direct control over the Nawab's officers or the Zamindars, Kazis, or other persons who administered justice. If those Judges refused to abide by their advice the only course open to the Supervisors was to report the matter to the Resident at Murshidabad who, in turn, was to urge the Nawab for action. This cumbersome process defeated the entire purpose. The successful interferences of Supervisors, with the Country Courts in the interest of justice were, therefore, very few and far between. Hence the institution of Supervisors failed to bring any improvement in the chaotic state of the judiciary in Bengal.

While the state of the Province deteriorated fast under the "dual administration" begun in 1765, the Company did not become affluent either, which had been the primary motive behind the

[1] Bengal Secret Cons., 13th March 1775, quoted in 6th Report of Select Committee, Parl. Branch Colls., 1782, Vol. 14, Appx. 15.

* Banias were Indian agents employed by Englishmen for conducting their private trade in the interior.

[2] 7th Report of Committee of Secrecy, Parl. Branch Colls., 1772-3, Vol. 7, pp. 324-26.

arrangement of 1765. The yield from revenue was very disappointing. Within five years of the grant of Diwani they faced bankruptcy, to tide over which they had to apply to Parliament for a loan of £100,000.

Under such circumstances the Company decided to assume the Diwani in 1772. This implied the direct management of the revenue and the administration of Civil justice. Warren Hastings formulated a plan for executing the Diwani functions. Under it, the Civil judiciary in the interior was consigned to Collectors of revenue. A Civil and a Criminal Court was established in every District. The Collector was to sit as Judge in the former. The Criminal Court was to be presided over by the Nawab's servants, the kazis and Muftis[1], but the Collector was also required to supervise their conduct. Two superior Courts of Civil and Criminal justice were established at Calcutta. They were to be known as the Sadr Diwani Adalat and Sadr Nizamat Adalat respectively. The former was to be conducted by the Governor-General and his Council. The latter was left in the hands of the Nawab and his officers.

It is apparent from the arrangements of 1772 that the administration of Civil justice in the mofussil was made a subsidiary function of the revenue officer. This in fact was the continuation of the system prevailing from before. Hastings actually made no innovation in organising the judicial administration in 1772. This system survived in essence until 1793, though some outward changes were made.

For various reasons the Collectors were withdrawn in 1774.[2] They were replaced by six Provincial Councils of Revenue, established at various Divisional headquarters, which succeeded to the Collectors' judicial functions. A Diwani Adalat (Civil Court) was attached to each Council. One of the Council members was to sit in this Court by rotation. In the Districts the Naib Diwans or Amils, who were now restored[3] to do the work of collection in lieu of the European Collectors, were given authority to decide Civil suits of small amount.

[1] The Mufti expounded the law and the Kazi pronounced the judgment.

[2] For details regarding the withdrawal of Collectors in 1774 and their reinstatement in 1781, see Chap. IV.

[3] The Naib Diwans were previously employed by Reza Khan and Shitab Rai before the assumption of the Diwani by the Company, They used to collect revenue and decide revenue disputes. See above.

In 1780 the judicial functions of the Provincial Councils were separated by employing distinct officers to preside in the Civil Courts hitherto annexed to them. They were designated Superintendents of Diwani Adalats. But all causes concerning revenue were reserved to the cognizance of the Provincial Councils. In 1781, the separated Diwani Adalats were established in eighteen Districts into which the territory under the Company's management was then organised. The Provincial Councils were simultaneously abolished and Collectors were restored to all eighteen Districts. Separate Judges were appointed to preside in the Diwani Adalats of all except the four sparsely populated Districts of Chatra, Bhagalpur, Islamabad and Rangpur. In those four Districts the Collector was also to act as the Judge—as the position had been in 1772.[1] Even the Collectors of the other fourteen Districts were not completely divested of judicial authority. All cases relating to demands and undue exaction of rent and those relating to public revenue were reserved to their exclusive cognizance in their own Courts, styled *Mal-Adalats*. The District Judges were also made Magistrates of their respective areas in 1781. In this capacity they were entrusted with supervisory authority over the rural police, a function hitherto exercised by the Faujdars. In 1787, the Judges were withdrawn from all the Districts except Patna, Dacca and Murshidabad. The Collectors were now to discharge the judicial and magisterial functions as well. Between 1787 and 1793, Collectors of the Districts remained Judge, Magistrate and Collector, all in one.

So far the outlook of the Company had been purely commercial. In 1772 the administration of Civil justice had been undertaken primarily because it was a part of the functions of the Diwani and because a better administration of justice was essential to the prosperity of the people, on which the collection of revenue largely depended. The entire judicial policy of Warren Hastings's administration was determined more by this attitude than by any sense of responsibility of the Government towards the people. The result had been a subservience of judiciary to revenue. Hastings's successor, Cornwallis, who assumed office in 1787, analysed this situation correctly: "Upon our first obtaining possession of the

[1] The changes in the judicial powers of Collectors have been discussed in detail in Chap. IV.

Country, it was expected to be rendered as immediately advantageous as possible . . . . In the civil branch of government, all the early arrangements were framed chiefly with a view to mere collection of revenue."[1]

There had been nothing like a judicial department until 1793. All Regulations respecting the administration of justice had been passed in the revenue department although, as Cornwallis observed, "No two departments of Government can be more unconnected than finance and judicial."[2]

The judicial functions annexed to the Collectors after 1772 have been noticed above. All salaries and allowances were, however, attached to the office of Collector only. They were paid nothing for their services as Judges or the Magistrates, which were considered as appendages to their fiscal office. They were also allowed a commission on the amount of revenue collected by them. Under such circumstances those officers were bound to give first importance to their revenue duties. "Neither his [Collector's] exertion nor his omissions in the capacity of Judge meet the public eye, but the least failure in realising the revenue is immediately noticed, and subjects his character to imputations besides occasioning a diminution in his commission."[3]

The Zamindars took advantage of this situation. They deterred the Collectors from paying heed to the complaints of the raiyats for undue exaction by alarming them with the prospect of failure of collection. The raiyats fully realised this and therefore looked upon the Collectors as parties against them from whom they could expect no redress. The feeling of justice being subordinated to revenue had gone so deep that as late as 1782 the Zamindars were found insisting upon their exemption from prosecution in the Courts by their creditors, on the plea that they were under contract to collect revenue for the Government.[4]

Cornwallis brought about a revolution in the Company's policy by introducing the liberal whig concepts into the Indian administration. He started from the basic principle that the Government

[1] Minute of Cornwallis, 8th Feb. 1793, para. 27, Bengal Revenue Cons., 11th Feb. 1793, No. 1.

[2] Cornwallis's Minute, 8th Feb. 1793, para. 28, Bengal Revenue Cons., 11th Feb. 1793, No. 1.

[3] *Ibid.*

[4] Minute of Cornwallis, 8th Feb. 1793, para. 29. Bengal Revenue Cons., 11th Feb. 1793, No. 1.

which collected revenue was obliged to secure full protection to the rights and the properties of the people against the invasion of individuals or the Government itself. This protection was to be guaranteed by a system of "rule of law" which was to replace the discretionary rule of revenue officers hitherto in force. A set of Regulations was accordingly framed in 1793, which sought to define the powers of the Government officers on the one hand and the rights of the private individuals on the other. The judiciary was given the role of the protector and enforcer of the "rule of law". This became the fundamental philosophy behind judicial administration in India for all time to come. The structure of Civil judiciary erected by Cornwallis was in the following order.

Sadr Diwani Adalat
|
Provincial Courts of Appeal
|
Courts of District Judges
| |
Courts of Registers Courts of Munsiffs

It had two salient features. The first was the exclusion of Indians from all situations of trust and responsibility on account of their lack of character and ability, the second, separation of the judiciary from revenue and executive branch of administration. The association of Indians with the judicial administration was permitted only at the lowest level. In the Districts the Collectors were completely deprived of judicial authority, all judicial powers having now been lodged in the Judge-Magistrate. But this principle of 'separation of powers' was not implemented above or below the District level. The highest tribunal, the S.D.A., was to be conducted by the Executive body, the Governor-General-in-Council. The Indian Judgeships in the interior of the Districts were to be conferred upon the official and unofficial agencies employed in the collection of revenue.[1]

Between 1793 and 1800 the only change of significance made in judicial administration was the revival of the system of institution

[1] For details see Chaps. II and VI.

fees on cases, for discouraging litigation. This system had been originally established in 1781 by Hastings but was discontinued by Cornwallis for making justice inexpensive. But apprehension of frivolous litigation led to its revival in 1795 by Regulation XXXVIII of that year.

The changes in the form of Cornwallis's structure as well as in its salient features came between 1800 and 1831. They form the theme of the present work.

Chapter II

THE INDIAN JUDGES

Origin of Indian Judges under Company's Administration

AFTER ASSUMING THE direct management of the Diwani in 1772 Warren Hastings organised a Civil judiciary for the Provinces.[1] The only Indians then allowed a share in the Civil judicial administration were the Zamindars.[2] They were allowed to decide causes up to Rs. 10.00 in amount. The European Collector was to be the Civil Judge in the Mofussil. In 1774 the Collectors were withdrawn from the Districts. Indian Officers called Amils or Naib Diwans were appointed in their place for collecting the revenue. The latter were also given authority to decide petty Civil disputes.[3] Judicial authority was granted to the Zamindars and the Amils in order to make justice in small causes more accessible to the people. In 1780 Civil Courts presided over by European Judges were established in all the Districts. The judicial functions of Amils ceased. The judicial authority of the Zamindars was however extended. By Regulation XIV of 1780 they were authorised to adjudicate causes up to Rs. 100.00.

In reorganising the judicial structure in 1793, Cornwallis started from the assumption that Indians, from their character and bearing, were incapable of holding any position of trust and responsibility. He remarked. "I conceive that all regulations for the reform of that department, [Judicial], would be useless and

[1] This, in fact, was a continuation of the judicial authority already being exercised by the Zamindars, See Chap. I.

[2] Progs. of President-in-Council, 23rd Nov. 1773.

[3] The administration of Civil Justice was a part of the functions of the Dewan under the Moghul Constitution.

nugatory whilst the execution of them depends upon any Indian whatever . . . "[1]

As a result the association of Indians with the new judicial organisation was kept at the lowest level. They were entirely excluded from the administration of Criminal justice. On the Civil side provision was made for the appointment of some Indian functionaries for deciding petty disputes.[2] They were to be generally classified as 'Native Commissioners'. They were to be appointed by the S.D.A. on the recommendation of local District Judges. Their power was to be limited to causes of personal property not exceeding Rs 50.00 in amount or value. They could be employed in the following three capacities :

I As Amins or Referees, who were to carry out investigations in particular cases and submit their report to the Judge, on the latter's requisition.

II As Salisans or Arbitrators, who were to adjudicate in a particular case after the plaintiff agreed before the District Judge to refer his complaint to their arbitration, or if the Judge chose to refer any suit to them of his own accord.

III As Munsiffs, who were empowered to decide cases up to Rs. 50.00 when referred to them by the Judge or when preferred directly to them by the parties. Any person commissioned as Munsiff became automatically entitled to act as Amin and Salisan as well.

Of the above three officers, the Munsiffs alone acted as regular judicial officials. The Amins had no power of decision. They were only to submit a report after an investigation if called for by the Judge. The Salisans could pass a judgment on cases submitted to them by consent of the parties or on those referred by the Judge. But cases could be referred to them only through the agency of Judges. The plaintiff had to repair to the District headquarters to institute his complaint before the Judge. And once he travelled all the way to the Sadar station he preferred to have his dispute settled by the Judge or the Register instead of having it referred to the Salisan of his locality. The reasons for this tendency were correctly analysed by William Douglas, Judge of Rajshahi.[3]

[1] Letter from Bengal, 2nd Aug. 1789, *Cornwallis Correspondence,* (ed). Ross, Vol. I, p. 548.

[2] By Regn. XL of 1793.

[3] Douglas to S.D.A., 8th Aug. 1798, S.D.A. Progs., 29th Aug. 1798, No. 74.

The first was the expectation of fairness and impartiality from the European Judges. The person seeking redress was led to this conclusion by the Pleaders of the District Courts who actually acted from self-interest. The second reason was the desire of subjecting the defendant to the same hardship as he himself had undergone in leaving his occupation and going to the Sadar Station. Hence very few cases could be referred to the Salisans. In 1797, 504 suits referred to the Arbitrators by the Judge of twenty-four Parganas had to be withdrawn and transferred to the Register in response to a general clamour of the suitors to have their suits decided where they were filed, i.e. at the District Court.[1]

The Munsiffs, on the other hand, constituted regular judicial tribunals in the interior. Parties were not obliged to repair to the Sadar to institute their complaint before the Judge before obtaining a reference to the Munsiff of his area. The case, if within Rs. 50.00 could be instituted direct before the local Munsiff, who was to try and decide it like any other Judge. Hence for the purposes of the present analysis, of the three classes of Indian Commissioners, the Munsiffs alone have been considered as Judges.

Powers of Munsiffs under the arrangements of 1793.

Although the jurisdiction of Munsiffs extended up to causes of Rs. 50.00, their authority even within this limit was restricted in certain ways. In the first place they were to try suits for money or personal property* only. Besides, their cognizance was to be confined to cases against under-renters and raiyats or cultivators only.[2] By implication all other persons were exempt from being sued in their Court. Regulation VII of 1799 entitled the Zamindars to have the property of the defaulting raiyats distrained. The Munsiffs were authorised by section 7 of that Regulation to issue such a process of distraint on application from the Zamindars. This provision had been introduced to help the Proprietors make timely collections. The question arose whether the Munsiffs could afford a reciprocal redress to the raiyats in cases of undue restraint of their property by the Zamindars. On the principle of reciprocity, the individual (i. e. the Zamindar) who instituted a complaint

[1] Civ. Judl. Cons., 13th July 1798, No. 55.

[2] Regn. XL of 1793, S.5, Cl. 6.

* Personal property connotes movable property like cattle, crops, trees and other articles, as distinguished from immovable property, like lands, buildings, water reservoirs etc., which were classified as real property.

before the Munsiff, simultaneously rendered himself amenable to the same Court, and a Court which afforded redress to a Proprietor against his raiyat ought not to refuse to hear the complaint of the latter against the former. But in spite of the ethical propriety S.5 of Regulation XL of 1793, remained a bar to any reciprocal action by the raiyats against the Zamindars in cases under Regulation VII of 1799. This view was taken by J. Melville, the Judge of Jessore, in 1799.[1] The S.D.A., though refusing to enter into any abstract discussions, did not contradict Melville's interpretation.[2] But a different construction was put on the matter by Arbuthnot, the Judge of Tirhoot.[3] While applying for the sanction of more Munsiffs for his District, in view of the promulgation of Regulation VII of 1799, he assumed that those officers would also provide easy redress to the raiyats against the Zamindars for injuries sustained by undue distraint of their property. Technically, the former interpretation of Melville was correct so long as Cl. 6, S.5 of Regulation XL of 1793 was not rescinded. But the S.D.A. either overlooked or declined to contradict the latter assumption of Arbuthnot. The issue was therefore left unclarified until 1803, when the jurisdiction of Munsiffs as regards persons was considerably widened. The Munsiffs were also not allowed to enforce their own Decrees or orders. This was to be done by the Judge.

Extension of Indian agency (1803-31)

(a) Creation of Sadr Amins and improvement in the situation of Munsiffs (1803)

As arrears started mounting before the District Courts[4] the need for a more extended employment of Indians in the judicial administration was felt. In 1801, acting on an initial proposal from Tufton, Judge of Zillah Behar[5], the S.D.A. recommended the appointment of a new class of Indian Judges in all the District headquarters.[6] They were to be called Sadr Amins, or Head Native Commissioners, and were to be authorised to decide causes up to

[1] Melville to S.D.A., 12th Oct. 1799, S.D.A. Progs., 30th Oct. 1799, No. 76.

[2] *Ibid.*

[3] Arbuthnot to S.D.A., 15th Oct. 1799, *ibid.*, No. 96.

[4] See Chap. III.

[5] Civ. Judl. Cons., 6th Jan. 1801, No. 11.

[6] Civ. Judl. Cons., 27th June 1801, No. 7.

Rs. 200.00 referred to them by the Judge. The S.D.A. also simultaneously recommended the extension of the powers of Munsiffs up to cases of Rs. 100.00.

A consideration of this proposal was, however, deferred by the Governor General-in-Council, because they decided to wait for the answer to their interrogatories, before taking any decision on issues of judicial reform. These interrogatories were circulated in 1801 among the Judges of Provincial and District Courts. Their purpose was to form an estimate of the working of the existing judicial structure as well as to obtain individual opinions on ways of improving it. Question No. 6 ran : "Are you of opinion that it would be advisable to extend the jurisdiction of Native Commissioners to suits for sums or values exceeding Rs. 50.00 . . . ?"[1]

The replies received were conflicting.[2] Of the five Provincial Courts three opposed the extension, one favoured it and one reserved its opinion. Most District Judges were also opposed to any extension of the power of Munsiffs. The reason for opposing the extension ranged from dishonesty or incompetence of those officers to their encouragement of litigation for self interest.* Those who favoured the extension emphasised its practical utility in relieving the District Courts. A few also acknowledged the superiority of the Indian Judges in making better assessment of the circumstances of the cases and the character of the parties.

Among those who favoured the extension strongly were Henry Strachey, Judge of Midnapur, and William Douglas, Judge of Patna City. Strachey asserted that an Indian of common capacity would, after little experience, examine witnesses and investigate the most intricate cases "with more ability and effect than almost any European."[3] Douglas considered the extension of power of Munsiffs to be absolutely essential for expedition of justice.[4]

Prominent among those condemning the Munsiffs and emphatically opposing any extension of their power were J. Thompson,

[1] Civ. Judl. Cons., 29th Oct. 1801, No. 6.

[2] The answers are recorded under Civ. Judl. Cons., 8th July 1802, Nos. 19-75.

[3] Civ. Judl. Cons., 8th July 1802, No. 55.

[4] *Ibid.*, No. 37.

* From 1795 onwards the Munsiffs were allowed to appropriate the institution fees of the suits brought before them. Hence they had a natural interest in institution of more suits.

the Judge of Burdwan, and A. Pierrad, the Judge of Purnea. The former suggested the abolition of Munsiffs altogether because they were dishonest and corrupt and therefore, "hurtful to the Country."[1] The Purnea Judge called the Munsiffs of his District a "set of miscreants" and charged them with encouraging frivolous litigation for increasing their income.[2]

The S.D.A. were convinced of the absolute necessity of retaining the Indian Judges.[3] But apparently, in view of the majority opinion against the extension of the powers of the existing Indian Judges (the Munsiffs), they modified their former proposal.[4] The idea of extending the power of Munsiffs was dropped altogether. The scheme of creating a new order of Indian Judges, however, stayed though it was now proposed to give them a smaller jurisdiction than that originally intended (*i.e.* Rs. 200.00).

The modified proposal was passed into Regulation XLIX of 1803. It provided for the appointment of one Head Commissioner (to be designated Sadr Amin) for each District. They were authorised to decide cases of personal or real property up to Rs. 100.00 in amount or value, which might be referred to them by the Judge for trial. With a few exceptions* cases against any Indian could be referred to the Sadr Amin. British subjects of European descent, European foreigners and Americans were expressly exempted from their jurisdiction. Like the Munsiffs, these officers were not authorised to enforce their own decisions. Even their processes were to be issued under the signature of the District Judge or the Register.

The Sadr Amins had been created as a superior order of Indian Judges. They had more power than the Munsiffs but less independence. They could not receive cases directly. Their processes were to be issued under the signatures of the European officers. In fact it was intended to maintain a close supervision over the conduct of all the Indian Judges. The comparative independence of Munsiffs (in receiving cases direct and issuing their own processes)

[1] Civ. Judl. Cons., 8th July 1802, No. 45.

[2] *Ibid.*, No. 56.

[3] S.D.A. to Govt., 19th April 1803. Civ. Judl. Cons., 5th May 1803, No. 5.

[4] See above.

* Those were cases in which he himself or his relatives or dependants or Vakeels or officers of his Court were personally interested.

was based upon convenience. If the parties had to come all the way to the Sadar station to institute petty complaints, the main purpose behind the establishment of Munsiffs would be lost. The Munsiffs were allowed to issue their own processes because the alternative would be extremely impracticable and dilatory.

Though the pecuniary limit of the jurisdiction of Munsiffs was left unchanged Regulation XLIX of 1803 made a significant change in their jurisdiction with regard to persons. Under Regulation XL of 1793 their jurisdiction had been kept confined to certain specified classes of persons.[1] This situation was improved by the above Regulation. Now only those cases in which a European foreigner or an American was a party, or those in which the Munsiff himself, his relatives or a dependant or the Vakeels or officers of the Court, had a personal interest, were excluded from their cognizance. Cases against all other persons (including the Zamindars) were now made triable by them.

(b) Law Officers made Sadr Amins (1805)

The agency of Sadr Amins worked advantageously in relieving the District Courts. During 1805, 7160 suits were referred to them out of which they decided 6395.[2] The continuing pressure on the District Courts[3] made the authorities look for more aid. A further expansion of the Indian agency was the easiest and the cheapest solution. In 1805, therefore, it was decided to multiply the number of Indian Judges. By Regulation XV of that year all the existing Law Officers of the District Courts were constituted ex-officio Sadr Amins. One Hindu and one Muslim Law Officer, called Pandit and Maulvi respectively, were attached to every District Court. Their function was to expound the laws from the holy scriptures, on a particular case, when called for by the Judge to do so. They were to discharge this new function in addition to their duties as Law Officers. Their powers were to be the same as the other Sadr Amins.

The Law Officers had been respected functionaries in the judicial department. They enjoyed a fixed salary from the Government.

[1] See above.

[2] I.O. Library. Parl. Branch Colls. 1832, Vol. 77, Table in Appx. V. No. 16.

[3] See Chap. III.

From their experience in the Courts, witnessing the proceedings and interpreting the laws, they were generally considered well suited to act as Judges. They might even have had plenty of time to spare because their services as Law Officers were required by the Judge only when a particularly complicated question of Hindu or Mohammedan Law arose.

Regulation XV of 1805 also authorised the appointment of one or more Sadr Amins in a District, whenever found advisable, in addition to the Law Officers. After 1805, the Law Officers were called Sadr Amins and these Sadr Amins who were not Law Officers were designated Additional Sadr Amins.

(c) Sadr Amins granted appellate authority (1810)

By Regutation III of 1800, an appeal was allowed to the Register from decisions of Munsiffs in all causes up to Rs. 25/-. This authority was withdrawn from the Registers in 1803. By Regulation XLIX of 1803, all appeals from the decisions of Munsiffs and Sadr Amins were made triable, by the District Judge himself. The idea was to keep a direct supervision of the District judicial officer over the conduct of the Indian Judges. But the operation of this Regulation led to a large accumulation of appeals from decisions of Munsiffs on the files of many Judges[1]. In some District Courts they constituted the bulk of arrears.[2]

It was, therefore, considered necessary to provide some relief to the Judges in this direction. By Regulation XIII of 1810, S. 11, they were authorised to refer appeals from the decisions of Munsiffs to the Sadr Amins. The latters' decision on these was to be final unless the Judge found sufficient reasons to admit a Second or Special Appeal himself.

[1] For example, on 1st Jan. 1809, the number of appeals from decisions of Munsiffs pending on the files of some of the Judges were :—

Before Chittagong Judge	676
,, ,, Assistant Judge	710
,, Nuddea Judge	996
,, Purnea Judge	1,008
,, Rungpur Judge	913
,, Midnapur Judge	887

Civ. Judl. Cons., 17th Nov. 1809, No. 1.

[2] For instance, of the total of 1,036 units pending on the file of Judge of Rungpur, on that date, 913 were such appeals. *Ibid.*

(d) Factors leading to the extension of Indian agency in 1814.

The institution of Indian Judges was being assessed from time to time by the European officers. In 1813, J. T. Shakespear, Judge of Nuddea, expressed deep appreciation of the conduct of the three Sadr Amins of his District. He observed : " . . . in such of their proceedings as I have had occasions to inspect . . . I have had frequent occasions to admire the great perspicuity and ability with which their Decrees are drawn out, particularly those of Maulvi Wazid, which would do credit to the most experienced judicial character . . . .[1]"

In 1814, R.O. Wynne, the Judge of Jaunpur, recommending the extension of the powers of Sadr Amins, remarked :

" . . . they are, in general, respectable and well educated men and are extremely serviceable to the community by their superior knowledge of the habits and customs of the people . . . . the Head Commissioners usually determine a suit within four months of its institution [reference], owing to their superior knowledge of Hindu and Mohammedan Law."[2]

There was no doubt about the usefulness of the Sadr Amins. The position with regard to the Munsiffs was somewhat different. In spite of the fact that they had been accounting for a large share of the disposal of suits, their utility was doubted by some. Between 1806 and 1814, three District Judges recommended their total abolition on grounds of corruption, inefficiency and misconduct.[3] C. Dumbleton, the Judge of Gorakhpur, observed : "The low and petty intrigue carried on in their [Munsiffs'] Courts may be more readily conceived than described, . . . the District is plundered through their means . . . [4]"

But on the contrary, their services were appreciated by a number of other Judges.

T. Fortescue, the Judge of Allahabad, informed the Government that on the average only one-seventh of the decisions of Munsiffs

[1] Civ. Judl. Cons., 18th Sept. 1813, No. 2.

[2] Report of Jaunpur Judge, para. 123, H.M.S. Vol. 775, pp. 667-75.

[3] They were H. Cornish, Judge of 24 Parganas in 1806; C. Dumbleton, Judge of Gorakhpur in 1810; and J. T. Shakespear, Judge of Nuddea in 1813. Quoted in S.D.A. to Govt. 11th July 1814, Civ, Judl. Cons. 19th July 1814, No. 6.

[4] Report of Allahabad Judge, paras. 62 and 73, H.M.S. Vol. 776, ff. 9-66.

were appealed against. They were all referred to the Sadr Amins from whose decisions only one-twenty-eighth were specially appealed to the Judge. In the ultimate analysis only one-twenty-fifth of the decisions passed by the Munsiffs were reversed or altered. The Judge regarded such a small fraction of error as being extremely creditable to the Munsiffs.[1] Besides, he remarked, "I think they reach the truth and unravel the cases, . . . better than we can, owing to their superior knowledge of habits and customs of the people."[2] The Judges of Jaunpur and Nuddea expressed identical opinions on the utility of Munsiffs.[3]

Considering the practical problems of judicial administration the S.D.A. consistently and emphatically advocated the continuation of these officers. In 1809, they remarked.

"A difference of opinion exists upon the utility of the present establishment of Native Commissioners. But considering the limited number of European officers that are, or can be employed in the judicial department, it is evident that without the aid of the inferior judicatures, it must be utterly impossible to provide for the complete administration of Civil justice . . , '[4]

In 1814, referring to the recommendations for the abolition of Munsiffs,[5] the S.D.A. contended that it would defeat one of the principal objects of the arrangements of Cornwallis, which was to provide against the inconveniences and expenses of parties in going a long way to the Sadar for legal redress.[6] They asserted that a fair trial had not been given to the Munsiffs yet, because it was wrong to expect honesty and uprightness from a class of Judges so long as their remuneration was most inadequate and uncertain.[7]

It was indeed absurd to think of abolishing the Munsiffs. The already overburdened District Courts would have been overwhelmed with petty suits and a large number of people would have gone without legal redress, if the Munsiffs were not retained. The situation actually called for a further expansion of the powers of Indian Judges. The arrears before the District Judges had been

[1] Report of Allahabad Judge, paras, 62 and 73, H.M.S. Vol. 776, ff. 859-66.

[2] *Ibid.*

[3] H.M.S. Vol. 775, ff. 176 and 667.

[4] Civ. Judl. Cons., 17th Nov. 1809, No. 1.

[5] See above.

[6] S.D.A. to Govt., 11th July 1814, Civ. Judl. Cons., 19th July 1814, No. 6.

[7] *Ibid.*

gradually mounting.[1] More aid was required. The easiest means of bringing relief to the District Judges would be to place more causes within the jurisdiction of the Sadr Amins and Munsiffs. Their numbers could be increased without any significant* financial liability to the Government. The only obstacle to a large increase in the powers of the Indian Judges was a doubt in their competence. But there could be no objection to a gradual enhancement.

A series of judicial reforms was adopted by the Bengal Government in 1814 with the object of making the judicial machinery equal to the demand. Under this scheme the powers of Indian Judges were enhanced. By Regulation XXIII of 1814, the pecuniary limit of the jurisdiction of Munsiffs was raised to Rs. 64.00 and that of the Sadr Amins to Rs. 150.00.

(e) Directors' plan of 1814, and its consideration

From 1814 onwards strong pressure was exerted on the Bengal Administration by the Directors for the expansion of the agency of Indians in judicial administration. The Directors' attitude on the issue had largely been moulded by Thomas Munro, whose ideas had a very strong influence both on the Board and the Court between 1808 and 1815.[2] Munro advised the Directors : "As much as possible of the administration of justice should be thrown into the hands of Natives, and the business of European Judges should rather be to watch over their proceedings and see that they execute their duty, than to attempt to do all things themselves."[3] The Directors were also influenced in favour of extending the participation of Indians by Henry Strachey, a former Bengal civilian.[4]

[1] The number of pending causes on the files of the District Judges at the end of 1805 was 15,291. By 1811 it had accumulated to 29,341. Parl. Branch Colls. 1832, Vol. 77, Table in Appx. V, No. 16.

* The only financial liability that the Government incurred on account of the Indian Judges was a small establishment allowance which was granted to the Additional Sadr Amins after 1805.

[2] A detailed discussion about Munro's influence at London has been presented in Chap. IV.

[3] Munro to Court in 1813, Selection of Papers from records of E.I. House. Vol, II, p. 105. Quoted in B.S. Baliga "influence of Home Government on Revenue and Judicial Administration in Bengal", Unpublished London Ph.D. thesis, 1933.

[4] Strachey's opinion on Indian Judges (see above) was quoted by Directors in Judl. Despatch to Madras, 29th April 1814.

In 1814 the Directors forwarded a scheme of judicial reforms to the Bengal Government. It was based upon the idea that the expansion of Indian agency was the only possible way of making the judicial machinery equal to the demand.[1] "Double [sic] the number of Zillah Judges would do little more than palliate most feebly the evil [of accumulation of arrears]."[2] The Directors were also motivated by the political consideration to strengthening the loyalty of Indians to the Company's Government and preventing discontent by giving them a larger share in the administration. Recommending the employment of Indian Judges in the administration of Criminal justice, they observed, " . . . there are considerations of general policy which would strongly recommend a liberal admixture of native with European authority in the Magisterial department, as in the other departments of civil administration."[3]

The salient features of the Directors' plan were as follows :—

I Heads of Villages (known as Mandals, Patwaris or Gomashtas) were to be constituted village Munsiffs for deciding petty Civil disputes.

II At least four Indian Judges of a superior order were to be employed in every District. They were to be designated District Munsiffs. One of them was to be stationed at the Sadar station and the other three were to be distributed in the interior. They were to have original jurisdiction in causes up to Rs. 200.00 and appellate jurisdiction over cases decided by Village Munsiffs and Panchayats. These Judges were also to have Criminal jurisdiction in petty offences.

III The system of Panchayat or assembly of Indian jurors for settling disputes was to be officially organised. The Village and District Munsiffs were to be authorised to assemble the Panchayats, for deciding a case, with the consent of the parties.

The Bengal Government had already enhanced the powers of the Indian Judges[4] prior to the arrival of the Directors' despatch. But those reforms apparently fell short of the Directors' suggestions. In 1816, the Directors pointed this out to the Bengal

[1] Judl. Despatch, 9th Nov. 1814, para. 55.
[2] *Ibid.*
[3] Judl. Despatch, 9th Nov. 1814, para. 161, Vol. 3.
[4] See above.

Administration and desired them to make the changes suggested under the Judicial despatch of 9th November 1814.[1]

But before considering whether to adopt the Directors' suggestions, the Bengal Government called for the opinion of the S.D.A. on their practicability. The latter forwarded the proposals to the Judges of Provincial and District Courts and called for their views.[2] After receiving their replies the S.D.A. submitted a report to the Government.[3] On the proposal for the appointment of Village Munsiffs, the S.D.A. reported that, while none of the Judicial officers had favoured the idea, several had strongly objected to it. The greatest objection was that it would be impossible to exercise a proper control over such a huge number of petty tribunals, scattered over thousands of villages.[4] Besides, it was argued that the impartiality of the Village Heads could not be relied upon in any cases between the Zamindars of the area and the raiyats. This was because these village authorities (i. e. Mandals, Moccudums and the Gomashtas) were directly subordinate to the Zamindar for whom they collected rent. Thus, people could never have confidence in their impartiality. The S.D.A., therefore, doubted the expediency of vesting the Village Heads with any regular judicial authority. As the idea of appointing a superior class of Munsiffs in the interior largely depended on the creation of the village Munsiffs (whose decisions the latter were to revise) the S.D.A. decided against that proposal too.

In 1818, the Bengal Government also called for a report from the Madras Administration on the working of the new judicial system established there in 1816, in conformity with the Directors' suggestion.[5] The report from Madras revealed that in the two years since the establishment of village Munsiffs in 1816 (by

[1] Judl. Despatch, 10th April 1816.

[2] Circular letter of S.D.A. to Provincial and District Courts, 23rd Nov. 1815. Civ. Judl. Cons., 24th March 1820, Nos. 48-50.

[3] S.D.A. to Government, 9th March 1818, Papers on the Judicial system of Bengal, Reg. (71) 197.

[4] In 1816 there were 150,748 villages in the 28 Districts of Lower Provinces (Bengal, Bihar and Orissa), which gave an average of 5,823 villages per District. Vide report of J. Shakespear, Superintendent of Police for Lower Provinces. Civ. Judl. Cons., 7th Nov. 1817, No. 12.

[5] The plan recommended to Bengal had also been sent to Madras. Vide Judl. Despatch to Madras, 14th April 1814.

Regulation V of 1815 of Madras Government) the 32,228 village Munsiffs in that Presidency had disposed of 10,744 causes.[1]

There had also been a general opposition among the judicial authorities in Bengal to the establishment of Panchayats on an official basis. One of the senior District Judges, Henry Shakespear (Judge of Rajshahi) remarked : "I am of opinion that the Panchayet can never be established to form an integral part of our judicial system . . . although I am in favour of every encouragement being held out to the natives, to submit their disputes to its investigation and adjustment."[2] The S.D.A. advised that the encouragement to be given to the Panchayats should be indirect. No statutory provision should be made for the same. The Panchayats organised on an official basis in Madras (under Regulation VII of 1815, of that Presidency) had not been successful. Between 1816 and 1818, Panchayats had been called only 457 times by the Village and District Munsiffs.[3] In theory Panchayats could be assembled by all the 32,328 Village and 95 District Munsiffs. The figure of only 457 assemblies showed that the Panchayats were summoned very rarely.

In view of the S.D.A.'s opinion and the Madras report the Bengal Government shelved the proposals for creating Village Munsiffs, Superior Indian Judges and an officially regulated system of Panchayats.

The Directors too, though remaining convinced of the need of expanding the Indian agency, seem to have abandoned their specific proposals of 1814. It is particularly interesting to note how they transformed their views on the question of Panchayats. This change was apparently influenced by the objections of the Bengal authorities and the failure of Village Munsiffs and Panchayats in Madras. Thus in 1827, when the Board expunged a certain paragraph from the draft (No. 424) of a Judicial Despatch to Bombay, cotaining certain observations against Panchayats, no less than

[1] Madras Report recorded under Civ. Judl. Cons., 24th March 1820, Nos. 52-55.

[2] Quoted in the report of S.D.A.

[3] Madras Report referred to above. Civ. Judl. Cons., 24th March 1820, Nos. 52-55. The Panchayats did not gain in popularity even later. Between 1822 and 1827, vlllage Panchayats disposed of 199 causes and the District Panchayats, 215. Report of Madras Sadar.-Adalat. Civ. Judl. Cons., 15th June 1830, Nos. 7-10.

eight Directors dissented from the Board's interference.[1] N. B. Edmontone and H. G. Tucker defended the paragraph in question by arguing strongly for the unsuitability of the Panchayats. The main premises of Edmontone's arguments were that the ancient system of Panchayats was a device for administering justice in the absence of regular tribunals established by the Government. The Panchayat was an occasional, not a fixed, court, acting under no fixed code of laws, and its members were continually changing. Under such a tribunal there could be no security for a regular and impartial administration of justice.

Tucker recalled that the object of the arrangements of 1793 had been to interpose, between the Government and the people, an independent authority which could decide issues between them "Fairly and fearlessly." He argued that it was vain to expect that the Panchayat, an assembly of natives as it was, could guard the rights of the subjects against the encroachments of the Government and its officers.

Tucker's reasoning seems to have been based upon the wrong assumption that the Panchayats were to function as an alternative to the established Courts of justice. He failed to realise that the Panchayats could very well function as a subsidiary branch of judiciary for settling petty disputes. It might never be required to provide protection against official oppression. That job could be left to the regular judicial tribunals.

The Panchayats remained a dying institution in Bengal. In 1830 R. D. Mangles, the ex-Deputy Secretary of the Judicial Department in Bengal, informed the Parliamentary Committee of enquiry that the Panchayats had not been of much use in any part of the Bengal Presidency.[2]

The Panchayats had been in common use during the Nawab's administration. This was noticed by Holwell in the 1750s.[3] In 1773, the Parliamentary Committee of Secrecy also bore evidence to their popularity.[4] In fact, the Panchayat, as a system of adjudicating Civil disputes and minor offences among the Hindus was

[1] Court Minutes, 14th Feb. 1827, Vol. 134, pp. 623-29.

[2] Evidence of Mangles, 4th March 1830, Parl. Papers, 1830, Vol. 6, pp. 40-41.

[3] Holwell, *India Tracts*, pp. 203-4.

[4] 7th report of Committee of Secrecy, 1773, Parl. Branch Colls., 1782, Vol. 7, pp. 324-25.

an institution of great antiquity. It survived the Muslim and Moghul administrations because of the latters' general non-interference with the village communities and the customary system of adjudication among the Hindu rural population. The village communities retained much of their corporate character and acted as instruments of justice particularly under conditions of anarchy and lawlessness "when no government existed outside the village capable of giving authority to Court or Judge."[1] Under the Moghul Government Courts presided over by secular Judges like the Diwan, the *Mir 'Adls*, and the revenue officers functioned only in the urban areas. Kazis were the only judicial officers employed by the Government in the interior. But the kazis applied the Koranic laws only. Hence the Hindus could not approach them for the decision of their Civil disputes, which were guided by their own distinct laws, customs and usages. The Zamindars who usurped the judicial authority from the kazis were expected to decide the cases of both Hindus and Muslims according to their respective laws and usages, upon the advice of Brahmins and kasis, but people could have little confidence in their justice.[2]

The situation was greatly changed after the Company took over the administration. Courts of various grades presided over by professional judges and acting upon fixed rules and procedure were distributed throughout the Province and were thrown open to Hindus and Muslims alike. The Panchayats were casually constituted tribunals. Their members were continually changing. They acted upon no fixed principles or laws and their members were most amenable to pressure from the powerful persons of the locality. Their justice was often crude, and tribal in concept.[3] Under these circumstances a general preference for

[1] Henry Maine, *Early History of Institutions*, pp. 389-90. Quoted from B.B. Misra *op. cit.*, p. 223.

[2] See Chap. I.

[3] Many instances were reported by the Judges of the Panchayats either having failed to do justice, or having acted in the most arbitrary and tyrannical manner. For example, in Bundelkhand, the settlement of boundary disputes by Panchayats was frequently attended by armed clashes resulting in loss of several lives which again opened fresh sources of disorder and bloodshed. Instances were reported by the Judges of Allahabad and Ramgarh, of prominent persons of the village assembling to try women accused of witchcraft and assuming in their own persons "the character of prosecutors, magistrates, judges, jury and executioners." Judl. Letter, 22nd Feb. 1827, paras 26-60.

the Company's Courts naturally developed among the rural population, even though it meant a sacrifice of time and money. In spite of its inadequacy the Company's judicial system marked a distinct advance over the indigenous institutions.

There could be another plausible reason for the decline of Panchayats. Under the previous Governments the rights of the individual villages were guaranteed only by public opinion enforced by the collective will of the village community. Hence the individual was made to depend completely upon the latter for protection. This position was entirely changed under the Company's rule. The rights and properties of individuals were now protected by a set of Regulations to which all were equally subject. Those Regulations to be enforced through a system of Courts whose decision had the full backing of the governing authority. The establishment of the "rule of law" liberated the individual from his dependance upon the corporate authority of the village community, fostered the growth of individualism in society, and infused a common desire among people to have their rights tested and confirmed by a Court of law.

Edmonstone's above observation[1] that the Panchayat was a device for administering justice in the absence of regular tribunals established by Government, therefore, holds a good deal of truth.

The revival of Panchayats under proper supervision and as an integral part of Company's judiciary could have been very beneficial. By settling the numerous petty disputes on the spot they could bring great relief to the existing judicial tribunals. Besides, Ram Mohan Roy asserted that : ". . . it is the only system by which the present abuses consisting of perjury, forgery and corruption, can be removed."[2] But the system could be revived only by the following measures. In the first place it had to be organised on an official basis. The Panchayats had to be given the full support and backing of the Government. But this alone was not enough. It was also necessary to make it obligatory for the inhabitants of a locality to settle certain kinds of disputes through this agency or go without legal redress. So long as it remained optional for the parties to resort to the Panchayats, there would be a tendency in

[1] See above.

[2] Evidence of Ram Mohan Roy before Parliamentary Committee, 19th Sept. 1831. Parl. Papers 1831, Vol. V, pp. 726-36.

them to resort to the Courts to which they had now become accustomed. It was because of the absence of this element of compulsion that the system failed to gain popularity in Madras in spite of the official backing.[1]

(f) Increase of Powers of Indian Judges (1821)

Though the new judicial agencies suggested by the Directors in 1814 were not created, the authorities in Bengal had not been against an extension of powers of the existing Indian Judges. In 1815, Lord Hastings, the Governor-General, had observed that the jurisdiction of Sadr Amins could be safely enlarged to the limit cognizable by the Registers (i.e. up to Rs. 500.00) because their decisions were not only easily amenable to the District Judges' revision but could be said to be passed under the latter's own vigilance.[2] But nothing was immediately done.

In 1821, W. B. Bayley, the Chief Secretary, advocated an increase of the powers of the Indian Judges on account of the shortage of European officers.[3] He remarked that :

> "Even with the contracted powers at present vested in the native judicial officers, most essential assistance is acknowledged to have been derived from them . . . . Of the chief defects at present incident to the judicial administration, a great part may be remedied by the employment of natives to a sufficient degree . . . "[4]

Bayley proposed the enhancement of the jurisdiction of Munsiffs to Rs. 150.00 generally, and that of specially qualified Sadr Amins to Rs. 500.00. The Sadr Amins were to be authorised to issue their own orders and execute their own Decrees as well as those of the Munsiffs referred to them by the Judge for execution.

[1] Lack of the element of compulsion was actually nominated as one of the reasons for the unpopularity of the Panchayats in Madras. Report of Madras Commission for revision of judicial system, recorded in Civ. Judl. Cons., 24th March 1820, Nos. 52-55.

[2] Hastings's Minute, 2nd Oct. 1815, Papers on the Judicial system of Bengal, Reg (71) 197.

[3] Memorandum of Bayley, 1st Jan. 1821. Civ. Judl. Cons., 19th Jan. 1821, No. 22.: He showed that the working strength of European judicial officers in Bengal was much below the required number of 191. The number actually employed in 1821 was only 156. Of these, 14 were absent on leave, and 8 on special missions. Bayley remarked that the number of European officers actually functioning in the judicial department, at any one time, seldom exceeded 130.

[4] *Ibid.*

The Law Officers were to be authorised to decide petty criminal cases on reference from the Magistrate. All these proposals were accepted by the Governor-General-in-Council and enacted in Regulations II and III of 1821.

(g) *Enhancement of Powers of Sadr Amins (1827)*

The Directors had ceased to insist on the adoption of the arrangements suggested by them to the Bengal Government in 1814. But their basic views about the extension of Indian agency as the only solution to the problems of judicial administration remained unchanged. In 1824, they came out with a fresh proposal for transferring the entire original jurisdiction to the Indian Judges, leaving the European officers only to try appeals from their decisions and to exercise a general supervision over their conduct.[1] They argued that the existing system of restricting the powers of Indian Judges to suits up to Rs. 500.00 only was wrong because a suit of Rs. 500.00 may be "more difficult to decide and with reference to the circumstances of the litigant parties, of more importance than a suit involving ten times that amount."[2]

Cornwallis's idea of not entrusting Indians with positions of responsibility still held a strong influence in Bengal. As the above proposal involved a fundamental change in the system adopted by him, the Amherst Government were hesitant to implement it. They argued that the existing system had not been originally framed with a view to such an extensive employment of Indians in the judicial department.[3] In fact, even the extent to which the Indians were then being employed had not been contemplated. In 1793, it was thought that except for petty disputes and matters of inferior importance, the agency of European officers would be adequate. This arrangement had not operated to develop a class of Indians, qualified by education, experience and influence in the society, for holding situations of high responsibility in the judicial department.

The successful transfer of almost the entire original jurisdiction to the Indian Judges during Bentinck's administration only proved that the conservatism of the Amherst Government had been ill founded. It is true that the system of 1793 did not contemplate any drastic increase in the powers of Indian Judges. But practical

[1] Judl. Despatch, 23rd July 1824, para 10.
[2] *Ibid.*
[3] Judl. Letter, 5th Oct. 1826, paras 7-9.

necessities had already forced many modifications in Cornwallis's structure. The powers and functions of Indian Judges had been enlarged in 1803, 1814 and in 1821. The transfer of the entire original jurisdiction would be in keeping with the trend already established. It would certainly mean a major compromise of Cornwallis's system. But it was necessary for the Bengal authorities to discard traditions and lean more on practical solutions for their judicial problems.

The majority of the Judges of S. D. A. also opposed such a vast increase in the powers of Indian Judges.[1] Their argument was the same as that of the Government. The only exception was Alexander Rose, the fifth Judge. He favoured the idea because the Indian Judges were already accounting for 95 per cent of the disposals.[2] But the Government were not inclined to accept Ross's advice.

Nevertheless, a provision was enacted by the Bengal Government for increasing the powers of Sadr Amins. By Regulation IV of 1827 the S. D. A. was authorised to vest the Sadr Amins, upon the recommendation of the District Judges, with special powers to try cases up to Rs. 1,000.00. This was done both to pacify to some extent, the Directors in their demand for the extension of the Indian agency, as well as for expediency. The number of cases between Rs. 500.00 and Rs. 1,000.00 on the files of many Judges had been heavy.[3] In a large number of Districts the assistance of Registers was also not available due to the shortage of European civil servants.[4] Authorisation of one or more Sadr Amins in the District to try causes up to Rs. 1,000.00 would relieve the Judge's file and make up for the absence of the Register.

Regulation IV of 1827 also removed the restriction on Sadr Amins trying causes in which a British subject, a European foreigner or an American might be a party. In fact this was done in

[1] S. D. A. to Govt., 18th May 1827, Civ. Judl. Cons., 12th Sept. 1827, Nos. 20-25.

[2] Ross's Minute, enclosed in S. D. A. to Govt., 18th May 1827, Civ. Judl. Cons., 12th Sept. 1827, Nos. 20-25.

[3] For example the number of such cases on the files of some of the Judges on 1st July 1827 was as follows: Allahabad—137; Kanpur—197; Ghazipur—147; Chittagong—102; Mymensingh—100; Tirhoot—295; Patna —158, and Gorakhpur—147. Civ. Judl. Cons., 12th Sept. 1827, No. 25.

[4] See Chap. III.

response to a demand from some European residents of the interior themselves.[1]

h) Bentinck's reforms—1831

With the arrival of Bentinck the stage was set for some revolutionary changes in the judicial structure of Bengal. Bentinck had no hesitation in sacrificing tradition for the sake of economy and practical needs. His approach was that of a practical reformer. He fully agreed with the Directors' suggestion of transferring the entire original jurisdiction to the Indian Judges. Replying to a correspondence from William Astell, Chairman of the Court, on the subject of extending the Indian agency, Bentinck wrote : "I entirely agree with you on the subject of native agency. I have been always of this opinion . . . . We cannot govern the Country without them. The most we [Europeans] can attempt is control."[2] Nevertheless, Bentinck appears to have started with an unfavourable opinion about the quality of Indian judicial officers. His friend, James Young, remonstrated with him on this point : "I have never ceased to ruminate on some things which fell from your Lordship on Saturday. One, in particular, both surprised and grieved me. It was the very contemptible opinion you expressed of the natives as Munsiffs and Sadar Ameens."[3] But his prejudice seems to have been short-lived. In 1831, he justified making a large extension of the powers of the Indian Judges, saying :

"... being fully satisfied that native probity and talent may immediately be found ... in abundance to justify the introduction of the present system I should have deemed myself criminal, had I any longer delayed to concede to the people of this country, a measure so eminently calculated to facilitate their access to justice . . . "[4]

Later he wrote to Charles Grant :

"We make a prodigious boast of our liberality in now giving the native Judges of the first instance, a salary of Rs. 400.00 per month, while your wretched Writer has as much. There will be no want of ablest and most virtuous men [Indians] if only proper increase of salary is held out."[5]

[1] On 17th April 1826 a petition had been presented to the Government by Messrs. Mercer, Thomas Rush and other European residents of Zilla Fatehgarh, representing against the inconveniences they had to suffer in recovering their debts, on account of the Sadr Amins not being authorised to take cognizance of their cases. Civ. Judl. Cons., 12th Sept. 1827, No. 13.

[2] Bentinck to Astell, 8th June 1829, Bentinck MSS.

[3] J. Young to Bentinck, 4th July 1830, Bentinck MSS.

[4] Judl. Letter, 15th Sept. 1831, paras. 13—15.

[5] Bentinck to Grant, 22nd Dec. 1832, Bentinck MSS.

The detailed plan for the extension of the Indian agency was, once again, formulated by W. B. Bayley. It was incorporated in Regulation V. of 1831. Its salient features were as follows :

1. The pecuniary limit of the jurisdiction of Munsiffs was now doubled (to Rs. 300.00). They were now, for the first time, allowed to take cognizance of causes for "real property" as well. They were prohibited, as before, from entertaining suits for personal damages, those instituted as Paupers, and those in which a British Subject, a European foreigner or an American may be a party. The Munsiffs were not given authority to try suits for personal damages because their decision called for a greater discretionary authority than it was considered safe to entrust to them. They were not allowed to take cognizance of cases of British Subjects, Europeans and Americans because of the danger of their being swayed by the prestige and influence which the latter enjoyed in the Mofussil. But the restriction on their trying suits instituted in *forma paupris* appears to have had no valid reason. This reservation had originally been made because the source of income for the Indian Judges was the institution fees. Since it was now decided to provide a fixed salary for the Munsiffs, there seemed no justification for that restriction being continued. The Munsiffs were now given the power to try suits for real property but they were not allowed to take cognizance of cases concerning *lakheraj* or rent free lands. The reason for this restriction was that the value of rent free lands being assessed at eighteen times their annual produce, few suits would come within their cognizable limit of Rs. 300.00.[1]

   A significant provision concerning the Munsiffs was the withdrawal of the option to the parties of instituting before the District Courts suits that were within the competence of Munsiffs. Suits cognizable by Munsiffs now had to be instituted before the local Munsiff (under S. 7 of Regulation V of 1831) unless the Judge saw some special reasons to make an exception. This was done to prevent the growing practice of rich plaintiffs compelling poor defendants to attend the District Courts just for the sake of harassing the latter.[2]

[1] Marginal note on the resolution of Governor-General-in-Council on the proposed changes in judicial administration (n.d.). Bentinck MSS Colls. in Folder No. Pw Jf. 1828, Nottingham University Library.

[2] *Ibid*.

II The Sadr Amins were empowered generally to try causes up to Rs. 1,000.00 Regulation IV of 1827 had provided for such extension to specially chosen Sadr Amins. But that provision had been very sparingly used.[1] Now the grant of increased powers to Sadr Amins was not left to the discretion of the District Judges. By S. 15 of Regulation V of 1831, the authority granted to the Sadr Amins by Regulation IV of 1827 to try cases in which British Subjects, Europeans or Americans might be a party, was withdrawn. No reason for this was assigned in the contemporary discussion. From the vehement opposition that the proposal for a revival of authority of superior Indian Judges to try cases in which Europeans were concerned received in 1836 from the Europeans of Calcutta,[2] it may be conjectured that the thinking of Calcutta Europeans might have been behind the withdrawal of that authority in 1831.

III A new class of superior Indian Judges was created. They were Principal Sadr Amins,[3] with jurisdiction on cases between Rs. 1,000.00 and Rs. 5,000.00. Every District was to have one Principal Sadr Amin. These officers were to supply the gap created by the abolition of Registers, provision for which was now made. The Principal Sadr Amins were also subjected to the same restrictions as the Munsiffs and Sadr Amins with regard to trial of causes in which Europeans were concerned.

It had been intended to transfer nearly the whole original jurisdiction to the Indian Judges and reserve the entire appellate Jurisdiction for the European District Judge. Hence the former authority of Sadr Amins to try appeal from decisions of Munsiffs was withdrawn. The Principal Sadr Amins were also constituted as a court of primary jurisdiction. Only when the District Judge found his file clogged with appeals from Munsiffs and Sadr Amins, could he refer some of them to the Principal

[1] Judl. Letter 18th Aug. 1830.

[2] Minute of Macaulay, (no date). Parl. Papers, 1837-38, Vol. 41, pp. 219-20.

[3] The appointment of a superior class of Indian Judges with powers similar to Registers (i. e. over suits between Rs. 500.00 and 1,000.00) had originally been suggested by the Directors in 1828. Judl. Despatch, 23rd July 1828, para 23.

Sadr Amins, and that too after seeking the permission of the S. D. A. The original jurisdiction of the Principal Sadr Amins was limited to Rs. 5,000.00* because Bentinck preferred a gradual extension instead of a "sudden and violent change".[1]

Qualifications of Indian Judges :

a) Munsiffs

It had been laid down by Regulation XL of 1793, which initially established the Indian branch of judiciary, that in the selection of Munsiffs preference was to be given to Zamindars, *Suberkars* (i. e. Managers of Estates of disqualified landlords) and to the *Tehsildars* or *Sejawals* (who were officers employed by the Government for collecting revenues from *khas* lands, i. e., the lands not settled with any private individual). This preference, in favour of Landlords and Managers of revenue, was withdrawn by Regulation XLIX of 1803, which laid down character and ability as the only criteria for selection. In 1814, a class preference was again sought to be established. By Regulation XXIII of that year it was provided that preference was to be given to kazis, in the selection of subordinate Indian Judges. In actual practice, however, these statutory provisions could never be strictly adhered to.

Under the system of 1793 no remuneration was provided for Munsiffs. Actually the Indian Commissionership was intended to be a subsidiary occupation for those profitably employed otherwise. Hence for supplying these posts a search had to be made for persons who would not look for the remuneration from these offices, but only to their respectability. The landed aristocracy and those managing the collection of revenue were expected to answer this description best. Another consideration might have been to continue the Civil judicial authority of the Zamindars[2] in the new set up. The notion of allying powerful Indians with Government might also have worked. Accordingly, the semi-official (the Zamindars etc.) and the official (*Tehsildars* and *Sejawals*) agencies employed in the collection of revenue were preferred as Munsiffs.

[1] Resolution of Governor General-in-Council, Bentinck MSS, Folder no. Pw Jf. 1828, Nottingham University Library.

[2] See *above*.

* In 1838, the pecuniary restriction on the jurisdiction of Principal Sadar Ameens was withdrawn and they were authorised to try suits irrespective of amount or value.

Cornwallis had withdrawn the judicial authority of the Collectors at the District level[1] on the principle of 'Separation of Powers'. But that principle does not seem to have descended further down.[2]

The withdrawal of the preference in favour of Zamindars and revenue officers in 1803 might have been made for several reasons. First, the post of Munsiff had been made remunerative in 1795. This precluded the necessity of seeking persons with other established sources of income.

Secondly, on practical considerations, most District Judges had already kept the selection open to some other kinds of persons too, like kazis, respectable inhabitants and former ministerial officers of the judicial Courts, etc., rather than confine their choice to Zamindars and Managers of revenue.[3] In Zilla Chittagong, for example, twenty one Munsiffs were appointed in 1795, who were all kazis.[4] The difficulty of forming compact jurisdictions with the Zamindars (because they were so unevenly distributed) and the absence of Tehsildars and Sejawals in that district (because there were no unsettled khas lands there) were advanced by Judge Thompson as the reasons for not appointing either. The fitness of Zamindars to be Munsiffs was also in doubt. T. Brooke, Judge of Birbhun, refrained from recommending any Zamindar for the commission because he thought that very few of them would hesi-

[1] See Chap. IV.

[2] There was no 'Separation' even at the top. The Company's highest tribunal, the S.D.A. was to be conducted by the Governor General-in-Council. See Chap. VI.

[3] This can be deduced from the list of recommendations (recorded in the proceedings of the S.D.A. submitted by the several District Judges to the S.D.A. for the appointments. In very few Districts were the appointments made exclusively from the Zamindars and revenue officers. Such Districts were Mymensingh, Purnea, Ramgarh, and Tirhoot. In the rest of the Districts the selection has been primarily from kazis, respectable inhabitants, former ministerial officers etc.

[4] S.D.A. Progs., 15th April, 1795, No. 49. Under the Moghul system the kazis were Civil and Criminal Judges. Besides, they drew and authenticated deeds for transfer of property and mortgages and conducted religious ceremonies like marriages and adoptions. But the judicial authority of the kazis in Bengal declined after the weakening of the Nawab's power (See Chap. I). Between 1772 and 1770, some of the superior kazis were employed as Judges in the District Criminal Courts. Their judicial functions were formally abolished by Regulation XXIX of 1793.

tate in converting the judicial authority for private gain.[1] The nomination of such unworthy men, he stated, would not only increase the business of the District Judge by engaging a good deal of his time in correcting their decisions, but would also open a source of "fraud and peculation" in the Mofussil. James Pattle, the Judge of Burdwan, considered the Zamindars unsuitable for that employment because the majority of suits cognizable by them would be those in which they themselves or their dependants would have a direct or indirect interest.[2] Some of the Zamindars who were commissioned as Munsiffs were found to have abused their authority. One such example was Prithvi Chand, the Zamindar Munsiff of Pargana Umbaur, in Bhagalpur District. He had resorted to the practice of manipulating to get fake complaints instituted against persons who incurred his displeasure and then passing the Decree against the latter. He had also been seizing the persons or properties of persons, pretending that to be within his authorised powers.[3]

The institution of Munsiffs was also gradually ceasing to be a subsidiary occupation. It was becoming a full time profession. Already the number of causes disposed of by the Munsiffs in some of the Districts indicated that they must have been almost fully occupied with that function alone.[4] In 1803 it was decided to reduce the number of Munsiffs.[5] This would mean the distribution of a greater load per Munsiff. And that in turn would demand more time for this function. This could be a very valid reason for not preferring the revenue servants, the Tehsildars and Sejawals, for the appointments, because their revenue duties would not leave enough time for undertaking the additional assignment.

It has not been possible to trace the actual effect upon the recruitment of Munsiffs of the stipulation in Regulation XLIX of 1803 that preference should no longer be given to Zamindars and revenue officers. The appointment of Indian Judges was vested

[1] S.D.A., Progs, 21st May 1795, No. 27.

[2] S.D.A. Progs., 23rd April 1795, No. 11.

[3] J. Fombelle, Bhagalpore Judge, to S.D.A., 20th April 1799, S.D.A. Progs, 2nd May, 1799, No. 15.

[4] For instance, the average disposals per Munsiff in some of the Districts in the month of June 1796 were as follows :

Jessore–65; Rajashahi – 30; Bihar – 60; Ghazipur–37; Nuddea–35 ; S.D.A. Progs., 30th Sept. 1796, No. 16.

[5] See below.

with the S.D.A. The detailed correspondence concerning the selection of Munsiffs is, therefore, solely to be found in the S.D.A. Proceedings. And that series of records is available only up to 1801. Only a few scattered appointments are incidentally mentioned from time to time in the proceedings of the Government.

Nevertheless, it seems reasonable to conjecture that the practical effect of opening the employment to all persons of character and ability was to exclude the revenue servants completely and reduce the number of Zamindars in the rank of Munsiff, and increase the preference for persons otherwise unemployed. Those who would fit best into this category were respectable inhabitants by descent, education and wealth, former ministerial employees of judicial Courts and persons belonging to the hereditary learned classes such as the *Maulavis* or *Brahmins.* It is quite likely that a number of Zamindars were also retained as Munsiffs because better substitutes answering to the requirements of character and ability could not be found. Their employment had not been prohibited by the above Regulation. Availability would also be an important factor determining the choice.

In 1814 it was ruled that, subject to their ability, preference was to be given to the Pargana and city kazis for selection as Munsiffs. The main intention behind this provision was, perhaps, to improve the monetary situation of the Munsiffs. In spite of the reduction in their number in 1803 (which could be expected to improve their income by distributing a greater share of cases per Munsiff) the average income derived by them from the institution fees had been pitiable.[1] By combining the office of kazis with that of Munsiff, it could be hoped that the joint income from the two offices would provide them an adequate income. Besides, the kazis, as a class, had some background of legal experience which made them preferable to others, like the Zamindars, having an extra source of income.

In 1825, H. Shakespear, an officiating Judge of S.D.A., observed in the course of a minute on the qualification of judicial officers that the Pargana kazis and Munsiffs were very frequently the same persons.[2] As the appointment of Munsiffs was still not made by

[1] No salary had been provided for the Munsiffs, Instead (under Regn. XXXVIII of 1795). They were allowed to appropriate the institution fees' paid on the cases tried by them.

[2] Committee of Public Instruction to Government, 17th March 1825, Civ. Judl. Cons., 22nd Sept., 1825, No. 15.

the Government * the official judicial consultations rarely make any mention of their qualifications or antecedents. It has not been possible to discover exactly what kinds of persons were actually appointed to those situations in the period following 1814. All the same, it has been possible to check the correctness of Shakespear's above statement. In 1828, as a preliminary to reforming the office of Munsiff, the Government had called for a report on the income derived by these officers from their employment as Munsiffs, and from the kaziships. The returns from the various Provincial Courts give the exact number of Munsiffs who were also kazis.[1] Of the 111 Munsiffs in the Calcutta Division, only fifteen held the additional employment of kazis, In 1795 all twentyone Munsiffs of Chittagong had been kazis.[2] In 1828 there were fifteen Munsiffs functioning there. Only five, or thirty per cent of them, were kazis.[3] In Murshidabad Division twenty-six out of 136 Munsiffs were kazis, in Baraiily only seven out of seventy-three, and in Benares only two out of seventy-four. The highest proportion of kazis employed as Munsiffs was in the Patna Division where thirty out of seventy-nine, or approximately 37 per cent of the Munsiffs were kazis.

It is obvious from the above figures that Shakespear's statement that Munsiffs and kazis "were very frequently the same persons" is not borne out by facts. The ignorance of a Judge of S.D.A. about the personnel of Munsiffs indicates that the Company's highest tribunal had almost ceased taking any interest in those appointments, after that function had been delegated to the Provincial Courts in 1814.

The reason for kazis not having been given a general preference in the selections must have been that their situation was gradually getting dislocated. Their loss of judicial authority must have greatly reduced their consequence. Their other extra-religious functions (like drawing and authenticating deeds), the gratuities**

[1] The reports from the Provincial Courts are recorded under Civ. Judl. Cons. 12th Oct. 1830, Nos. 14-44.

[2] S.D.A. Progs., 27th May 1795, No. 3.

[3] Civ. Judl. Cons., 12th Oct. 1830, No. 27.

* In 1814 that function was transferred to the Provincial Courts in order to relieve the S.D.A. of a portion of its Miscellaneous duties.

** The kazis were prohibited from demanding any fees for such services (by Regn. XLVI of 1803), but they were allowed to receive the considerations voluntarily submitted.

from which formed a major source of their livelihood, were also usurped by the Zamindars in some areas.[1] Most kazis were now reduced to the position of priests performing marriages and other religious ceremonies. Under these circumstances most of them were left without any significant income. T. Fortescue, the Judge of Allahabad, remarked in 1814 : "The functions of kazis have almost solely subsided . . . , their former name and influence have both sunk to the lowest pitch . . . "[2] Hence, combining the office of kazis with that of Munsiffs would neither bring an addition to the latters' prestige nor to their income.

In Benares Division only two kazis were appointed Munsiffs. The reason given by the Provincial Courts was that most kazis of the Parganas (sub-divisions of the Districts) had left their stations and taken up residence in the cities, in search of a better livelihood. Though officially those persons still continued to be the kazis of their respective Parganas their duties were being performed, by proxy, by others.[3]

In general, therefore, only those kazis seem to have been preferred for the appointments who were available at their station and were earning a sizeable income from that situation. The reason for the employment of a higher percentage of kazis as Munsiffs in the Patna Division, was exactly the same. For instance, in Zilla Behar, many of the Pargana kazis enjoyed a small fixed salary from the Government and also earned some income from fees. They had all been appointed Munsiffs. The net income (salary and fees) of some of the kazis (for example those of Hulasganj, Jehanabad and Baur) considerably exceeded their emoluments from the Munsiffship.[4] In Shahabad District seven out of ten Munsiffs were also kazis. Most of them derived considerable income from that office.[5]

The selection of Munsiffs in the post-1814 period continued to be kept open to all classes of persons in spite of the class preference laid down by Regulation XXIII of 1814. Kazis were

[1] Dacca Provincial Court to Govt., 13th June 1828, Civ. Judl. Cons., 12th Oct. 1830, No. 27.

[2] Fortescue to Govt., 1st Sept. 1814, H. M. S. Vol. 776, ff. 659-666.

[3] Benares Provincial Court to Government, 13th June 1828., Civ. Judl. Cons., 12th Oct. 1830, No. 43.

[4] Civ. Judl., Cons., 12th Oct. 1830, No. 42.

[5] *Ibid.*

appointed where they were available and where the union of their office with that of Munsiff was expected to improve the latter's income. The position regarding employment of kazis as Munsiffs must have been very nearly the same between 1803 and 1814. The low income of the office would not usually attract men of education and talent. Hence while making the appointments the Judges must often have compromised standards with availability.

The variety in the selection is borne out by a couple of isolated instances of these appointments, incidentally referred to in the official consultations. In 1818 Ayodhya Prasad, a former Persian Mohurrir (writer) of Benares City Court, was appointed Munsiff of Pargana Sunda in the District of Gorakhpur.[1] In 1826 one Khundkar Muzibuddin was nominated Sadar Munsiff of Junglimahal. The latter had never held any public employment. He had been educated in the Calcutta Madarsa, was versed in Mohammedan law and read both Persian and Bengali.[2] In 1828 Danwar Singh, a small Zamindar, was functioning as Munsiff at Chatra in the District of Ramgarh.[3] He was described as the most efficient Munsiff of that District. In Zilla Behar too there were a number of Zamindars acting as Munsiffs.[4] An instance of a Government Pleader having been appointed Munsiff is also found. He was Maulavi Ghulam Ibrahim, the ex-Government Pleader of Mymensingh who was appointed the Munsiff of Thana (Police jurisdiction) Netrokona in 1825.[5] But such instances of a Pleader being selected Munsiff were very rare. In 1832, Holt Mackenzie, a distinguished ex-civilian of Bengal, stated that seldom, "if at all", were Indian Judges selected from the Pleaders.[6] Lack of confidence in, and respect for, the Pleaders in general must have been the reason for not establishing a link between the Indian Bar and the Bench. Ram Mohan Roy stated in 1831 that the Pleaders, particularly of the District Court, were "treated as an inferior

[1] Civ. Judl. Cons., 14th Aug. 1821, No. 11.

[2] Civ. Judl. Cons., 22nd June 1826, No. 38.

[3] Civ. Judl. Cons., 12th Oct. 1830, No. 42.

[4] *Ibid.*

[5] Judge of Mymensingh to Government, 21st April, 1825, Civ, Judl. Cons., 27th March 1826, No. 17.

[6] Evidence of Holt Mackenzie before Parliamentary Committee of Enquiry, 16th March 1832, Parl. Papers 1832, Vol. 12, pp. 15-16.

caste of persons."[1]

b) *Sadr Amins*

When the office of Sadr Amins was created in 1803, no specific qualification was laid down for it. The appointment was made open to all persons of ability and character. No change was made in this criterion for the rest of the period under review. Like that of Munsiffs, the appointment of Sadr Amins* was also originally vested with the S. D. A. on the District Judge's recommendation. In 1814 this duty too was transferred to the Provincial Courts. Hence, once again; it is not possible to discover in detail the numbers or qualifications of the Sadr Amins that were appointed in the period following 1803. From 1817, the Bengal Government adopted the practice of compensating those Additional Sadr Amins whose incomes averaged below Rs. 100.00 per month, in spite of their reasonable efforts in disposing of cases. The recommendations forwarded from the District Judges to the Government (through the S.D.A.) for compensation to individual Sadr Amins give some idea of the type of persons who were holding those posts. In 1824, the Sadr Amins were made regular salaried servants of the Government.[2] Sanction of Government now became necessary for every appointment. Hence, after that date, their selection was recorded in the official consultations, from which full details are available concerning their experiences and qualifications. In general, the selection of Additional Sadr Amins was made from those who had formerly held ministerial offices of Peshkars, Nazirs and Sheristedars in the Provincial or District Courts, and from persons of recognised academic attainments. Sometimes ex-Munsiffs were also selected for the post. But such appointments were very rare. The system of promotion had not come into being in respect of Indian Judges. Not one instance of a Pleader having been appointed Sadr Amin in to be found. The reason which must have weighed against their selection as Munsiff would have advocated even more strongly against their

[1] Evidence of Ram Mohan Roy, 19th Sept. 1831, Parl. Papers 1831, Vol. V, pp. 728-29.

[2] Resolution of Gov.-Gen.-in-Council, 18th March 1824, Civ. Judl. Cons. 18th March 1824, No. 8.

* From 1805 "Additional Sadr Amins" because from the.. onwards the Law Officers became sadar Ameens, See *ante*. p. 17.

recruitment to a superior rank. A few city kazis were also appointed.

Selection of additional Sadr Amins was not confined to Indians only. A few Anglo-Indians and Europeans were also appointed. In 1814, Peter Turnbull, son of an Englishman by an Indian wife, was acting as the Additional Sadr Amin of the Suburbs of Calcutta.[1] In 1823, one Henry Cooper had been functioning in the same capacity at Ghazipur, and another, Benjamin Bart, at Murshidabad.[2] James Riley was acting at Mymensingh and Herklots at Burdwan.[3] After the Sadr Amins were made salaried servants in 1824, a number of Civil and Assistant Surgeons posted in the Districts, were nominated to hold the office of Additional Sadr Amins as an extra duty. For example, in 1825, Henderson, the Assistant Surgeon of Zilla Behar, was appointed Additional Sadr Amin for that station.[4] In 1826, Richard Shaw, Assistant Surgeon of Shahabad, was appointed Additional Sadr Amin for that District at his own request.[5] In the same year, Reynolds, the Assistant Surgeon of Dinajpur, was appointed likewise.[6] In 1828, J. Morton. the Civil Surgeon of Zilla Rungpur, was similarly commissioned.[7] The extra income from salary for the appointment must have been the attraction for the Surgeons, who were lowly paid. Like the Law Officers, the Surgeons too must have had sufficient leisure to undertake this additional occupation. As to legal training, they had none. But neither had many of the Indians who were recruited. The expectation of the British educated surgeon's ability to apply the Regulations and form reasonable judgements was probably the justification for his selection. His efficiency was never doubted. On the contrary, Jackson, the Judge of Behar, reported to the Government that Assistant Surgeon Henderson was the most efficient of the four Sadr Amins of his District and that the local inhabitants had more confidence in him than in the three Indians acting in the same situation.[8]

In 1805, the Law Officers were constituted *ex-officio* Sadr

1 Civ. Judl. Cons., 12th Jan. 1816, No. 2.
2 Annual Report for 1823, Civ. Judl. Cons., 10th March 1825, No. 20.
3 *Ibid.*
4 Civ. Judl. Cons., 19th Jan. 1826, No. 11.
5 Civ. Judl. Cons., 31st Aug. 1826, Nos. 6 and 7.
6 Civ. Judl. Cons., 5th Oct. 1826, Nos. 5 and 6.
7 *Ibid.*, Nos. 14-16.
8 Jackson, Behar Judge to Government, 15th Jan. 1828, Civ. Judl. Cons., 31st Jan. 1828, No. 26.

Amins.[1] The duty of a Law Officer was to expound the Laws applicable to the cases (mainly of inheritance and succession) which had to be decided in accordance with the Hindu or Mohammedan Laws. They were, therefore, required to be versed in the laws of their respective religions. Their knowledge of the Hindu and Mohammedan Canons was certainly a very desirable qualification in deciding cases of inheritance and succession. But this very asset tended to become a disqualification when they were called upon to decide cases not governed by the religious laws. This was particularly true of some of the Muslim Law Officers who tried to decide all cases according to their religious convictions rather than in conformity with the Regulations or "justice, equity and good conscience." For example, in 1828 the Judge of Behar reported that although Sayfulla was a very able Muslim Law Officer of his Court, the latter's decisions as Sadr Amin were deeply influenced by his religious prejudices and were, therefore, often objectionable.[2] Mohammad Mazid, the Maulvi Sadr Amin of Bhagalpur had refused to grant interest to the creditors because it was repugnant to the doctrines of *Koran*, in spite of the latters' being entitled to it by the Regulations.[3]

These reasons led the Government discontinue the system of constituting Law Officers as *ex-officio* Sadr Amins. It was provided by Regulation V of 1831 that only those Law Officers were to be appointed Sadr Amins who were found fit to hold the latter assignment.

(c) Principal Sadr Amins

For Principal Sadr Amins, too, no statutory qualification was prescribed. The office was open to "natives of India of any class or description."[4] Nevertheless, the selection of these Judges was made mostly from Indians with a sufficient amount of experience as Sadr Amins.

Number and Distribution of Indian Judges :

a) Munsiffs

According to Regulation XL of 1793, the distribution of Munsiffs was to be such that no one would have to travel more than

[1] See *above*, p. 17.

[2] Civ. Judl. Cons., 12th Oct. 1830, No. 80.

[3] Civ. Judl., Cons., 31st Jan. 1828, No. 26.

[4] Regulation V of 1831, S. 17.

five *kos* (about ten miles) to reach a Munsiff's tribunal. A minimum scale was thus laid down. No limit was, however, fixed for the appointment of more than one Munsiff within the same radius of ten miles. For this reason, the District Judges, in general, did not bother about limiting the number of Munsiffs. A large number of Munsiffs were, therefore, commissioned in the years following 1793. For example, in Zilla Jessore alone 134 Munsiffs had been initially appointed,[1] in Rungpur 98[2], in Tipperah 83,[3] in Midnapur 43,[4] and in Purnea 41.[5] In twenty-two Districts for which detailed figures are available 622 Munsiffs were appointed between 1794 and 1797.[6] This gave an average of twenty-eight Munsiffs per District. It was impossible to maintain an efficient supervision over such a large number of Munsiffs. Besides, with a number of them functioning in the same area, great confusion over jurisdiction often ensued. For these reasons their number was reduced in 1803 by more than one half. A new rule for the distribution of Munsifis was adopted by Regulation XLIX of 1803, which remained in force until 1831. It laid down the general scale of one Munsiff per Thana or area of Police jurisdiction.* Exceptions could be made under special circumstances by appointing more than one Munsiff in the same Thana or by putting more than one Police jurisdiction under one Munsiff. In actual practice the latter exception seems to have been more frequently made. The total number of Munsiffs commissioned in Bengal fell considerably short of total number of Thanas. In 1825 there were 539 Munsiffs[7] in the forty-six Districts

[1] S.D.A. Progs., 8th June 1797, No. 57.
[2] S.D.A. Progs., 8th April 1795, No. 7.
[3] S.D.A. Progs., 16th April 1795, Nos. 73-75.
[4] *Ibid.*, Nos. 73-75.
[5] S.D.A. Progs., 6th April 1797, No. 33.
[6] Figure compiled from the recommendations for appointments recorded in the proceedings of S.D.A.
[7] Civ. Judl. Cons., 12th Sept. 1827, No. 20.
* There was no uniform system of distribution of Thanas either. Variations existed from District to District. For example, in Zilla Chittagong the average area covered by each Thana was 196 square miles, in Hooghly 133 square miles, in Jessore 345 square miles, in Rajshahi 188 square miles, and in Mymensingh 583 square miles. The population under the control of each also accordingly varied. The Thanas of Mymensingh had, on the average, a population of 121,222, those of Jessore 78,906, of Chittagong 46,720, of Burdwan 91,352. Data compiled from a table of areas and population of the Districts of Bengal, recorded in Parl. Branch Colls., 1832, Vol. 77, Appx V, No. 1.

which gave an average of 11.7 Munsiffs per District. The total number of Police jurisdictions, at the same time, was 828,[1] making an average distribution of eighteen per District. As the Government did not pay the Munsiffs it had no financial inducement to keep their number low. The purpose behind keeping the number below the permitted level was to provide a better distribution of income per Munsiff. Nevertheless, the scale of one Munsiff per Thana was very nearly followed in the Calcutta and Patna Divisions. In the former there were 120 Munsiffs in 162 Police jurisdictions, in the latter 79 in 101 Thanas.[2] In most Districts of Patna Division the number of Munsiffs exactly coincided with the number of Police jurisdictions. For example, Behar had eleven Munsiffs for eleven Thanas, Shahabad ten for ten and Saran* had fifteen for the same number of Thanas. The net ratio was kept down by the figures of Barailly and Benares Divisions. Barailly had only 74 Munsiffs for 179 Thanas, and Benares had 73 for 174.

b) Sadr Amins

According to Regulation XLIX of 1803, one Sadr Amin could be appointed to each District. In 1805 all the Law Officers were constituted *ex-officio* Sadr Amins and provision was made by Regulation XV of 1805, for the appointment of as many Additional Sadr Amins in any District as were considered necessary. This rule of distribution survived for the rest of the period under review. The number of Law Officer Sadr Amins can be easily assessed by multiplying the total number of Districts (44 in 1805) by two.[3] But it is possible to discover the exact number of Addi-

[1] Figure obtained from the reports of the Provincial Courts on the establishment of Munsiffs, recorded in Civ. Judl. Cons., 12th Oct. 1830, Nos.14-43.

[2] *Ibid.*, Nos. 14 and 43.

[3] In the years following 1805 all the Law Officers may not always have been functioning as Sadr Amins. For example, in 1816 neither of the Law Officers of the Patna City Court was acting as Sadr Amin. The Hindu Law Officer was considered unfit for the assignment and the Muslim Law Officer was unwilling to undertake the office. Patna City Judge to Patna Provincial Court, 12th Dec. 1816., Civ. Judl. Cons., 10th Jan. 1817, No. 19.

After 1816 there were 46 Districts in Bengal. The established strength of Law Officer Sadr Amin fluctuated between 88 and 90. Civ. Judl. Cons., 18th March 1824, No. 7.

* Dr. B. B. Misra has erroneously stated the number of Munsiffs in Saran in 1828, to be only ten, which actually was a revised establishment proposed by the Judge of Saran and not the existing one which consisted of fifteen Munsiffs. B.B. Misra, *Central Administation of East India Company*, p. 278.

tional Sadr Amins employed only for the post-1817 period.[1] From 1817 evidence regarding the number of Additional Sadr Amins employed in Bengal Presidency is available in the recommendations for their compensations and in a report of the S.D.A. on the issue of instituting a fixed salary for them. During 1820 there were thirty-five Additional Sadr Amins functioning, during 1821 forty-one and during 1822 forty-two.[2] On the average about forty of those officers were being employed in the forty-six Districts. Many Districts were without any Additional Sadr Amins. In 1822 there was no such officer in twenty out of the forty-six Districts.[3] In 1824 the Sadr Amins were granted a fixed salary. The total number of those officers then was 130. The number of Additional Sadr Amins still remained flexible. About ten more such officers (including some Civil and Assistant Surgeons) were added to the establishment between 1824 and 1830, so that by 1831 the total number of Sadr Amins was about 140.

Working of the Indian Judges

In 1827 A. Ross, Judge of S.D.A., presented a statement showing that during 1825, out of a total of 154,563 suits disposed of by the company's tribunals, the Munsiffs and the Sadr Amins had accounted for 147,268.[4] This meant that 19 out of 20 disposals had been made by the Indian Judges. But even earlier the proportion of suits disposed of by them had been nearly as high. On account of their large number, acquaintance with the language and customs, and less formal proceedings, the Munsiffs in particular were able to dispose of a very large number of suits from the very beginning. During 1797, 134 Munsiffs of Jessore disposed 64,067 causes, or about 485 cases each.[5] This gave an average monthly disposal of forty causes per Munsiff. The average was about the same for Munsiffs of Behar, Dacca City, Ghazipur and Nuddea, for June 1826.[6] During 1800 the Munsiffs accounted for 93 per cent of the total disposal.[7] The number of Munsiffs was

[1] The reasons have been dealt with earlier, see ante p. 40.
[2] S.D.A. to Government, 6th Feb. 1824, Civ. Judl. Cons. 18th March 1824, No. 7.
[3] Annual Report for 1822, Civ. Judl. Cons., 23rd Dec. 1823, Nos. 10-25.
[4] Civ. Judl. Cons., 12th Sept. 1827, No. 20.
[5] From a table in Judl. Despatch, 8th Dec. 1824, para 18.
[6] Civ. Judl. Cons., 14th Oct. 1796, No. 12.
[7] Judl. Despatch, 8th Dec. 1824, para 18.

reduced in 1803, but their reduction was, to an extent, compensated by the employment of Sadr Amins from that year onwards. The share of Indian Judges in the total disposal remained the same. During 1805 Munsiffs and Sadr Amins accounted for 92 per cent of the net disposal, during 1810, 86 % during 1815, 89 % and during 1820, 90 per cent.[1] As per Ross's above statement they accounted for 95 per cent of the disposals of 1825. During 1830 their contribution was 93 per cent.[2] The average of the above averages is 91 per cent, which may be taken to represent roughly the overall share of disposals by the Indian Judges between 1800 and 1830.

From the above figures it is clear that the Indian Judges bore the brunt of the judicial administration in the Districts. But all the same, a general feeling of distrust towards them, or, at least, one of reluctance in allowing them to exercise extended authority, seems to have consistently prevailed among the European District Officers during the entire period under review. This is amply illustrated by a study of working of the Sadr Amins.

Until 1831 the exercise of the authorised powers of the Sadr Amins was left to the discretion of the District Judges. The Sadr Amins had no authority to receive suits on their own. They were only to try those cases which the Judge chose to refer to them.

By Regulation III of 1810, S. II, the Sadr Amins were authorised to try appeals from the decisions of Munsiffs. But the Judges refrained from making any extensive use of this provision. The S.D.A. reported in 1814 that in spite of their files being heavy, Judges of most Districts had abstained from referring any considerable number of appeals from the decisions of Munsiffs to their Sadr Amins.[3] The only exceptions were the Judges of Purnea, Patna City and Burdwan, who had been referring most of the appeals from the decisions of Munsiffs to their Sadr Amins.[4]

At this, the Government desired the S.D.A. to circulate an instruction requiring all those District Judges, whose files may have

[1] Percentage calculated from table of disposals presented in Parl. Branch Colls. 1832, Vol. 77, Appx. V. No. 16.

[2] Civ. Judl. Cons., 31st May 1831, Nos. 7-11.

[3] Civ. Judl. Cons., 19th July 1814, No. 6.

[4] *Ibid.*

more than 220 suits, to refer *all* appeals from the decisions of Munsiffs to their Sadr Amins.[1]

But James Stuart, a Judge of the S.D.A., opposed this proposition.[2] He advocated that a portion of such appeals must be retained on the files of the Judge and the Register, to enable the European officers to keep a watch over the conduct of the Munsiffs. This was a sensible approach. The other Judges of S.D.A. concurred with Stuart and the Government also conceded the wisdom of his reasoning.[3] An order was accordingly circulated in 1816 to the District Judges directing them to retain a fraction of appeals from Munsiffs on their own files and on those of their Registers.[4]

The tenor of the above instruction seems to have been followed in the succeeding period. From the statements of the number of appeals retained on the files of Judges and Registers annexed to the Annual Reports for 1820 onwards, it appears that only 5 to 7 per cent of those appeals were annually kept on the files of the Judges and Registers.[5] The rest were apparently being referred to the Sadr Amins.

By Regulation II of 1821, selected Sadr Amins were authorised to be vested with the power of deciding causes up to Rs. 500. Under this provision at least one Sadr Amin in every District was vested with the "special" power by 1824.[6] On enquiry it was discovered that during 1827 in nine of the Districts for which the actual figures were available, the Judges had retained a large number of suits of less than Rs. 500.00 on their own files.[7] The Vice-President-in-Council apprehended that on further enquiry many more Judges would be found to be following the same practice. They regretted this tendency and observed : "Such a practice, if carried to any considerable extent must, of course, render nuga-

[1] Government to S.D.A., 28th June 1815, Civ. Judl. Cons., 28th June No. 17. 1815, No. 2.

[2] Minute of Stuart, 23rd Sept. 1815. Civ. Judl. Cons., 24th Oct. 1815,

[3] *Ibid., No. 18.*

[4] Civ. Judl. Cons., 10th Jan. 1817, No. 9.

[5] Percentage calculated from the Statements marked 'M', enclosed in the Annual Reports of 1820 to 1830.

[6] The total number of specially empowered Sadr Amins in 1824 was 65. Civ. Judl. Cons., 18th March 1824, No. 7.

[7] Annual Report for 1827, Statement 'R'. Civ. Judl. Cons., 3rd March 1829, Nos. 32-37.

tory every attempt to relieve the Judges' files by enlarging the powers of the Native Judges:"[1]

By Regulation IV of 1827, the Sadr Amins were further authorised to be vested with the power to try causes up to Rs. 1,000.00. But once again, this enactment remained ineffective due to the reluctance of the Judges to make use of it. The Bengal Government wrote to the Directors in 1830.

"We were in hopes that this inconvenience (paucity of Registers) would have been remedied in some degree . . . by the operation of Regulation IV of 1827, which gave the Judges the power of transferring to specially nominated Sadar Ameens, suits to the amount of Rs. 1,000.00. Few of the Judges, however, availed themselves of their services and we are sorry to observe an apparent disinclination among Zillah Judges to entrust Native Officers with extended powers authorised to be vested in them."[2]

To take a concrete example, the Judge of Rajshahi had 130 suits of between Rs. 500.00 and 1,000.00 on his file, on 1st July 1830.[3] One of the Sadr Amins there had been especially empowered to try suits up to Rs. 1,000.00. But not a single suit of more than Rs. 500.00 had ever been referred to him.[4]

The above phenomenon was apparently the result of a feeling of distrust towards the Indian Judges, which in turn was largely the legacy of Cornwallis's thinking.

[1] Government to S.D.A., 3rd March 1829, paras 8 and 9, *ibid.* No. 37.

[2] Judl. Letter, 18th Aug. 1830.

[3] Civ. Judl. Cons., 16th Nov. 1830, No. 9.

[4] *Ibid.*

CHAPTER III

THE DISTRICT JUDGES

Origin

THE JUDICIAL ADMINISTRATION of the Company began in 1772, but the separate institution of District Judges did not come in to being until 1780. Between 1772 and 1780 the civil judicial administration had been consigned first to the Collectors and then to the Provincial Councils of Revenue.[1] In 1780 separate officers with exclusively judicial functions were appointed by the Government to preside in the Civil Courts attached to the six Provincial Councils. They were called "Superintendents of Dewani Adaluts." This was the origin of District Judgeship. In 1781, under a plan of judicial reform formulated by Sir Elijah Impey, the area under Company administration was divided into eighteen Districts and a Civil Court was set up in each. In fourteen of these Courts similar separate judicial officers were to preside, but they were now to be designated "Judges" instead. In the remaining four Districts the Collectors were to act as Judges as well. In 1787 the office of District Judge was abolished in all except the Districts of Patna, Murshidabad and Dacca. Their functions were transferred to the Collectors.[2]

Finding a combination of revenue and judicial functions repugnant to the principle of 'separation of powers', Cornwallis withdrew the judicial authority of the Collectors in 1793.[3] District Judges were reappointed to the twenty-six Districts into which the territory under the Company's administration was now

[1] See Chap. IV.

[2] For a discussion of the reasons for this change see Chap IV.

[3] This change is considered in detail in Chap. IV.

organised. To provide for the new territorial acquisition, and for the sake of administrative convenience, additions and modifications were subsequently made in the above establishment of Districts. In 1795 the Benares Division was brought under the Company's administration. It was divided into four Districts: Benares City, Mirzapur, Ghazipur and Jaunpur. A District Judge was naturally placed over each. In 1797 a new District was carved out of the area under the existing District of Dacca-Jelalpur. It was to be known as the District of Bakarganj.* This was done because the vast area that the District of Dacca-Jelalpur originally covered was unmanageable for one Judicial and one Revenue Officer. Seven Districts were formed in 1803, in the territory ceded by the Nawab of Awadh. In 1805 the area surrendered by the Peshwa and Daulat Rao Sindhia was organised into six Districts under Barailly Division. A District Court was established at Cuttack in the same year. In 1806, for the sake of economy, the Murshidabad Zilla Court was abolished and its jurisdiction was divided between two neighbouring Districts, Murshidabad City and Birbhum. In 1814 two new Districts were created by rearranging the territories around Calcutta.

As a result of all the above additions and alterations, by 1830 there existed under the Bengal Presidency a total of forty-six District Courts, twenty-seven in the Lower Provinces, eighteen in the Western Provinces, and one in Cuttack.**

The extent and population of these Districts, over which the Judge had to dispense, or supervise the administration of, justice were extremely varied.[1] To take a few examples, the District of Ramgarh had a huge area of 22,430 square miles and a population of 2,252,985. Rajshahi had nearly twice that population (4,087,155) over only about one-fifth the above area (3,950 square miles). Behar (modern Gaya) had an area of 5,235 square miles and a population of 1,340,610. Saran had 1,464,075 inhabitants

[1] This can be deduced from the report of a survey made in 1822 by H. Shakespear, the Superintendent of Police of the Lower Provinces, printed in Parl. Branch Colls., 1832, No. 77, Appx. V. No. 1.

* Dr. B.B. Misra has stated that in 1797 'two' new Courts were established at Bakarganj and Dacca-Jelalpur. But in fact only one new Court was established. The Court of Dacca-Jelalpur had already been functioning since 1793. B.B. Misra, *Central Administration of the East India Company*. p. 266.

** See map.

over 5,760 square miles. Burdwan had 1,187,580 inhabitants in an area of 2,000 square miles. Patna was the smallest District of all. It had an area of only 667 square miles and a population of 255,705.

The size and population of the District had a natural bearing on the business before its Civil Court.

Powers and Functions

Cornwallis had intended to make the Judge the central and dominating figure in the District. He was to be the Magistrate of his territory. He was to manage the police and he was to be the Civil Judge of his realm. In the latter capacity he was not only to dispense justice himself but also to control and supervise the conduct of all the other subordinate agencies of judicial administration in his District. In short, he was responsible for the distribution of justice to every one who lived within his jurisdiction. The Judge's Court was to have an European establishment of Register* and an Assistant, and an Indian establishment of one Hindu and one Muslim Law Officer besides a host of such servants as clerks, writers, administrators of oaths and peons. The Register and the Assistant were to assist the Judge in running his office. The former was also to help the Judge in the disposal of Civil suits. The Law Officers were there to advise the Judge on questions relating to Hindu or Mohammedan Law.

The local jurisdiction of the District Judges' Courts was, according to Regulation III of 1793, to extend to all places within the limits of the Zilla or city where they operated. Certain exceptions were, however, made. Thus, in Zilla Cuttack, the estates of certain Rajas were made immune from the jurisdiction of the local Judge's Court.[1] So were the territories and Jagirs (Estates) in actual possession of several Chieftains.[2] Their jurisdiction in respect of persons extended over all Indians as well as Europeans, not being British subjects, residing outside Calcutta.[3] All British subjects, except King's Officers and Covenanted Civil Servants of the Company, who took residence beyond a radius of ten miles from Calcutta,

[1] By Regn. XII of 1805.

[2] By Regn. VII of 1816.

[3] By Regn. III of 1793, Ss. 7 and 9.

* In 1814 provision was also made for employment of additional Registers in the Courts where it was considered necessary. See Chapter IV.

were required to execute a bond rendering themselves amenable to the local Judge's Court in all Civil suits instituted against them by Indians or Europeans alike, provided the amount or value of the suit did not exceed Rs. 500.00.[1] A special privilege in respect of the amount or value of the suit was granted to the *khasias* and other tribal people living on the border of Zilla Sylhet. The reason was that the British traders used to make regular purchases of *chunam* (lime) and other articles from them. Those transactions often involved sums exceeding Rs. 500.00. Hence, to save those tribes the trouble of repairing to Calcutta for settling their claims of more than Rs. 500.00, it was provided by Regulation 1 of 1799 that they could institute their claims against the British subjects, irrespective of the amount, before the Judge of Sylhet.

In 1794 T. Brooke, Judge of Burdwan, sought instruction from the S.D.A. whether a British subject, residing in Calcutta. who had extensive business transactions in the Mofussil, should also be required to execute the bond (making himself amenable to the local Judge's Court) under Regulation XXVIII of 1793.[2] Brooke thought that as the intention of the Regulation was to provide protection to Indians against injury or oppression committed by any British subject, persons of the above description should also be required to execute the bond and make themselves amenable to the Mofussil judicature. But the S. D. A, held that under the meaning of Regulation XXVIII of 1793, only those British subjects could be required to execute the bond who actually lived under the jurisdiction of a District Court and not those who merely had trading connections there.[3] The S. D. A. also considered such a step unnecessary as the transactions of such British subjects must be carried on in the Mofussil through agents who would always be amenable to the local Judge's Court for all their acts.

In 1805 W. W. Massie, Judge of Nuddea, reported to the Government the case of one John Farquhar, who had refused to sign the required bond after taking up residence in Nuddea as the Company's Salt Agent.[4] The Judge held the view that as

[1] By Regn. XXVIII of 1793, Ss. 2.8.

[2] Burdwan Judge to S.D.A., 11th June 1794, S.D.A. Progs., 24th July 1794, No. 7.

[3] S.D.A. Progs., 24th July 1794, No. 8.

[4] Civ. Judl. Cons., 18th April 1805, No. 11.

Farquhar was neither a king's officer nor a covenanted servant of the Company he could have no exemption from submitting to the jurisdiction of the local Court. The Government agreed with the Judge and ordered Farquhar to sign the bond or leave his situation and quit the District.[1]

In 1813 by St. 53 Geo. III., Cap. 155., Cl. VII, the system of making a British subject amenable to the Mofussil Courts by a bond was made redundant. By the Act all British subjects who were in "occupation or possession of any immovable property, or who were carrying on any trade or business in any part of British India at a distance of more than ten miles of Calcutta," were made generally subject to the Civil jurisdiction of the local District Judge. This Statute was intended to facilitate legal redress from Indians against British subjects. It had two specially significant features. First, it withdrew the exemption of king's officers and covenanted servants of the Company from being amenable to the Mofussil Courts. Secondly, even those British subjects who resided in Calcutta, but had trading or other establishments in the interior, were made liable to the District Court under whose jurisdiction such establishment existed.

By Regulation III of 1793, the District Judges were empowered to take cognizance of Civil suits of any nature. Their jurisdiction had no pecuniary limit. By Regulation XIII of 1808, a pecuniary limit of Rs. 5,000.00, was put on the District Judge's jurisdiction. Suits above that amount were made cognizable in the first instance by the Provincial Courts.[2] By Regulation XIX of 1817, parties were given the option of instituting suits of between Rs. 5,000.00 and Rs. 10,000.00, in the local District Judge's Court instead of in the Provincial Court. This was done for the convenience of those parties who might find it difficult to repair to the Divisional Headquarters for prosecuting their claims. In 1831 it was decided to abolish the Provincial Courts. Hence by Regulation V of that year all causes of above Rs. 5,000.00 were transferred back to the original jurisdiction of the District Judge. But at the same time causes of less than Rs. 5,000.00, were made cognizable in the first instance by the Indian Judges.[3] More than 90 percent of the causes fell under the latter limit. Hence in 1831

[1] Civ. Judl. Cons., 9th May 1805, Nos. 15-16.

[2] The reasons for this change have been dealt with in Chap V.

[3] See Chap. II.

the District Judge's tribunal virtually ceased to be a Court of primary jurisdiction.

Among the Civil causes cognizable by the District Judges there was a class specially known as Summary suits. They were suits connected with complaints for forcible dispossession from lands, crops, or water courses, and for arrears or undue exaction of rent. These were distinguished from the regular suits because they were required to be disposed of with top priority and by a Summary process, that is without the formal procedure of pleading, answer, reply, rejoinder etc. This process was evolved because the peace of the rural society and the collection of revenue both depended on a speedy termination of such disputes.

Besides their original jurisdiction, the District Judges were given the appellate authority over the decisions of all the subordinate judicial officers of the District, i.e. the Indian Judges and the Registers.[1] But they were prevented from trying appeals from the decisions of those Registers who were specially empowered under Regulation XXIV of 1814 (S. 9) to try cases of more than Rs. 500.00.[2] Those appeals were to go direct to the Provincial Courts. The Judges were also authorised to try Second or Special Appeals from the decisions of Registers on appeals from the Munsiffs and Sadr Amins, and from the decisions of Sadr Amins on appeals from Munsiffs.

Under the arrangements of 1831 the appellate authority of the District Judges was greatly enhanced. They were now to try appeals from all decisions of the Indian Judges who had been authorised to try causes up to Rs. 5,000·00.[3]

Experience and Qualifications.

After its establishment in 1800,* all Civil Servants appointed to Bengal were required to spend three years in the College at Fort William before commencing their official careers. The curriculum of the College included a training in the languages and the laws of India and the study of sciences and humanities. But no specific rule about the requisite experience or qualification of District judicial officers was laid down until 1807. As a result, between

[1] By Regulation XXIV of 1814, S. 6.

[2] See below.

[3] See Chap. II.

* The College was founded by Wellesley for the purpose of providing a better training for the Company's Civil Servants.

1793 and 1807, civilians with little or no judicial experience were often called upon to act as a District Judge. For example,[1] John Becher began his official career in 1781 as Assistant to the Commercial Chief at Murshidabad. He subsequently served as Deputy Paymaster to troops at Rohtas and then as the Superintendent for the collection of market duties at Kanpur. In July 1797 he was suddenly elevated to the position of District Judge and Magistrate of Murshidabad. John Battaye, a Civil Servant who began his career in 1792, was appointed Judge of Zilla Rungpur, after hiving served in the situations of a Commissioner of Court of Requests for one year, assistant to Collector for two years, Deputy Post-Master General and Post-Master General for two years, and Collector of Revenue for one year. There were many more instances of officers with very little judicial experience having been appointed District Judges.

Lord Minto was the first Governor-General to give serious consideration to the experience of men appointed to District Judgeships. He observed.

> "... it can not be pretended that the knowledge obtained in the public schools in England and in the College at Fort William, ... is calculated to qualify a young man, without further aid and instruction, to discharge the important duties ... and to qualify them, in fact, for the responsible and arduous situation of Judge and Magistrate."[2]

To improve the academic qualifications of judicial officers Minto appointed J.H. Harington, a Puisne Judge of the S. D. A., as Professor of Law to instruct them in the principles of jurisprudence at the Fort William College.[3] And to insure adequate practical experience for the prospective Judges, he decided to separate the judicial branch of service from the revenue branch.[4] Civilians, after completing their initial training in the College of Fort William, were to make a choice between joining the judicial or the revenue branch of service. Those choosing the judicial line were to be

[1] These examples have been gathered from Dodwell & Miles. List of Civil Servants in Bengal.

[2] Minto's Minute, 3rd Jan. 1807, Civ. Judl. Cons., 3rd Feb. 1807, No 32.

[3] Judl. Letter, 7th April 1807, paras. 81-83.

[4] Minto acknowledged to have done this on the advice of G. Dowdswell, the ex-Judicial Secretary, and H.T. Colebrooks, the Chief Justice of S.D.A. Minto to G.H. Barlow, 11th April 1809, Minto MSS, National Library of Scotland, Edinburgh.

attached to the S.D.A. and S.N.A. at least for one year before being posted out in the Districts as Registers.[1] Every six months these Assistants were to be examined in their knowledge of the Laws and the Regulations, the practical duties of Judges and Registers, and the general principles of jurisprudence. They were also required to prepare reports of cases adjudged by the S.D.A. and S.N.A.[2] This was for giving them an idea of how cases were tried and decided.

To prevent those trained for the judiciary from changing over to another department and thereby wasting their legal knowledge and training, the Minto Government decided that once an officer was selected for the judicial or revenue service, he was to stay and receive promotions in that department alone.[3] A change-over was to be allowed only in very exceptional circumstances. Thus Minto refused to accept a personal recommendation from John Lumsden for transferring T. Richardson from the commerce department, in which the latter had a very distinguished record of service, to the judicial, stating that it would be "against the general principle of separation of revenue and judicial authorities which I think too important to admit of any exceptions."[4]

The sole idea behind the above arrangements was to provide a better legal knowledge for those who would become District Judges. As Minto put it.

"They will pass through the situation of Register only, and it is hoped that one year's attendance on S.D.A. and S.N.A., together with some instruction in the elements of legal science, . . . may afford such a preparation for the discharge of the first duties of that line, and such a foundation for experience and practice to build upon, as may supply a good choice of future [Judge] Magistrates."[5]

The plan for training Civil servants for the situations of District Judges was provided with a statutory basis in 1814. Regulation XXIV (S. 5) of that year laid down that no person was to be appointed a District Judge unless he had previously officiated as Assistant Judge. or Register or Joint or Assistant Magistrate, for at least three years or had held any other employment in the judicial department, or any other office implying the

[1] Judl. Letter, 7th April 1807, paras 81-83.
[2] *Ibid.*
[3] Judl. Letter, 7th April 1807, para 84.
[4] Minto to Lumsden, 28th July 1808. Minto MSS.
[5] Minto to C. H. Barlow, 11th April 1809. Minto MSS.

discharge of judicial functions for at least the same number of years.

The arrangements adopted in 1807 and the rule of 1814 secured better qualified and experienced persons for the situation of District Judge. But a strict adherence to the provisions was not possible on account of the shortage of Civil Servants, particularly after 1820. Even during Minto's regime two officers, W.B. Martin and David Campbell, with past services only in the political and revenue departments, were appointed Judge-Magistrates of the twenty-four Parganas and Hooghly respectively.[1] This was done in 1809, only two years after the adoption of the principle of keeping the judicial service distinct from the revenue line. The rule of 1814 was often disregarded between 1825 and 1832. In no less than six instances persons without the required experience were appointed District Judges.[2]

The impracticability of a rigid separation between the revenue and judicial services was pointed out by the Directors in 1827[3], and was simultaneously appreciated by the Bengal Government as well.[4] After 1820, certain enactments had also been passed which ignored the principle of separation of services.[5]

Besides, the Collectors had been acquiring judicial experience by making investigations in the Summary suits for rent.[6] In 1824, they were empowered to pass judgements on such suits.[7] Henceforth the office of Collector could by interpretation be regarded as one implying the discharge of judicial functions in conformity with the requirement of experience by Regulation XXIV of 1814. This position was indirectly admitted in Regulation V of 1825, which authorised the Collectors to be appointed District Judges when found expedient.

The total length of service of an officer promoted to the rank

[1] Dodwell and Miles, *op. cit.*

[2] These appointments were those of B. Taylor in 1826; W.N. Garret in 1827; R. Macan in 1828; C. Phillips in 1830; J. Fraser in 1830, and J. Dunsmere in 1831. Dodwell and Miles, *op. cit.*

[3] Judl. Despatch, 31st Jan. 1827. pp. 37-38.

[4] Judl. Letter, 22nd Feb. 1827. pp. 198-99.

[5] These were in particular Regulations IV of 1821 (which authorised Collectors to exercise powers sf Magistrate or Joint Magistrate) and V. of 1825 (which authorised them to act as District Judges).

[6] See Chap. IV.

[7] See Chap. IV.

of District Judge was normally ten or eleven years.[1] But, depending upon availability of officers and individual merit, some were promoted earlier. For instance, J. Ewing, G.R. Boddam and J.N. Halhead, all starting their official careers in 1807, became District Judges in 1814, after only seven years' service.[2] W.B. Bayley, a very able officer, who started his service in 1803, was promoted to the rank of District Judge after six years only, in 1809.* On the other hand some had to wait longer than the average period of ten to eleven years. For example none of the officers appointed in 1817 could become District Judges before 1830.

In spite of the arrangements of 1807 and 1814, the ability of the District Judges in general remained in doubt. The Directors observed in 1824 : "Your civil servants, unprepared by education [in England] for the judicial offices have many difficulties to contend with in the exercise of their functions . . ."[3] The Bengal Government replied that lack of English legal training was more than made up for by the practical education which the judicial officers of the Company obtained by a long course of service in the interior.[4]

Though there was some truth in the Bengal Government's assertion, it could not be denied that the Judges had to face some practical handicaps in the discharge of their functions. The depositions of witnesses were made in the local languages, and the proceedings were recorded in Persian. The Judge needed a perfect knowledge of the local languages as well as of Persian. The Directors had considered this to be the "indispensable qualification for a Judge".[5] Though the curriculum of Fort William College included a study of the Indian languages and Persian, there seems to have prevailed a general gap between academic knowledge and practical proficiency. In 1809 very few Judges were reported to be

[1] Judl. Letter, 5th October 1826, para 2.

[2] Dodwell & Miles, *op. cit.*

[3] Despatch from Court to Bengal, 23rd July 1824, para 35, Despatches to Bengal.

[4] Judl. Letter, 5th Oct. 1826, para 88.

[5] Judl. Despatch, 28th Feb. 1805, Para 6.

* Bayley had even distinguished himself as a trainee at the Ft. William College. On that account a "Degree of Honour" was conferred upon him by the Gov. General in 1803 at the time of his leaving the College. Report on examination at Ft. William College, 29th March 1803, *Wellesley Papers*, (ed.) M. Martin, Vol. 3, p. 66.

able to speak or understand the local languages.[1] This continued to be a serious handicap for most judicial officers. Ram Mohan Roy stated in 1831 that on account of his ignorance in the local languages, "the Judge is apt to be induced to transfer a great part of his business to native officers, who are not responsible and who, being ill-paid, may bargain justice with self interest."[2]

This difficulty was removed to a great extent in respect of civil cases by the transfer of all original trials to the Indian Judges after 1831, for it was at that stage that an intimate knowledge of the local dialects was necessary for the Judge in following the deposition and cross-examination. The Courts of appeal decided mostly on points of law and on the basis of the records prepared at the original trial. The European Judges sitting in them could, therefore, manage even with an academic knowledge of the Indian languages. By a series of enactments from 1835 onwards, Persian was replaced by English as the language of record and legal proceedings. This made things still easier for the European Judges.

Working

Administering Civil justice was not the only function of the District Judge. He was also the Magistrate of his area in which capacity he was to control and supervise the Police, apprehend criminals and commit them for trial to the Court of Circuit, and try and punish petty offences himself.[3] Apart from these functions he had a number of miscellaneous duties. These consisted of correspondence with the superior Courts, fulfilment of the latters' precepts in connection with cases under trial before them, passing interlocutory orders, executing Decrees, not only of his own Court but also of the subordinate Courts* and the superior Courts, disposing of petitions concerning the redemption of mortgages and succession to intestate Estates, and dealing with acts of corruption

[1] Judl. Despatch, 10th Aug. 1811, para 9, quoting a recent report from Bengal.

[2] Evidence of Ram Mohan Roy before Parliamentary Committee of Enquiry, 9th Sept. 1831. Parl. Papers, 1831, Vol. V, Appx. 39.

[3] The functions of Magistrates have been enumerated in detail in Chap. IV.

* Some relief was provided to the Judges in this respect by Regulation II of 1821. By S. 7 of that Regn. Registers were empowered to execute Decrees of Indian Judges. By Regn. XIII of 1824, Sadr Amins were authorised to execute their own Decrees.

or misconduct of Indian judicial officers. These miscellaneous duties occupied a good portion of the time of the Judge. Complaints were often made about their being a serious obstacle to the despatch of the regular business of trying cases.[1]

In fact, the miscellaneous and Magisterial duties of the District Judge absorbed about half his time. As a result, the time he could devote to the disposal of Civil cases became very limited. The District Judges were hard worked. They had to sit in Court for six, eight or often even ten hours a day, six days a week. But the time they could devote to the disposal of Civil cases seldom exceeded two or three days in the week. For example, J.T. Shakespear, the Judge of Nuddea, had been able to devote only two and a half days in the week to Civil cases in 1813.[2] The Judge of Zilla Burdwan, which was always one of the heavy arrears Districts, could afford only three days in the week for Civil suits.[3] The rest of his time was spent on Criminal and miscellaneous business.

For these reasons the District Judges in general lagged behind in the disposal of Civil business. In 1795 the Judge of Burdwan alone had 30,000 cases pending on his file.[4] In 1805 the total arrears of Civil suits before all the District Judges were 15,291; at the end of 1815 they were 16,898. The figure climbed to 29,963 in 1825[5] and by 1830 it had reached 27,233.[6]

The District Judges remained unequal to their task throughout the period under review. Attempts were made from time to time to reduce their work load by devising other agencies, European as well as Indian, to share their burden. The failure of the District Judges to cope with their business, and the European* agencies devised for their relief have been studied

[1] For example, complaints were made by T. Brooke, Judge of Hooghly in 1800 (Civ. Judl. Cons., 13th July 1800, No. 7) and in 1814, by the Judges of Nuddea, Tirhoot and Murshidabad (Home Misc. Series, Vol. 775, ff 5, 79 and 169).

[2] Charge note of J.T. Shakespear, 4th Sept. 1813, Civ. Judl. Cons., 18th Sept. 1813, No. 2.

[3] Report of W.B. Bayley, Burdwan Judge, 20th June 1814, Civ. Judl. Cons., 12th Aug. 1817, No. 18.

[4] 5th Report of Select Committee of House of Commons, Parl. Branch Colls., 1812, Vol. 56, pp. 63-65.

[5] Parl. Branch Colls., 1832, Vol. 77, Appx. V, No. 16.

[6] Civ. Judl. Cons., 31st May 1831, Nos. 7-11.

* The Indian agency has been dealt with in the preceding chapter.

hereafter in three phases, 1793-1803, 1803-14 and 1814-31.

Under the arrangements of 1793, the agencies available for the assistance of the Judges in the disposal of Civil business were the Registers and the Munsiffs. Under Regulation XIII of 1793 (S.6) the Registers were empowered to try causes up to Rs. 200.00 referred to them by the Judge. By Regulation III of 1800, the District Judges were also permitted to refer to their Registers appeals from the decisions of Munsiffs in cases upto Rs. 25.00. The relief obtained from the Registers was considerable. Between July and December 1801, a total of 6,375 suits had been transferred from the Judges' files to those of Registers.[1] But still the existing aid was not adequate. The arrears of pending cases before the then existing twenty-eight District Judges were 12,262 in 1802.[2] In some Districts the arrears before the Judge on 1st January 1803 were even higher than the total disposals of the preceding five years.[3] At the same time in Tirhoot, the file of the District Judge had more pending cases than the aggregate disposals of the past seven years.[4] Concerned at the heavy accumulation of arrears the Directors had already desired the Bengal Government to take immediate steps for reducing them.[5]

The need for increasing the aid available to the Judges was realised. In 1803, the S.D,A. worked out a scheme which was passed into Regulation XLIX of 1803.[6] This sought to provide extra relief to the Judges from three directions—first, by authorising the appointment of Sadr Amins to whom causes up to Rs. 100.00 could be referred;[7] secondly by extending the original jurisdiction of Registers from Rs. 200.00 to Rs. 500.00 and

[1] Civ. Judl. Cons., 22nd April 1802, No. 5.

[2] 5th Report of Select Committee, Parl. Branch Colls. 1812, Vol. 56, pp. 63-64.

[3] Such Districts were Behar, Dacca-Jelalpur, Patna, Jessore, Birbhum, and Tirhoot. Civ. Judl. Cons., 5th May 1803, No. 12.

[4] On 1st Jan. 1803 the arrears before the Judge of Tirhoot were 2,041. The total number of causes decided in the past 7 years (1796-1802) was only 20,40. *Ibid.*

[5] General Despatch to Bengal, 23rd March 1801, paras 6-8, Despatches to Bengal, Vol. 35.

[6] Civ. Judl. Cons., 5th May 1803, No. 12.

[7] See Chap. II.

thirdly, by authorising the appointment of Assistant Judges in the heavy arrears Districts.

The creation of Sadr Amins and the enlargement of the power of Registers were intended to be permanent features of District judiciary. But the institution of Assistant Judges was designed as a temporary relief operation. The Assistant Judges were to be appointed at the recommendation of the S. D. A. by the Government in the Districts where the judges' files were particularly, heavy, and were to be withdrawn as soon as the arrears before the Judges reduced to manageable limits.

The Assistant Judges were to have the same powers as the District Judges but they could try only cases referred to them by the Judge. As those called upon to fill the situation of Assistant Judges were mostly junior Civil Servants with some experience as Registers, the practice adopted was to refer to them original causes of inferior importance and appeals from the decisions of Indian Judges and Registers.[1]

The first four appointments of Assistant Judges were made to the Districts of Tirhoot, Dacca-Jelalpur, Behar and Patna City, where the arrears before the Judges had been very heavy.[2] In 1807 all four appointments were withdrawn because the arrears had been substantially reduced.[3] But no extensive employment of Assistant Judges could be made on account of the continued reluctance[4] of the Directors to sanction it for reasons of economy.[5]

To obviate the objection of increased expenditure the S.D.A. advanced a new proposal in 1809.[6] This was to authorise those Collectors who had previous experience as Registers to act as Assistant Judges. Under the existing provisions of Regulation XLIX of 1803, the Assistant Judges were to function under the absolute control of the District Judges. They were to try only those suits which the Judges referred to them. Even their processes and orders were to be issued under the seal of the District Judges. The S.D.A. thought that the above provisions would be

[1] Govt. to S. D. A., 5th Dec. 1808, para 3, Civ. Judl. Cons., 9th Dec. 1808, No. 2.

[2] Judl. Letter, 30th Sept. 1803, para 25.

[3] Judl. Letter, 7th July 1807, paras 5 and 6.

[4] This is apparent from the following Judl. Despatches : 28th Feb. 1805. 25th April 1806, 2nd June, 1812.

[5] For a detailed discussion of the Company's finances in this period see Chap VI.

[6] S.D.A. to Govt. 7th April 1809, paras 14-16, Civ. Judl. Cons., 28th April 1809, No. 1.

an adequate safeguard against abuse, if the Assistant Judgeship was conferred upon the Collector. But Governor-General Minto rejected this proposal outright on the ground of its being repugnant to the principle of "separation of powers".[1]

Arrears before Judges in many Districts were still heavy.[2] Hence, in spite of the Directors' reluctance to approve the measure occasional appointments of Assistant Judges continued to be made. In 1809 Assistant Judges were appointed in Chittagong, Nuddea, Jessore, Jaunpur and Midnapur.[3] Further appointments were made in 1814 to the Districts of Murshidabad, the twenty-four Parganas, Saran, Burdwan, Gorakhpur, Tirhoot, Patna City and Rajshahi.[4] The Assistant Judgeships of Saran, Midnapur and Jaunpur were discontinued towards the end of 1813, because the purpose of the appointments had been fulfilled.[5] In 1814 the office of Assistant Judge was abolished altogether.

There is no doubt that the Assistant Judges provided substantial relief to some of the overburdened District Judges from time to time. But no extensive employment of this agency could be made on account of the attitude of Directors. Besides, from the very beginning this institution was intended to be a temporary relief operation. The accumulation of arrears, on the other hand, was a steady and permanent feature. It was often found that the arrears having been reduced in a particular District Court, after the employment of an Assistant Judge, mounted again once that assistance was withdrawn.[6]

Regulation XLIX of 1803, had provided two other means for securing aid to the District Judges—the extended power of

[1] Govt. to S.D.A., 28th April 1809, para 6, Civ. Judl. Cons.. 28th April 1809, No. 8.

[2] On 1st Jan. 1809 arrears before the Judges in some of the Districts were : Chittagong-2166; Jessore-1661; Purnea-1211; Nuddea-1206; Midnapur-1156; and Jaunpur-1028. Civ. Judl. Cons., 7th April 1809, No. 1.

[3] Judl. Letter, 7th April 1809, para 69, and Judl. Letter. 21st Aug. 1809, para 11.

[4] Judl. Letter, 30th Jan. 1813, Vol. 3, pp. 149-50.

[5] Judl. Letter 2nd Oct. 1813, para 109.

[6] For instance, in Tirhoot and Patna City the Assistant Judgeships were discontinued in 1807, because the arrears before the Judges had been reduced (see above.). But then the arrears in both Districts accumulated again. By 1812 the Judge of Tirhoot had arrears of 1521, and that of Patna 627. Assistant Judges had therefore to be reappointed to both Districts. Civ. Judl. Cons., 11th Nov. 1812, No. 4.

Registers and the appointment of Sadr Amins.[1] But, at the same time, it withdrew the authority of the Registers to try appeals from the decisions of Munsiffs.

It is not possible to calculate how far the Judges used the extended power of Registers because the available records do not state the number of cases between Rs. 200.00 and Rs. 500.00, that existed on the files of the Judges, or the number of such cases that the Judges referred to their Registers. But it is certain that the relief enjoyed from the additional references (i.e. of cases between Rs. 200.00 and Rs. 500.00 was bound to be offset to a considerable extent by the withdrawal of the authority of Registers to try appeals from the decisions of Munsiffs. Besides, some of the Registers were themselves already overloaded with pending business[2] and therefore their ability to absorb the load of additional references would be very limited.

A few more reforms were made for increasing the aids available to the District Judges. By Regulation XIII of 1808, suits of Rs. 5,000.00 and above were made cognizable, in the first instance, by the Provincial Courts. But such cases were few.[3] Hence, the relief to the Judges from the operation of this provision must have been negligible.

In the same year provision was made for the appointment of Assistant Magistrates (by Regulation X of 1808) for providing relief to the Judge in his Criminal duties.

In 1810 the aid withdrawn from the Judges in 1803 by the rescission of the authority of Registers to try appeals from the decision of Munsiffs was sought to be replenished by authorising Sadr Amins to try those appeals.[4] But no extensive use was made of this provision.[5] Hence no significant relief could be obtained by this measure.

[1] See above.

[2] By the end of 1801, a total of 7,231 suits was pending before the Registers. The arrears were particularly heavy before the Registers of some Districts, viz. in Behar, Burdwan, Backerganj and Birbhum. Civ, Judl. Cons., 8th July 1802. Nos. 50-81. At the end of 1805 the arrears before Registers were 9.160. Arrears before Registers of some of the Districts were : Jessore-782; Chittagong-770; Burdwan-933; Backerganj-840; Behar-1 041 and Hooghly-840, Civ, Judl. Cons., 1st May 1806, No. 20.

[3] S.D.A. to Govt., 7th April 1809, para 11. Civ. Judl. Cons.- 28th April 1809, No. 1.

[4] By Regn. XIII of 1810.

[5] For details see Chap. II.

In spite of all the above reforms the District Judges remained unequal to their task.[1] In 1812 the Select Committee of House of Commons reported :

"Expedients have been reported to for relieving the Judges by enlarging the limits of causes referable by him to the Registers and Native Commissioners [Indian Judges] . . . Something, however, is still wanting to complete that system of speedy justice, . . . which Cornwallis was so desirous of introducing . . . "[2]

Worried over the failure of the judicial structure to cope with the incoming business, the Directors sent a plan for its reform to the Bengal Government in 1814.[3] Its salient features concerning the District Judiciary were the transfer of Magistracy from the Judges to the Collectors[4] and the extension of Indian agency.[5] Both measures were calculated to reduce the load of Judges.

But the Bengal Government had in the meantime already adopted a series of reforms for making the judicial machinery equal to the available business.

For the piecemeal aid of Assistant Judges was substituted a more stable assistance through the enlargement of the agency of Registers. The ordinary jurisdiction of Registers remained the same, over cases up to Rs. 500.00. But under Regulation XXIV of 1814, S.9, Cl.6, provision was made for investing any of them with special powers to hear appeals from the decisions of Munsiffs and Sadr Amins and to try all original suits cognizable by the Judge.

The same Regulation also provided for the appointment of one or more Additional Registers to the District Courts. An Additional Register could also be stationed at some place away from the District headquarters. Like the other Registers, they too could be vested with special powers.

Under Regulation XXIV of 1814, both the regular and Additional Registers were allowed to try only the cases referred to them by the Judge. But in 1821 (by Regulation II of that year) the Additional Registers stationed away from the Sadr were authorised to receive and try on their own all original suits and

[1] See above.

[2] 5th Report of Select Committee, Parl. Branch Colls., 1812, Vol. 56, p. 59.

[3] Under Judl. Despatch, 9th Nov. 1814, Vol. 3.

[4] For a detailed discussion of this change see Chap. IV, part II.

[5] For details of Directors' plan and its consideration see Chap. II.

appeals within their competence. This was done to save the time of the Judge as well as the trouble that the people living under the jurisdiction of such Registers had to undergo in instituting their suits before the Judge at the District headquarters. Regulation II of 1821, also provided for the transfer of a portion of the miscellaneous duties of the District Judges to the Registers. The Additional Registers holding Court away from the Sadr Station were authorised to receive, and dispose of on their own, the applications for the execution of Decrees by Indian Judges. The Registers holding office at the Sadar station could also be authorised by the District Judges to execute such Decrees.

By Regulation IX of 1819, S. 8, judicial authority was also conferred on the six Registers of the Provincial Courts. The Judges of the Districts in which the Provincial Courts sat were authorised to refer original suits up to Rs. 500.00 to the Registers of the Provincial Courts for trial. But this provision was of little effect as the office of Registers of Provincial Courts was abolished in 1821.[1]

Efforts were made to use fully the extended agency of Registers in the post-1814 period. During 1815 the existing Registers of Chittagong, Nuddea, Etawa, Tirhoot, Patna City, Dacca and Gorakhpur were vested with "special power" under Regulation XXIV of 1814, S.9.[2] Subsequently, such investments became a routine affair. By 1828 the number of Registers vested with special power had risen to thirty, which was nearly the entire existing establishment of those officers.[3]

In a number of Districts Additional Registers were appointed at stations away from the Sadr. Initially, five such separated Registerships were established at Monghyre, Futehpur, Shahjehanpur, Sindose and Ghazipur.[4] Five more were established later at places like Malda, Sherpur, Buggora, Nugwan and Bhagandih.[5]

These separated Registerships were virtually independent units of judicial administration. They had their own establishment of

[1] By Regn. II of 1821, S. 14.

[2] Civ. Judl. Cons.. 14th Feb. 1815, No. 4; Civ. Judl. Cons., 2nd May 1815, No. 14; Civ. Judl. Cons., 9th May 1815, No. 15; Civ. Judl.. Cons., 14th Nov. 1815, No. 10.

[3] This can be ascertained from the Annual Report for 1828, Civ. Judl. Cons., 26th Jan. 1830, No. 19.

[4] Civ. Judl. Cons., 12th June 1815, No. 13.

[5] Parl. Branch Colls.. 1832. Vol. 77, Appx. V, No. 1.

ministerial officers. They had Sadr Amins* and Munsiffs functioning under their direct control. Regulation II of 1821, rendered their situation very independent by authorising them to receive direct all suits and appeals within their competence. These officers must have rendered great relief to the District Judges, whose exertions in respect of the areas where these Registers functioned must have been reduced to merely a general control and supervision and hearing of appeals.

Additional Registers were provided at a few Sadr Stations as well. But such appointments had to be very limited on account of a great shortage of Civil Servants, which even prevented the adequate supply of regular Registers. Only a few stations like Allahabad, Baraílly, Benares and Saharanpur South could have a steady assistance of an Additional Register between 1815 and 1831. Such officers were rarely made available to other Districts, whose needs were no less pressing.[1] The maximum number of Additional Registers entertained at any one time on the establishment of the forty-six District Courts was nine, in 1825.[2] In 1821, there was not a single Additional Register functioning in any of the District Courts. In 1831 the number of those officers employed was only two.[3]

The reforms of 1814, nevertheless, showed some encouraging results in the initial years of their operation. The number of pending causes before the District Judges fell from 16,898 on 1st January 1815, to 13,875 at the end of 1820.[4] According to the S.D.A. the main factors that had contributed to the above reduction were the extension of the agencies of Sadr Amins** and Registers.[5]

[1] Applications for appointment of Additional Registers were frequently made by the District Judges, but most of them were rejected by the Govt., particularly in the period after 1820, on account of shortage of officers. In 1822, seven Judges had made requests for such appointments, but all were refused by the Govt. Vide: Civ. Judl. Cons., 13th June 1822, Nos. 2 and 3: Civ. Judl. Cons., 9th May 1822, Nos. 1 and 2; Civ. Judl. Cons., 15th March 1822, Nos. 2-4.

[2] Data collected from *India Register* for the years 1814-31.

[3] *India Register* for 1831.

[4] Parl. Branch Colls., 1832, Vol. 77, Appx. V, No. 16.

[5] Civ. Judl. Cons., 4th July 1817, No. 12.

* Provision for stationing Sadr Amins with Additional Registers holding Court at separate stations was made by Regn. II of 1821.

** The power of Sadr Amins was extended in 1814 to cases up to Rs.150.00 in amount or value.

There was a significant increase in the disposal by the Registers during 1816, the year immediately following the promulgation of the Regulations of 1814.[1]

The extended agency of Registers was more effective in aiding the District Judges than the previous agency of Assistant Judges. This is proved by the fact that the District Judges were able to dispose of more cases with the help of the enlarged agency of Registers during 1815 and 1816, than they could in 1813 and 1814, with the aid of Assistant Judges.[2] The S.D.A. remarked that only in one respect did the Registers and Additional Registers vested with special power not fill the gap left by the abolition of Assistant Judges.[3] This was that the Assistant Judges used to hear appeals from the decisions of Registers, which the existing Registers could not. Even this gap was sought to be filled later. By Regulation IX of 1819, individual Registers, with at least six years experience in the judicial department could be authorised by the Government to try appeals from the decisions of ordinary Registers in cases below Rs. 500.00. But this arrangement postulated the presence of more than one Register in the District which, as stated earlier, could rarely be assured. No mention is ever made, in the subsequent consultations, of a Register trying appeals from the decision of his colleague. Hence it is very unlikely that any use was made of this provision.

But the extra aid obtained by the Judges from the enlarged agency of Registers was short-lived. The scheme, successful initially, failed later on account of a great shortage of Civil Servants after 1820.[4] Not only were the requests for appointment of Additional Registers rejected but from time to time many Districts had to

[1] The disposal by Registers was: In 1813–4,751; in 1814—4,497; in 1815—5,533; in 1816–8,886. *Ibid.*

[2] The following table would illustrate the point:

Disposed of by Js. and Asst. Js. and Registers		*By Js. and Registers and Addnl. Registers*	
During	1813–10,173	During	1815–9,255
,,	1814– 7,914	,,	1816–13,484
Total	18,087	Total	22,739

Civ. Judl. Cons., 4th July 1817, No. 12.

[3] *Ibid.*

[4] In 1823 the Bengal Govt. was forced to request the Directors to supply eighty new officers for meeting the existing demand. Public Letter from Bengal to Court, 3rd July 1823, quoted in H.M.S. Vol. 530, f. 757.

do without even the regular Register. For example, during the whole of the year 1821, no Register was present in nine Districts, in another ten their services had been available for only a portion of the year and in four Districts, though the Registers were present, they had been officiating as Collectors.[1] On 1st May 1823 as many as twenty-two Districts had no Register at all.[2] During 1825 no Register had been present in six Districts, and the assistance of that officer was available only for a fraction of the year in eleven Districts.[3] During 1828 twelve Districts remained without any Register for the whole of the year.[4]

The result of this deficiency was naturally reflected in the arrears before the District Courts. The number of causes pending before the District Judges and Registers on 1st January 1822 was 28,837, an increase of 10,507 over the number pending on 1st January 1817. During 1821 the Judges and Registers disposed of 5,108 fewer causes than they had during 1817.[5] Arrears before the Judges were 23,170 at the beginning of 1824.[6] At the beginning of 1830 they had risen to 27,233.[7] Two more reforms for relieving the Judge had been in operation during this interval. They were the separation of Magistracy from some of the Judgeships, and empowerment of Collectors to decide Summary suits.[8] The net result of both seems to have been absorbed by the deficiency of Registers.

Hopes for providing relief to the Judges by extending the agency of Registers were given up by 1820. In reply to a number of requests from various District Judges for the appointment of Additional Registers the Government remarked in 1820 :

"In the present circumstances any augmentation of the European agency is not possible."[9]

The S.D.A. observed in 1823 :

"Due to there being no Registers in many Districts, the relief intended to be given to the Judges by them has been frustrated."

[1] Civ Judl., Cons., 1st May 1823, Nos. 4-27.
[2] *India Register* 1823.
[3] Civ. Judl. Cons., 29th Dec. 1826, Nos. 24-26.
[4] Civ. Judl. Cons., 26th Jan. 1830, No. 19.
[5] Civ. Judl. Con., 1st May 1823, No. 19.
[6] Civ. Judl. Cons., 19th Jan. 1826, Nos. 5-11.
[7] Civ. Judl. Cons., 31st May, 1831, 7-11.
See Chap. IV.
[8] Govt. to S.D.A., 29th Dec. 1820, Civ. Judl. Cons., 29th Dec. 1820, No. 17.
[9] Civ. Judl. Cons., 10th March 1825, No. 21.

Of the arrangements of 1814 for the extension of the agency of Registers, the one calculated to bring the greatest relief to the Judge was the provision for appointment of Additional Registers, whether at Sadar Stations or at stations away from the Sadar. A mere enlargement of the jurisdiction of existing Registers was not enough, because in the "heavy arrears" Districts, the Register, like the Judge, was often saturated with business and was already making the maximum effort towards disposal. The actual remedy lay not in the juggling of jurisdictions between the European tribunals of the District but in establishment of new ones. By providing for the employment of Additional Registers the architects of the reforms of 1814 had driven in the right direction, but they could not visualise that the paucity of European officers would frustrate the entire scheme of providing additional relief to the Judges through the agency of Registers.

Efforts to provide the required aid to the Judges through their Registers having been ineffective, the office of District Register was abolished in 1831 (by Regulation V of 1831), and its place was supplied by a class of Indian Judges called Principal Sadr Amins.[1]

[1] See Chap. II.

Chapter IV

THE COLLECTORS

Origin and growth of Civil Judicial Functions

THE JUDICIAL FUNCTIONS of Collectors date back to the days when the Company only held a Zamindari in the vicinity of Calcutta. The Zamindar, or landlord, under the existing set up, was not only a collector of revenue but was also responsible for the maintenance of law and order in his territory. As such one member of the Council who held the office of "receiver of revenues" was not only a revenue collector, but also administered both Civil and Criminal justice in a Zamindari Court. Holwell, who had been the Revenue Collector of Calcutta from 1752 to 1756, held such a Court and administered justice to the Indians living under the Zamindary jurisdiction.[1] Bolts has also written about the existence of a Collector's Cutcherry (Court of justice) ever since the Company had anything to do with the collection of land rent.[2]

The problem of distributing judicial tribunals in the interior arose only after the Company directly assumed the functions of Diwani,* in 1772. Warren Hastings decided upon the simple solution of extending the Calcutta pattern of Collectors' Courts to the mofussil. In all Districts a Collector of Revenue was posted who in addition to his fiscal functions was to preside in the Civil Court of the District. The District Faujdari Adalat or Criminal Court was left in the hands of the Nawab's servants.

Thus, in 1772 the Collector was made the sole representative of

[1] Holwell, *India Tracts*, 1774, p. 20.

[2] Bolts, *Considerations on Indian Affairs . . .*, p. 81.

* According to Mughal constitution the functions of Diwani were collection of revenue and administration of Civil justice.

administrative authority in the interior. In those days of slow communication it was very difficult for the central authority at Calcutta to keep a watchful eye on the activities of that officer. In the absence of any local check there was a great danger of the Collector abusing his power for his personal gain. On this consideration, the Collectors were withdrawn in 1774 and replaced by the collective authority of Provincial Councils.[1] Their Civil judicial functions were distributed between the Amil, the Indian officer now appointed for supervising the collection in the Districts, and the six Provincial Councils, created at various Divisional headquarters. The former were to try the petty cases and the latter those of greater magnitude.

In 1780, the judicial functions of the Provincial Councils were withdrawn. The Civil Courts attached to them were now to be presided over by separate officers, known as Superintendents of Diwani Adalats.[2] In 1781, Diwani Adalats were established in the 18 Districts into which the territory under the Company's control was then divided.[3] The Provincial Councils were now abolished and the Collectors reappointed to all eighteen Districts.

But separate Civil Judges having already been appointed their former judicial function was not restored to them except in the four sparsely populated Districts of Chatra, Bhagalpur, Islamabad and Rungpur, where it was considered superfluous to maintain two officers. Even the Collectors of the remaining Districts where separate Civil Judges had been stationed were not completely divested of judicial authority. All cases relating to demands and undue exaction of rent, and all cases relating to public revenue, were reserved to the Collectors' exclusive cognizance in their revenue Courts, styled 'Mal Adaluts'.

The reasons for the restoration of the Collectors in 1781 might have been twofold. In the first place, it must have been in the interest of collections as the management of revenue by an individual on the spot could be more efficient than that by a centralised system of Provincial Councils. And, secondary, the danger of the Collector exercising an unrestricted tyranny and abusing his powers for personal gain was now lessened, in view of the reduc-

[1] Proceedings of G.G.-in-C., 23rd Nov. 1773, Bengal Rev. Cons., 12th Jan. 1774.

[2] See Chapter III.

[3] *Ibid.*

tion of his judicial functions, as also on account of the presence of another covenanted officer at the same place (i.e. the Civil Judge).

In 1787 the District Judgeships were reunited with the Collectorships in all the existing Districts except the cities of Patna, Dacca and Murshidabad. Simultaneously, the Magistracy was also joined with Collectorships. The Collector thus became the District Judge, Magistrate and Collector. The above arrangement had been carried out by Cornwallis under instruction from the Directors.[1] The latter had desired this change primarily for economy. They were also influenced by the 'one master theory' expounded by Sir John Shore who had thought that placing a single European officer in the District with all the powers would be the most suitable form of administration for the Indians as they had been used to looking up to a single despotic authority for the redress of all their grievances.[2] Besides, the separation of Judgeships from the Collectorships, made in 1781, had not worked well. The transfer of judicial authority to the Judge was not complete. The Collectors continued to exercise authority over the revenue cases. As cases concerning ownership and possession of land often involved questions of revenue and vice versa, there were very frequent clashes between the Collector and the Judge over jurisdiction. On this account the functions of both were obstructed, and the Governor General-in-Council had to waste a lot of time in deciding disputes over jurisdiction between the Judge and the Collector.[3] Hence, in 1787 it was thought that, " . . . the energy and simplicity would be much better consulted by the re-union of the functions of Civil Judge and Collector".[4]

But a combination of revenue and judicial functions in the same officer was against Cornwallis's principle of separation of powers, and his ideal of establishing the "rule of law" in place of the rule of men. He thought that :

"The Revenue Officers must be deprived of judicial powers. All financial claims of the public, when disputed, must be subjected to the Courts of

1 Letter from Court, 12th April 1786, para 7.

2 Remarks on the Administration of justice etc., by Sir John Shore, Bengal Revn, Progs., 29th May 1785.

3 Shore to Cornwallis, 15th March 1793, Revn. & Judl. Cons., 29th March 1793, No. 1.

4 Shore to Cornwallis, 15th March 1793, Revn. & Judl. Cons., 29th March 1793, No. 1.

justice, superintended by Judges, who from their official situation and the nature of their trust, shall not only be uninterested in the result of their decisions, but be bound, [by oath], to decide impartially between the Government and the Proprietors of land, and between the Proprietors and the Tenants.[1]"

Cornwallis sought to implement the Whig doctrine of reducing the executive role of the Government to the minimum. To him power in the hands of the Government and its officers seemed bound to be abused. Hence he decided to introduce a new order in which things would be regulated not by the personal discretion of individuals but by the impersonal agency of laws.[2]

Under the system established by Cornwallis in 1793, separate Judgeships were created for all the Districts and the judicial authority of Collectors was completely withdrawn. By Regulation II of 1793, the Mal Adalats or the Revenue Courts formerly attached to the Collector's office, were abolished and the cases cognizable by them were transferred to the jurisdiction of the District Judge. The Magistracy was also combined with the Judgeship.

There was another factor which facilitated the withdrawal of judicial powers from Collectors. Cornwallis's "Permanent Settlement" fixed the demands of the Government on the Zamindars on a permanent basis. The Zamindars, in turn, were required to fix their claims on their raiyats or tenants on a similar basis by issuing to them Pattas or title-deeds.[3] From this a great reduction of disputes relating to assessment of revenues could be anticipated. At least it could be presumed that the demands and obligations being committed to writing, most revenue disputes could be easily decided by the Judges like the other kinds of suits. The specialised knowledge of Collectors would no more be necessary in the trial of most revenue cases. The Regulations of 1793 were to be administered by the new District Judge and Magistrate. He was to be the pre-eminent figure in the District. His domination over the Collector was firmly established by the Regulations. The Collector was made amenable to the Judge's Court if he acted contrary to the Regulations. He was bound to render assistance and obedience to the Judge under pain of

[1] Preamble to Regn. II of 1793.

[2] 5th Report of Select Committee of House of Commons, Parl. Branch Colls., 1812. Vol. 56, p. 18.

[3] Regn. VIII of 1793.

penalty. In the following years those Collectors who could not be reconciled to the Judges' superiority and disputed their authority were fined by the Judges and/or reprimanded by the Government.[1]

Thus the Collectors were reduced to the position that their designation implied. But though their power of judicial decision was withdrawn certain judicial functions were left with them. They were in the form of investigation, distraint for default, and execution of decrees passed in favour of the Government, in cases connected with land revenue.[2] By regulation XXIV of 1793, the Collectors were entrusted with conducting investigations into matters relating to pensions,[3] and into the applications for separation of Taluks or small estates from their dependancies on Zamindaries to which they had been attached. They were also empowered to detain or attach or sell the property of persons defaulting in the payment of Government revenue.

Besides, by S. 13 Regulation VII of 1794, the District Judges were authorised to refer to the Collectors for report and adjustment any matters of account connected with suits concerning demands, arrears and undue exaction of rent, or any other matters formerly cognizable by the Revenue Courts. When such a suit was referred to the Collector for investigation and report the parties and the Vakeels had to appear before him for examination before he made his report. It is true that the Judge was free to reject or alter the recommendation of the Collector. But the above procedure in many cases rendered the Collector the person whose opinion directed the decision though he did not actually pronounce the judgement.[4] By Regulation V of 1812 all suits concerning distraint or attachment of property of raiyats, for arrears of rent

[1] Between 1793 and 1811, a number of Collectors, such as Armstrong, Deane, Leycester and Macarab were fined or chided by the Govt. for disobedience or disrespect to the Judge.

[2] These Judicial functions of the Collectors were noticed in the 5th Report of the Select Committee of House of Commons. Parl. Branch Coll., Vol. 56, 1812, p. 26.

[3] It had been the practice of the previous Govt, (of the Nazim) to grant pensions to various descriptions of Hindus and Muslims, like Mullas, Pandits and Faquirs. This was continued by the Company administration.

[4] The Directors also made a similar remark in their Judl. Despatch to Bengal, 19th Nov. 1814, para 78.

were required to be referred by the Judges to the Collectors for investigation and report. Any party dissatisfied with the decision of the Judge on the basis of a Collector's report was free to institute a regular suit in the Civil Court for a more formal investigation into the merits of the case.

The delegation of the aforesaid judicial function to the Collectors was, in fact, a concession to the practical necessity of providing assistance to the District Judges for a quicker disposal of such suits and also a recognition of the superior fitness of the Collector, in the investigation of suits connected with revenue.[1]

But this dual process of institution and decision before one tribunal and investigation by another was bound to be inconvenient to the suitors and their Vakeels; nor could it be expected to ensure a speedier disposal of those suits. By 1814, several Judges had complained of those difficulties.[2]

The Judge of Nuddea recommended in 1814 that "either the Collectors should be empowered to decide entirely in these cases, or that their intervention be dispensed with."[3]

A substantial relief could be provided to the Judges only by authorising the Collectors to decide such suits instead of merely investigating and reporting upon them. This was realised soon by the Bengal authorities. But the Minto Government kept averse to making any extension of the judicial powers of the Collectors. The only concession they made in this direction was to make it incumbent upon the Judges to refer a particular class of Summary suits to the Collectors investigation. This was done by Regulation V of 1812, which has been noticed earlier.

In their Judicial despatch of 9th November 1814, the Directors suggested[4] the transfer of disputes for demands and undue

[1] It may be recalled that all suits connected with rent and revenue were to be given a top priority in disposal by the Judges. They were to be disposed of by a summary process, leaving the party dissatisfied with the Summary investigation to file a regular suit. See Chapter III.

[2] They were, for example, H. Shakespear, Judge of Rajshahi, (Civ. Judl. Cons, 12th July 1814, No. 4.); T. Fortescue, Judge of Allahabad (Home Misc. Series, Vol. 776); & the Judge of Nuddea (H.M.S. Vol. 775, pp. 168-9).

[3] Answer to interrogatories of Moira by Nuddea Judge, para 36, H.M.S., Vol. 775, pp. 168-9.

[4] Judl. Despatch, 9th Nov. 1814, para. 93.

exactions of rent to the "bonafide cognizance" of Collectors, subject to a revision by the regular Courts of justice, by way of appeal. This, they thought, would benefit both Zamindars and raiyats. As for the above measure being a departure from Cornwallis's principles, the Directors argued[1] that such departure had in effect been made in past by providing for reference of cases connected with rent to the Collector's investigation (under Regulations XVII of 1794 and V of 1812). Besides, as the provision of Regulation VIII of 1793, requiring the Zamindars to grant *Pattas* or title-deeds to their under-tenants, had hardly been adhered to, the Directors held that the position of the raiyats, vis-a-vis (the oppression of) the Zamindars, remained unchanged.[2] The demands over the raiyats not having been conveyed in writing could be and were being, made arbitrarily by the Zamindars. It is true that the provisions requiring the issue of *Pattas* remained ineffective. This was due to a general reluctance on the part of the Zamindars to issue the *Patta,* as also a deliberate neglect on the part of the raiyats to demand it. Actually, neither party wanted to commit the demand or obligation to writing because that would have closed the door for one to demand more and for the other to claim to pay less. Under such circumstances disputes over arrears or undue exaction of rent went on adding to the files of the already overburdened Civil Courts of the District. In the absence of documentary attestation their investigation became complicated and cumbersome. As early as 1795, the Judges of Burdwan and Birbhum had complained of the inconveniences and delays in the decision of the Summary suits due to the general absence of *Pattas*.[3]

But in spite of the Directors' suggestion and the actual inconvenience of the existing system the constitutional position of Collectors regarding summary suits was retained unchanged by the Bengal Government. In fact it deteriorated further when by Regulation XIX of 1817, the choice of referring to Collectors summary suits relating to distraint of property for arrears of rent was restored to the District Judges. This discretion had been withdrawn earlier by Regulation V of 1812, which had made it imperative

[1] *Ibid.*, paras 78-80.
[2] Judl. Despatch 9th November, 1814 para. 75.
[3] S.D.A. Progs., 16th April, 1795, No. 71.

on the Judges to refer all those suits to the Collectors for investigation and report. This was apparently done on account of the various inconveniences that had been felt by the Judges in referring all such suits to the Collectors.[1]

Though the Hastings Government did not nominate it as a reason for not investing the Collectors with judicial powers, the ability and experience of the Collectors to exercise a power of judicial decision was, nevertheless, doubted by some. Commenting on the proposal of extending the power of Collectors to decide upon Summary suits, the Chief Secretary, Dowdswell, observed :

"The plan generally rests on a basis, which I apprehend, is quite unsound. It supposes that the Collectors will bestow a considerable share of their time and trouble to the discharge of a duty of a most irksome nature, which is in a great measure, foreign to the ordinary functions ot their office . . . It supposes likewise, the knowledge of the course of judicial proceedings, which few of the Collectors possess . . . "[2]

In 1820, Stuart, a member of Hastings's Council, who had previously served as a Judge of the S.D.A. for six years (1810-16), commenting on the Directors' insistence upon extending the judicial power of Collectors, remarked :

"The office of the Collector in Lower Provinces, has come to be considered as one that requires less talent and activity . . . Hence the Government has been tempted to select the ablest of the British officers for the judicial branch in the Lower Provinces, and in consequence, the office of the Collector has been filled, generally speaking, with least capable and efficient of Civil servants . . . "[3]

That the Collector's office was bestowed on men of inferior capability or integrity is also demonstrated by the fact that Judges found guilty of corruption, neglect or misconduct, and in consequence, considered unfit to hold a judicial situation, were made Collectors, as a mark of punishment.[4]

Though finally, after all the discussions, the power of Collectors regarding Summary suits remained unaltered (and the Judges

[1] See above. The S.D.A. also advanced the same justification later in 1824, Civ. Judl. Cons. 2nd July 1824, No. 12.

[2] Chief Secy.'s report, 17th Nov. 1814, Civ. Judl. Cons., 29th Nov. 1814, No. 27.

[3] Minute of Stuart, 21st Aug. 1820, Civ. Judl. Cons., 1st Sept. 1820, Nos. 10-12.

[4] Thus Sir Alexander Seton in 1808, and J. V. Biscoe, in 1824, after having been found guilty of misconduct and negligence, and consequently having been considered unfit to hold their situations of Judge-Magistrates, were appointed Collectors.

were even freed from the Statutory obligation of referring all suits under Regulation V, of 1812, to the Collector's investigation), the Hastings administration became keen to see that the available assistance of the Collectors was utilised to the fullest practicable extent.

During 1818 out of the 35,521 Summary suits for rent disposed of by the Civil Courts, only 6,051 had been referred to the Collectors, out of which their reports had been obtained in respect of 4,377. In many Districts not a single suit of that nature had been referred to the Collector's investigation, while in some the number referred had been trifling.[1] In noticing these facts the Governor-General-in-Council directed the S.D.A. to draw the attention of the District Judges to the importance of their availing themselves of the aid of Collectors[2] whenever the circumstances would permit of a more speedy decision by the Collectors than by the Judge.[3] In the following year, the Government after analysing the annual Report of S.D.A. for 1820 again felt dissatisfied with the number of such references made to the Collectors during the year (which was only 6,220 of which the Collectors had reported on 4,613), and remarked that : "The judicial officers, in general, had not availed themselves of the assistance of revenue authorities, in the decision of Summary suits to the extent to which it was desirable."[4]

Collectors who showed any slackness in reporting upon the suits referred to them were called upon by the Government to explain the reasons for the delay in the submission of their reports.[5] For example, in 1819, explanations were demanded from the Collectors of Jessore, Midnapur, Twenty-four Parganas, Dinajpur and Murshidabad for the reasons for the delays which

[1] Annual Report of S.D.A. for 1818. The Dists. where no suits has been referred to the Collector's investigation were Hooghly, Birbhum Backorganj, Chittagong, Dacca Jelalpur, Sylhet, Rungpur and Behar. In some, very few suits were referred, e. g. in Bhagalpur—2 Dacca City-14; Rajshahi—27; Civ. Judl. Cons., 13th Aug. 1819. Nos. 13-22.

[9] Letter from Govt. to S.D.A., 13th Aug. 1819. Civ. Judl. Cons., 13th Aug. 1819, No. 34.

[3] Govt. to S.D.A. 13th Aug. 1819, Civ. Judl., Cons., 13th Aug, 1819, No. 34.

[4] Govt. to S.D.A., 17th Dec. 1821, Civ. Judl. Cons., 17th Dec. 1821, No. 30.

[5] Govt. to Board of Revenue, 27th Aug. 1819, Civ. Judl. Cons., 3rd Sept. 1819, No. 2.

seemed to have occurred in the investigation of the cases referred to them during the second half of 1818. The replies received from the Collectors were considered to be satisfactory. Still, such a practice was definitely calculated to make the Collectors more alert towards this branch of their duty.

Under the vigilant attitude of the Government and under the increasing pressure of business before the District Civil Courts from 1820 onwards,[1] there was an increase of the use of the agency of Collectors.

During 1822[2] the Collectors investigated and reported upon 6,946 such suits; this number increased to 7,466 for 1823.[3] The S.D.A. then had the satisfaction of reporting that the judicial authorities were "now generally availing themselves of the aid of Collectors in the disposal of Summary suits for rent."[4]

Meanwhile, the movement for extention of the Collector's judicial powers had again been gathering strength. The exigencies of revenue administration in the unsettled districts of the Western Provinces forced the Government to invest the Collectors of those Districts with power to determine suits arising from disputes relating to irrigation, boundaries, crops and other local rights connected with land.[5] The powers vested in the Collectors of the Western Provinces extended in 1825[6] to the Collectors of Khas-mahal, Sunderbans and such other areas as the hill lands of Bhagalpur and all other waste lands which had not been specifically included within the limits of the estates permanently settled in the Lower Provinces. The judicial functions of the revenue authorities were increased in a few more cases also in order to provide further relief to the Civil Courts. For example, Regulation II of 1822, which specified the conditions for the validity of sales for arrears of rent, and defined the nature of the title and interest conveyed to the person purchasing the estate, also vested the revenue officers with the powers to rectify any errors

[1] Board of Revenue to Govt. (No date), Civ. Judl. Cons., 7th Dec. 1819, No. I.

[2] Annual Report for 1822, Statement 'F', Civ. Judl. Cons., 23rd Dec. Nos. 10-25.

[3] Annual Report for 1823, Statement 'F', Civ. Judl. Cons., 10th March 1825, Nos. 21-40.

[4] *Ibid.* General remarks of the S.D.A. on the report.

[5] By Regulation VII of 1822.

[6] by Regulation IX of 1825.

that might be committed in respect of the above, at the time of the sale.

Between 1815 and 1819, there had been a general reduction of arrears of pending causes. This naturally produced a feeling of optimism in the existing system which made Hasting's Government more reluctant to make any basic change in the same. But after 1819, when the arrears started to mount again, the succeeding Governments of Adam and Amherst were persuaded to give a trial to some of the reforms suggested by the Directors.

Thus a proposal from the S.D.A.* was enacted into Regulation XIV of 1824, by the Amherst Government, which vested in the Collectors generally "authority to hear, investigate and determine, subject to a regular suit in the Civil Court, all suits concerning demands of rent, arrears or exactions of rent, between landholders or farmers of land, and their under-tenants, or between any other persons concerned in the receipt or payment of land revenue."[1] In the trial of those cases, the Collectors were given the same powers as were previously vested in the Civil Courts, for causing the attendance of parties and their witnesses.[2]

The operation of this Regulation was bound to provide more relief to the Judges, and at the same time, ensure a quicker disposal of the Summary suits. This is borne out by the increase in the number of disposals of such suits by the Collectors, after its promulgation.[3] By 1830, the Bengal Government had the satisfaction of noticing that the powers vested in the Collectors by the above Regulation generally relieved the District Courts.[4]

But Regulation XIV had not transferred the original Jurisdiction in respect of the Summary suits to the Collectors. Those suits still had to be instituted before the Judge, who had the discretion of referring all, any or none of them to the Collector for his decision. The power of executing the Collector's orders or decrees was also reserved to the Judges. This was probably done to avoid a clash over jurisdiction between the Judge and the Collector. Also the the administrative opinion in Bengal had not yet grown strong

[1] Preamble to Regulation XIV of 1824.

[2] *Ibid.* Section 4.

[3] Disposal by the Collectors increased as follows : in 1824–8, 173; 1825–9, 279; 1826–13166; 1827—10,860; 1828–11,349; 1829–12,743. Data compiled from the Annual Reports of those years.

[4] Judl. letter from Bengal, 9th Nov. 1830, p. 37.

enough to make a complete break with Cornwallis's principles. The delegation of the power of judicial decision to the Collectors does represent a compromise of Cornwallis's philosophy. But, at the same time, the retention of a complete control over the judicial function of the revenue authorities in the hands of the Judges demonstrates that the Bengal Government was not yet prepared to break completely with Cornwallis's ideals and "the deadweight of administrative traditionalism it had come to represent".[1]

The inconvenience of the system adopted in 1824 came under attack under the reforming tide of Bentinck's administration. Baley, a member of Bentinck's Council, remarked :

"... there seems no good reason, specially since all suits of this description [Summary suits] are, under the provisions of Regulation 14 of 1824, referred to, and tried by, the Collectors, for requiring that they should be instituted before the Judge. They clog the files of the Courts and serve greatly to increase the miscellaneous business, while withe the decision of them the Courts have nothing to do ... The imposition of an unjust demand on the one hand or the evasion of a just one on the other, being more easily detected, at first sight, by the revenue authorities than by the judicial, ... such claims would be less frequently brought forward, if their entire jurisdiction should be transferred to the Collectors".[2]

Ever since 1809 the S.D.A. had been consistently and strongly favouring the extension of Collector's judicial powers to decision over the Summary suits. In 1824 the S.D.A. won its point when the Collectors were given the powers to decide upon the suits referred to them by the Judges. But at the same time the S.D.A. was keen to maintain a firm control over the Collector's judicial activity in the hands of the regular Civil judiciary. This attitude was amply demonstrated by their vehement opposition to the proposal for the re-establishment of the *Mal Adalats* in 1817. They thought that the powers which had been granted to the Collectors in 1824, had catered to the practical necessity without sacrificing the sacred principles of separation of powers and of the supremacy of judiciary, which they were zealous to preserve. Hence the majority of the Judges of the S.D.A. opposed Bayley's proposal of vesting the Collectors with original jurisdiction in cases of rent. They saw in it an impious infringement of the

[1] Eric Stokes, *The English Utilitarians and India*, p. 157.

[2] Minute of W. B. Bayley, dtd. 5th Nov. 1829, Civ. Judl. Cons., 12th Oct. 1830, No. 69.

structure and spirit of Cornwallis's hallowed system as well as a breach of the privilege of the regular judiciary.[1]

But Bentinck seemed to entertain no such sentiments and he agreed fully with Bayley's arguments.[2]

Bayley's plan was accordingly incorporated in Regulation VIII of 1831, which authorised the Collectors to receive and decide Summary cases for rent. Any party dissatisfied with the Collector's award had the option of instituting a regular Civil suit before the Judge, who was authorised to reverse or alter the Collector's decision. The District Judges, at the same time, were forbidden to receive any claim for rent, unless it was preferred as a regular Civil suit. This removed the possibility of a clash of jurisdiction. The Collectors were also authorised to execute their own decrees.

Transfer of Magistracy to the Collectors

It has been noticed in Chapter III that the trial of regular Civil suits and appeals was not the only occupation of the Judges of the Districts. They had many additional duties to perform, of which the Magisterial functions were the most arduous.[3] It often required of them more time than they could give to the Civil business.

As early as 1801, Tufton, the Judge Magistrate of Zilla Behar, had advocated the appointment of a separate Magistrate to that

[1] Minute of Judges of S.D.A. on Bayley's proposal, Ross, the 5th Judge, criticised it as a "halfmeasure which ignored important questions of principle". P. B. Colls, 1832, No. 77, Appx. V, No. 2.

[2] Resolution of G.G.-in-C. 12th Oct. 1830, Civ. Cons., 12th Oct. 1830, No. 80.

[3] Under the Constitution of 1793, the functions of the Magistrate were control and supervision of Police, apprehension and prevention of Crimes, punishment of petty offences, and commitment of prisoners charged with heinous offences to trial before the Court of Circuit. The list of offences triable and punishable by the Magistrates was enlarged subsequently (by Regulations XII of 1818, I of 1822, and X of 1824) so that by 1824 offences like house-breaking, burglary, affrays not attended with homicide or grievous hurt, escaping from prison, etc., had been transferred to the cognizance of the Magistrates to ensure their quicker disposal. By Regulation XV of 1824 the power of Summary investigation and award, in cases of dispossession, was transferred to the Magistrate. By Regulation XIV of 1816, he had been entrusted with the maintenance of order and discipline in the Jails.

District so that he could devote his undivided attention to Civil business.[1] But the request was not sanctioned.

In 1810 Ernst, the Judge of Circuit for Benares Division remarked.

"... the Criminal business of our Courts claim their [Judge-Magistrate's] first care, and in most Districts it has always been so heavy and so much stress has been laid on the state of Police, that the Magistrates have had but very little time to spare for Civil Courts. The consequence has been that these have been overloaded with business [so] that it has been found almost in vain to seek legal redress in matters of property ..."[2]

In 1812 Shakespear, the Judge—Magistrate of Jessore, while stressing the necessity of continuing the services of an Assistant Judge there, had stated :

"I have regularly reported my inability to sit more than two days in the week, sometimes only one, in the Diwani Adalat. Heavy duties of the Criminal Court require the most unremitting attention".[3]

In 1813 the same gentleman, as the Judge-Magistrate of Huddea, had been devoting four of the six working days in the week to Criminal duties.[4] It may be recalled that by Regulation III of 1793, (S. 5), the Judges were required to sit at least three days in the week for the disposal of Civil business.

During the second half of 1814 Douglas, the Judge-Magistrate of Patna, had been so occupied with the trial of petty Criminal suits that he could decide only one regular and twenty-five Summary suits during those six months.[5] Likewise, in 1826, Vibrat, the Judge-Magistrate of Rajshahi, was so engaged with his Magisterial duties that he could decide only one Civil suit during the whole of that year.[6]

[1] The Judge suggested the above measure instead of the proposed transfer of portions of that District to the adjoining Districts of Ramgarh, Bhagalpur, Shahabad and Patna, for reducing the pressure of business before the Distt. Court of Gaya. Tufton to Patna Provincial Court, 7th June 1801, Civ. Judl. Cons., 9th Sept. 1801, Nos. 3 & 4.

[2] Ernst to Govt.. dtd. 12th May 1810, quoted in Judl. Despatch to Bengal, 28th Oct. 1814, para 40.

[3] Shakespear to S.D.A., 14th Jan. 1812, Civ. Judl. Cons., 10th Feb, 1813, Nos. 15 & 16.

[4] Charge note of Henery Shakespear, Civ. Judl. Cons., 18th Sept, 1813, No. 2.

[5] He had disposed of 104 petty Criminal cases in the same period. Civ. Judl. Cons. 29th Dec. 1814, Nos. 4-7.

[6] Judl. Letter 9th Nov. 1830.

The inexpediency of the union of Civil Judgeship and Magistracy was noticed in the 5th Report of the Select Committee in 1812, which commented :—"If as a Judge, he [the Judge-Magistrate] exerts [himself] to reduce Civil business, the Magistrate's office is in the danger of falling into arrears, and if he employs himself sufficiently in the latter, the file of the Civil business must swell."[1]

The incompatibility of these two offices was acknowledged by the Governor-General, Lord Hastings, in the following words,

'The business of Judge necessarily confines him to his court house. The duties of Magistrate can perhaps never be so properly executed as while he is engaged in a personal visit to every part of the District. Preservation of peace calls for all the active energy of youth . . . . A Judge should perhaps be abstracted from all private converse with the natives. A Magistrate must maintain a most intimate communication with them . . . . Justice should be blind, but Police requires the eyes of Argus."[2]

The first statutory provision for the separation of Magistracy from Judgeship was made by Regulation XVI of 1810, which besides providing for the appointment of Assistant Magistrates enacted that the Superintendents of Police for the Lower and western Provinces could be entrusted with the Magistracy of the Districts lying close to their headquarters. It was, however, not practicable to make any extensive use of this provision. Only the Magistracy of the twenty-four Parganas was transferred to the charge of the Superintendent of police for the Lower Provinces, and that for a very short period.[3]

The authorities, both in London and in Bengal, were agreed that the Magistracy should be transferred from the Judges, in the interest of an efficient administration of both Civil and Criminal justice. But, as to the mode of transfer, there existed a difference of opinion between the two. There were two alternatives. Either separate officers were to be appointed to hold charge of the Magistracy, or else the Magistracy was to be transferred to the second officer of the District—the Collector.

[1] 5th Report of Select Committee of House of Commons, Parl. Branch Colls., 1812, Vol. 56, p. 69.

[2] Minute of Lord Hastings, 21st Sept. 1815, para 96. Printed in Papers relating to the Judicial system of Bengal. Reg. 71 (197).

[3] The Magistracy was transferred back to the Judge of twentyfour Parganas on 31st Dec. 1811. Judl. despatch, 28th Oct. 1814, para. 172.

In 1814, the Directors, keeping in line with their proposal to the Madras Government of making a general union of Magistracies with the Collectorships, desired the Bengal Administration also to make a general transfer of Police and Magistracy to the Collectors.[1] They made their desire imperative on this point: "... our orders are pre-emptory that the powers of Magistrate shall hereafter be vested in the Collector, together with the superintendence of Police."[2]

But to such a proposal objections came from many sources in Bengal. The S.D.A., basing its views on the opinions expressed by the Provincial and District Judges on the issue, tendered the following main objections:[3]

(i) The Collectors of most Districts were fully occupied with their revenue and settlement duties. Hence they would be unable to share the new burden of Police and Magistracy.

(ii) It was doubtful whether even any of the Collectors of the Lower Provinces could perform the whole of the additional duties that the Magistracy would impose, without neglecting their revenue functions.

(iii) Many Collectors were without any previous judicial experience. Hence they might not be competent to discharge the duties of Magistracy.

(iv) Under the established system the Judge-Magistrate combined in him a greater authority to obtain the cooperation of landholders, proprietors, and other inhabitants, in the administration of Police, than would be possessed by the Collectors, if vested with Magistracy.

(v) There would be a risk of collision of authorities, as in the event of the transfer the Collector would have to be subject to two distinct authorities, i.e. to the Judge of circuit, in his Magisterial capacity, and to the Board of Revenue in his fiscal role.

The S.D.A., therefore, recommended the appointment of separate Magistrates to those Districts where the Civil business before the Judge was very heavy.

1 Judl. Despatch, 9th Nov. 1814, paras. 165-168.

2 Judl. Despatch, 10th April 1816, 37-38.

3 S.D.A. to Govt., 9th March 1818, para 166. papers on the Judl. system of Bengal, Reg, 71 (197).

Dowdswell, a member of the Supreme Council, made two new objections to the proposed measure. They were, first, that such union of Magistracy with Collectorship would be against the principles of Civil polity founded in 1793 by Cornwallis, and, secondly, that such union might be rendered a most intolerable instrument of oppression, as the Collectors, in their seal to improve the revenue collection, on which their credit mostly depended, might utilise their Police powers for that end.[1]

Salmon, a member of the Board of Revenue, who contested the measure, stated :

"The division of judicial and revenue lines has deprived all Collectors of the opportunity of learning the duties of Magistrate, and there is no public office which requires experience and practice more . . . If a Collector were to become a Magistrate, he would either turn out to be a good Police officer and a bad Collector; or a bad Poliee Officer and a good Collector; it is possible that he would continue to devote his attention to that branch which interests him more. . . . Very deep research or maturity of judgement are not essential qualities in a Magistrate but quickness of intelligence, activity of both mind and body . . . are almost indispensable. The habits and routine of a Collector's duties are not of such a nature . . . "[2]

The Bengal Government had called for a report from the Madras Presidency on the working of the new judicial system which had been established there in 1816 in accordance with the plan of the Directors.[3] The report submitted by the Board of Revenue of Madras in 1819 showed that on the whole the combination of Magistracy with Collectorship had not been very useful.[4] There was some difference of opinion among the Collectors of that Presidency on the subject.[5] For example, the Collectors of Nellore, Coimbatore and Bellary had found that duties of Magistracy had not interfered with their revenue duties ; the Collectors of Malabar, Salem, Guntur and Ganjam had stated no decided opinion while the Collectors of Rajamundhry, North

[1] Minute of Dowdswell, dtd, 22nd Sept. 1819, Civ. Judl. Cons., 5th Nov. 1819, No. 15 'A'.

[2] Board of Revenue to Govt. dtd. 5th May 1818, Papers relating to the Judicial system of Bengal, Reg. (71), 197.

[3] Under the new plan the Magistracy was generally united with the Collectorship in all the Dists. of Madras Presidency.

[4] The report has been recorded under Civ. Judl. Cons., 24th March 1820, No. 66.

[5] In reply to the query circulated by the Madras Revenue Board. Enclosed in the Board's report above mentioned.

Arcot, Chingleput, Trichi, Madurai, Tinnevelly, Tanjore, Masulipatam and Vizagapatam stated that the discharge of their Magisterial duties had materially interfered with their functions in the revenue department. The Madras Revenue Board gave its own opinion : "that the union of Magistrate's office in the several Districts had proved detrimental to the interests of the Revenue Department . . ."; and advised that there should be a separate District Judge, Magistrate and Collector in each District.

In considering the adoption of the Madras pattern in Bengal, another factor to be reckoned with was that the Magistrates of Madras had fewer duties to perform than their counterparts in Bengal. As shown in a report of the Sadr Adalat of Madras of 1830,[1] the Madras Magistrates or their assistants seldom interfered at all with preliminary investigations in the cases which were not triable by them. In those cases the information was for the most part taken by Indian Heads of Police, who either released the accused or committed him direct to the District and Sessions Judge. In point of fact, the exercise of Magisterial functions in Madras was limited to the trial of petty offences punishable without reference to the higher authorities. The Bengal Government rightly observed that the Magisterial powers of the Collectors in Madras did not exceed the powers of the Assistants to the Magistrates, under the Bengal Code.[2] This fact alone, apart from the objections stated by the various authorities in Bengal (noticed earlier), was bound to introduce an element of hesitation, or at least of a greater circumspection, on the part of the Bengal Administration, in deciding to transfer the Magistracy to the Collectors.[3]

It was natural, therefore, for the Bengal Government to be

[1] Qutoted in the letter of Judl. Secy. of Madras to Bengal Govt., 9th Feb. 1830, Para 60. Civ. Judl. Cons., 15th June 1830, Nos. 7-10.

[2] Judl. letter from Bengal, 15th June 1830, para 8.

[3] The Madras Collectors had no Civil judicial functions in 1818 (when the above report noticed on p. from that Presidency was submitted), while their Bengal counterparts already had some. But this could not be made a ground for not transferring the extra load of Magistracy to the Bengal Collectors. In 1822 the Collectors of Madras were entrusted with extensive Civil judicial functions. By Regn. V of that year (of the Madras Govt.) they were authorised to take primary cognizance of all suits connected with rent. In fact the Civil judicial responsibilities then entrusted to the Collectors of Madras were much more than what their colleagues in Bengal had until 1831.

inclined in favour of the employment of separate Magistrates, when necessary, instead of making a general transfer of Magistracy to the Collectors. But on account of the paucity of Civil servants, and on account of the insistence of the Directors to implement their plan, the Bengal authorities at first resolved upon adopting a moderate course. This was to resort to both the alternatives simultaneously, *viz.* : (1) to transfer the Magistracy to the Collectors of those Districts where the revenue business was light and the individual holding charge of the office was considered competent; and (2) to employ separate Magistrates in the other heavy arrears Districts, where the Collector may be fully occupied with his own revenue duties or may not have adequate judicial experience.

In 1823 Acting Governor-General John Adam created five separate Magistracies for the Districts of Hooghly, Jessore, Nuddea, Purnea and Tirhoot, where the arrears before the Judges had been very heavy.[1] On the question of transferring the Magistracy to the Collectors, the Governor-General made this policy statement :[2]

" . . . whether the general introduction of the system, even if it were practicable would be desirable, is a question which it is not necessary to discuss on the present occasion, but there is no sufficient reason why the experiment should not be tried in any particular District in which the Collector may not only be well qualified for the task but have sufficient leisure to execute it, without interfering with his duties in the revenue department, and where, at the same time, the business devolving upon the Judge and Magistrate is particularly laborious.[3]

The Collectors of Western Provinces, Benares and Bihar were very busy and so were the Collectors of most of the Districts of Bengal. Nevertheless, after due consideration, the Collectors of Rungpur, Ramgarh and Junglemahal were vested with the Magistracy of their respective Districts.[4]

But these arrangements were, according to the Governor-General, intended to be of a temporary nature. It was stated that after the arrears had been reduced in the Districts concerned, the Magistracy was to revert to the Judges there. The arrange-

1 Minute of Gov. Gen., 12th June 1823, Civ, Judl. Cons., 12th June 1823, Nos. 20-23.

2 *Ibid.*

3 *Ibid.*

4 *Ibid.*

ments of separation of the two offices could then be employed in the other Districts with heavy arrears.[1] Thus, in 1826 the Magistracies were reunited with the Judgeships in Hooghly and Rungpur, on the ground that the purpose of separation had been accomplished.[2]

In the two years following the separation in the several Districts, the files of the Judges of most of them were greatly reduced.[3] Thus, in Jessore, where the number of pending suits before the Judge on the 1st March 1824 (the date when the separation was actually affected) was 4,044, by October 1825, i.e. after eighteen months, the arrears had fallen to 2,744, a reduction of 1,300. In Nuddea, between October 1823 (the date of separation) and October 1825, the arrears on Judge's file had been reduced by 1,773; and, in Rungpur, by 1,385 in approximately the same period. Only in the Districts of Junglemahal, Purnea and Tirhoot had there been a slight increase in the arrears. But in Junglemahal the duties of Judge, Magistrate and Collector had for unavoidable reasons devolved on the same person for many months during the period of reckoning (1823-25). Likewise in Purnea, where the separation had been affected from December 1823, the functions of Judge and Magistrate had to be discharged by the same person since November 1824, due to the non-availability of another officer.

Owing to the shortage of Civil servants it was often found necessary to make the Judge officiate as Collector, or for the Collector to officiate as Judge and Magistrate. Regulation IV of 1821 provided a legal basis for such arrangements. No specific regulation was enacted providing for the transfer of Magistracy to the Collector, but the Government regarded Regulation IV of 1821* as the enactment covering such transfers. In 1826 Magistracy was transferred to the Collectors in Behar[4] and Sylhet.[5]

[1] Minute of Govn. Gen., 12th June 1823, Civ. Judl. Cons., 12th June 1823, Nos. 20-23.

[2] Civ. Judl. Cons., 19th July 1826, No. 13.

[3] Memorandum of Judicial Secy., 7th June 1826, in which a detailed statement of the increases and decreases in the file of the Judges, (who had been relieved of the Magistracy), in the two years following the separation, is enclosed. Civ. Judl. Cons., 12th June 1826, No. 7.

[4] Civ. Judl. Cons., 26th April 1826, No. 2.

[5] Judl. Letter 30th Aug. 1827.

* It authorised officers of revenue to be vested with the powers of a Magistrate.

The policy enunciated by Adam on the issue of transfer of Magistracy to the Collectors continued to be the policy of the succeeding Government of Amherst, which remained averse to a general transfer of Magistracy to the Collectors. In 1827 the Bengal Government emphatically objected to the proposal of making a general transfer of Magistracy to the Collectors. It stated : " . . . unless we could restore the ancient institutions of village communities and could employ the heads of Villages, the farmers, the landholders, or their agents, as officers of Police, little would be gained and much would be sacrificed by making Collectors, Magistrates generally."[1] It went on to submit, for the approval of the Directors, a plan for having three separate European Covenanted Officers in each District, i.e. the Judge, the Collector and the Magistrate.

But with the commencement of Bentinck's Governor-Generalship there was a shift in the attitude of the Bengal Administration. A general transfer of Magistracy to the Collectors came to be accepted in principle. A number of factors could be responsible for this. In the first place, it would save money to have only two officers in the District instead of three (a Judge, a Collector and a Magistrate). And economy in the administration was one of Bentinck's primary concerns.[2] Paucity of covenanted civil servants was another factor that discouraged the creation of new posts of District Magistrates. The doctrinal support for the union of Magistracy with Collectorship came from the authoritarian paternalism of the Munro school. Bentinck, who had known Munro from the days of his Governorship of Madras, was influenced by his philosophy. As the best means of improving the efficiency of the administration, he recommended to the London authorities that they should "confirm and persevere in the system long since recommended by them to the Madras Government, upon the authority of Sir Thomas Munro, of uniting the appointments of Collectors and Magistrates, . . . of making the Collector's great office consisting of Deputy Collectors, Joint Magistrates, and Assistants, subordinate to one head . . . "[3]

Union of Magistracy with Collectorship had also been strongly

1 Judl. letter 22nd Feb. 1827.

2 Bentick to William Astell, Chairman, Court of Directors, 17th Oct. 1828, Bentinck MSS.

3 Bentinck's Minute, 10th Nov. 1831, Parl. Papers, 1831-32 Vol. 9, p. 749

advocated by Holt Mackenzie, in whose abilities and judgment Bentinck had considerable trust.[1] Besides, Bentinck had an enthusiastic support for this reform from the Vice-President of the Supreme Council, C.T. Metcalfe. The latter had ruled in Delhi territory, exercising himself all the functions of the Government, executive, fiscal and judicial. From that experience he had become an ardent champion of Munro's paternalism. He even went to the extent of advocating that there should be only one officer in the District who should combine in himself the functions of Judge, Collector and Magistrate.[2]

Under these influences the Bengal Government resolved in 1831 to make a general transfer of Magistracy to the Collectors. The practical justification given by Bentinck was:

"It became necessary to divest the Judges of their Magisterial powers, and there was no alternative consistent with the dictates of financial necessity than to transfer those powers to the Collectors .... I do not consider the latter measure to require any apology. On the contrary I hold it to be admirably calculated to confer efficiency on the Police of the country ..."[3]

Between 1826 and 1831 Magistracies had already been united with the Collectorships of Bhagalpur, Birbhoom, Rajshahi, Purnea, Allahabad, Benares City, Tirhoot and Jessore.[4] A single Judge was placed in the joint charge of the two Divisions of Bundelkhand (North and South), but a separate Collector-Magistrate was posted in each.[5]

Regulation V of 1831 provided for the transfer of Criminal Justice to the jurisdiction of the District Judges. This implied the transfer of Magistracy from the Judges to the Collectors in the Districts where the operation of this Regulation was to be extended in due course.* Following the implementation of the

[1] Mackensie had been recommended to Bentinck by Malcolm, the Governor of Bombay, as the "cleverest man in Bengal". Bentinck MSS., Memo of Malcolm, 24th June 1828. Bentinck seems to have agreed with the above opinion. He described to Mackensie as by far 'the ablest of the Company's servants'. Bentinck MSS. Bentinck to Melville, 16th Dec. 1828.

[2] Minute of Metcalfe, 11th April 1831, Parl. Branch Colls., 1832, No. 77. Appx. IV. No. 6.

[3] Judl. letter, 15th Sept. 1831, para. 17.

[4] Judl. letter, 6th Sept. 1831.

[5] *Ibid.*

* This followed from the principle that the committing authority, i.e. the Magistrate, and the trying authority i. e. the Sessions Judge, could not be the same individual.

above Regulation in the Districts of Agra, Merrut, Moradabad, Saharanpur and the Central Division of Cuttack, Magistracy was united with the Collectorship in each of them on 17th June 1832.[1]

In 1814 the Directors had strongly recommended the union of Magistracy with Collectorship. But by 1832 there had been a complete transformation in their attitude. In their despatch of 1832 they fully agreed with the objections stated by the S.D.A. fifteen years earlier,[2] and in accordance with the three-officer plan submitted by the Amherst Government (in the Judicial Letter of 30th August 1827) they instructed the Bentinck administration: "He accordingly direct that in the existing Zillahs, the ordinary European establishment consist of a Judge, a Magistrate and a Collector, each having its separate proper functions with separate Assistants."[3]

This change in the Directors policy was not abrupt. To understand this it would be worthwhile examining the history of policy-making at the London end over this issue.

The judicial despatches to Madras and Bengal of 1814 which suggested the transfer of Magistracy to the Collectors, and the grant of certain Civil judicial powers to them. Marked the culmination of a reaction against Cornwallis's system. This had to a great extent been influenced by Munro. He was a strong critic of the Permanent Settlement and the over-concentration of power in the hands of District Judges, which had made the Collectors weak and inefficient. Munro had come to London on leave in 1808 and lived there until 1814. His ideas gained complete ascendancy at the Board through James Cumming, who had become the Head of the Revenue and Judicial Departments in 1807. Buckinghamshire, who became President of the Board in 1812, and the latter's friend and son-in-law, John Sullivan, who was appointed one of the Assistant Commissioners of the Board.[4]

The Directors, too, were impressed with Munro's reasonings. In 1810 they positively forbade Minto to extend the Permanent Settlement to the Ceded and Conquered Provinces. One of the Directors, Davis, who had personally observed the working of

[1] Civ. Judl. Cons. , 23rd Feb. 1833, No. 3.

[2] See above.

[3] Judl. Despatch to Bengal, 1st Feb. 1832.

[4] C. H. Philips, *East India Company*, pp. 202-4.

Cornwallis's system in India, was very critical of it.[1] The alarming state of arrests before the Civil Courts and the delays involved in the disposal of suits also convinced them of the necessity of reform in the Cornwallis system.

Thus, though hopelessly divided on other issues, in 1814 the Court and the Board found themselves in agreement over the need for reform in the Madras and Bengal administrations, particularly the judicial side.[2] The Directors, however, wished to call for reports from the Presidencies before suggesting reforms, but the Board insisted on rushing them through without delay, commenting that in view of the information elicited by the 5th Report of the Select Committee, they could not permit "without modification or improvement the continuance of a system which, however excellent in principle, has not only in practice proved inadequate to the beneficient purposes of its author, but has had the effect in some degree of increasing the evils which it was intended to remove."[3]

A special committee of the Directors drew up a draft in 1813 for the reorganisation of the judicial system in Madras. The same plan was suggested to the Bengal Government by the Judicial Despatch of 9th Nov. 1814. The salient features of the plan were the transfer of Magistracy to Collectors and the creation of village Munsiffs and officially regulated Panchayets. This was exactly what Munro had proposed in 1808 in a memoir written just after his return from Madras.[4]

In Madras the plan advocated by the home government was implemented immediately in 1816 under the personal supervision of T. Munro who was sent out to that Presidency in 1815 for the specific purpose of carrying out administrative reforms. But the Bengal Government, who just before the arrival of the London despatch of 9th November 1814, had adopted a scheme of reforms to reduce arrears and ensure speedy decision of suits, were keen to observe the working of their own reforms first. They adopted a cautious and go-slow policy over the Directors' instructions.

[1] Dissent of Davis, 9th August, 1817, I.C. Appx. Court. Minutes, Vol. 3.

[2] C.H. Philips, *op. cit.*, p. 200.

[3] Board to Court, 13th Jan. 1814, I.C. Letters from Board to E.I. Company, Vol. 4, pp. 1234-66.

[4] Memoir on the Judicial System by Munro, Edinburgh, 10th Sept. 1808, Melville Papers, National Library of Scotland, MS 12, ff. 187-9.

They called for opinions from the judicial and revenue authorities in Bengal on the practicability of their adoption. They also called for a report from the Madras authorities on the working of the system there. This has been noticed earlier.[1]

For several years the Directors seemed to adhere firmly to the instructions conveyed in the despatch of 9th November 1814.[2] But after 1824 they started drifting away from the stand they had taken in 1814. By 1828 the Directors had already become lukewarm in their insistence upon the transfer of Magistracy to the Collectors. Thus, while in 1824[3] they had strongly disapproved of John Adam's appointments of separate Magistrates, in 1828[4] they sanctioned such appointments whenever they were considered necessary. This was in response to the arguments advanced by the Amherst Government in 1827, against the union of Magistracies with Collectorships in general.[5]

The factors influencing the change in the attitude of the Directors were, apparently, the practical difficulties in the execution of their plan, which were expressed by the authorities in Bengal from time to time, and also the Madras Report[6] which showed that the system had not been very successful there. But a change in the personnel of the Direction was also responsible for the pull back towards Cornwallis's ideals. The retirement of Samuel Davis in 1818 had removed from the Court a very strong anti-Cornwallis influence.[7] The election of N. B. Edmonstone in 1820 and H. G. Tucker in 1826 to the Court,[8] on the other hand, introduced a very strong pro-Cornwallis influence in the Direction. Both of them had served in Bengal during the time of Cornwallis and both had shared his ideals.

The Board, on the other hand, remained rigid on the proposal of 1814. For the sake of consistency they desired to expunge anything from the Court's draft which involved any deviation from the tenor of the instructions conveyed to Bengal in 1814. In 1827

1 See above.
2 See above.
3 Judl. Despatch, 23rd July 1824, para 15.
4 Judl. Despatch, 30th April 1828, para 19.
5 See above.
6 See above.
7 See above.
8 Dodwell & Miles, *List of Bengal Civil Servants*.

Tucker, along with another Director, G. A. Robinson, strongly criticized this attitude of the Board.

Tucker said :

"The Board of Commissioners seem anxious to avoid inconsistency in the public correspondence; but if the authorities in this Country were led to adopt vague and erroneous notions in 1814 . . . it is surely their duty to get, as soon as possible, into the right path . . . "[1]

The Directors had become opposed to any major deviation from Cornwallis's principles. They found Bentinck's constituting the Revenue Commissioners into Judges of Circuit, or Criminal Judges highly objectionable in principle. In 1831 they were only prevented by the Board's interference from sending a strong disapproval of this measure to Bengal.[2] And, finally, in their despatch of 1832, mentioned above, they ordered the creation of separate Magistracies in each District, instead of joining them with the Collectorships. The desiring of such a measure in the face of financial difficulties of Company's administration and of an acute shortage of European Civil Servants indicated that Munro's ideas had become a spent force at the Directors, end while Cornwallis's ideas still held firm ground.

But at the time when the Directors were changing their views the Munro doctrine was dominating the Bengal administration, through Bentinck and Metcalfe. It was natural that the Bengal Government so constituted should have shown reluctance to put the clock back by divesting the Collectors of their Magisterial powers. This would have destroyed his image of the "benevolent autocrat", the Ma-Bap (father and mother) of the District, which the champions of Munro's authoritarian paternalism wanted to keep. Throughout his Governor-Generalship Bentinck remained opposed even to opening a discussion on the separation of Magistracy from Collectorship. He argued that the unification of the two offices had been effected after much deliberation, and a discussion for its revision could be opened with propriety only when it could be proved by positive evidence that the deterioration of Police could be attributed to the Magistracy being joined to the fiscal authority.[3]

Auckland, who succeeded Bentinck in 1836, accepted the

[1] Dissent of Tucker, Court Minutes, 14th Feb. 1827, Vol. 134, pp. 623-29.

[2] Court Minutes, 2nd Feb. 1831, Vol. 138 (n.p.)

[3] Judl. Letter, 21st June 1836, para 84.

"three officer" scheme approved by the Directors. But due to the practical difficulty of providing enough covenanted Civil Servants to fill the posts of Magistrates, the separation of Magistracy from Collectorship was very gradual. Besides, this separation was confined to the Districts of Lower Provinces only. Thus, by 1841, separate Magistrates could be provided for only eleven out of the twenty-nine Districts of the Lower Provinces.[1] The number increased to twenty-four in 1850 and to forty-five in 1856.[2] For various considerations Canning finally decided to reunite the Magistracy with the Collectorships in all the Districts after 1859. But simultaneously separate Superintendents of Police were appointed to every District. This made the burden of Magistracy lighter. The Collector henceforth came to be designated the District Magistrate and Collector, a position he has retained ever since.

[1] *India Register.*
[2] *Ibid.*

Chapter V

THE PROVINCIAL COURTS OF APPEAL

Origin

BEFORE 1793 THE only Courts of Appeal were the S.D.A. and S.M.A., which functioned at Calcutta. In 1793 the judicial tribunals in the Districts were considerably increased.[1] This in turn brought about the danger of a flooding of the S.D.A. by the appeals from their decisions. The S.D.A. might not be equal to the business coming up from the District Courts. Hence in 1793 Cornwallis established a number of Provincial Courts to buffer the flow of appeals from the lower Courts in the Mofussil. Another idea behind the creation of Provincial Courts was to make the facilities to appeal more accessible to the people living in distant areas. The S.D.A. functioning at Calcutta was beyond the reach of many on account of distance, delay and expense.

In 1793 four Provincial Courts, called "Provincial Courts of Appeal and Circuit" were established at Calcutta, Murshidabad, Dacca and Patna. A fifth Court was constituted at Benares in 1795. In 1803 the sixth and the last Court was created at Barailly to cater for the newly acquired area known as the Ceded and Conquered Provinces.

Constitution

The number of Districts under the control of each Provincial Court varied. Murshidabad, Dacca and Benares Divisions each had seven Districts under them. Calcutta and Barailly had nine each while Patna had only six.

Under Regulation V (Section 2) of 1793, the Courts were to be

[1] The number of District Courts was increased from 18 to 26 in 1793. See Chap. III.

constituted by three Judges. But this number was found inadequate. The Provincial Courts were also the Courts of Circuit or the primary Courts for Criminal trials. To discharge the latter duty one of their Judges, by rotation, had to be constantly on "Circuit" at the District Headquarters for performing the "Jail deliveries". These circuits had to be so arranged that there was one "Jail delivery" in each District at least once every six months. But the number of criminal trials were often very large and their investigation took a very long time. Hence the Judge going out on the Circuit seldom managed to return to his Station before it was time for his successor to commence his allocated Circuit.[1] In the Division of Dacca, on account of the heavy accumulation of trials during 1800-2, all the circuits considerably exceeded the duration of six months.[2] Disposal of prisoners held in custody awaiting trial being given top priority, it often became necessary for the next Judge to begin his Circuit on time, while the one performing before him was still away. This left only one Judge in the Court while at least two were required to sit on the Civil appeals. And in case of a difference of opinion the casting voice of a third Judge also became necessary.

To prevent the Court's business from being at a standstill when two Judges happened to be away on Circuit, a Regulation was passed in 1810, which allowed single Judges to sit upon the Civil appeals.[3] But this did not go far enough as the Judges sitting alone were only authorised to confirm the decision of the lower Court. The opinion of at least two Judges was still required to reverse or alter a decision.

It was becoming obvious that the Courts could not cope with its Civil and Criminal duties with only three Judges. Already in 1802 when the arrears of Civil appeals before the Dacca Court had become very high (538), a fourth Judge was temporarily provided for that Court.[4] But later a similar request from the Patna Provincial Court on identical grounds was turned down for financial reasons.[5] It was not until 1814 that the strength of the

[1] 5th Report of Select Committee of House of Commons, *Parl. Branch Colls.*, 1812, Vol. 56, pp. 67-69.

[2] *Ibid.*

[3] Regn. XIII of 1810.

[4] Civ. Judl. Cons., 22nd April, 1802, No. 3.

[5] Civ. Judl. Cons., 17th Dec., 1811, No. 3.

Provincial Courts was permanently raised to four Judges each. This was done on a proposal from the Chief Secretary, Dowdswell, which was incorporated into Regulation V of 1814.[1]

The above arrangement was continued until 1829 except for the fact that from 1826 onward a fifth permanent Judge was provided for the Calcutta and the Benares Provincial Courts. This was done on account of the heavy accumulation of business before those Courts.[2]

In 1829 the Criminal duties of the Provincial Courts were transferred to the Commissioners of Revenue and Circuit. The Provincial Courts being relieved of a major part of their business, the number of their Judges was cut down. Thus only two Judges were left in the Dacca, Patna, Murshidabad and Barailly Courts, while Calcutta and Benares which so far had Five Judges each were now left with three each.

Powers and Functions

In 1793 the Provincial Courts were constituted entirely as Courts of appellate jurisdiction. At first an appeal was allowed to these Courts from all decisions of District Judges and Registers. But such a wide scope of appeals having been found unmanageable, in 1795 appeals to the Provincial Courts were restricted to causes of more than Rs. 25.00 in amount or value.[3] The Decrees of District Judges were to be final on appeals from decisions of Registers and Munsiffs in cases of less than Rs. 25.00[4]

In 1800 the District Registers were empowered to hear appeals from the decisions of Munsiffs, who tried causes of up to Rs. 50.00.[5] A second appeal was allowed to the District Judge from the decision of the Register. As many of the causes tried in the first instance by the Munsiffs were of more than Rs. 25.00 in accordance with Regulation XXXVI of 1795, still another appeal lay to the Provincial Court, this time from the decision of the District Judge on the Second Appeal, The normal practice being to allow two appeals at the most, the

[1] Proposal of Dowdswell summed up in Edmonstone's (Member of Council) minute, 12th March 1814, Civ. Judl, Cons., 12th March, 1814, No. 13.

[2] Judl. Letter, 30th August 1827.

[3] By Regn. XXVI of 1795.

[4] *Ibid.*

[5] See Chapter II.

above Regulation had to be modified for the sake of preventing excessive litigation. By Regulation XLIX of 1803, the appellate authority of the Registers was withdrawn and appeals to the Provincial Courts were restricted to those cases only which were tried in the first instance by the District Judges, or to second appeals from the decisions originally passed by the Registers and Sadr Amins. This rule was further modified by Regulation XXV of 1814, by which an appeal from the decision of the Registers in causes above Rs. 500.00 lay straight to the Provincial Court instead of going through the District Judge. The Provincial Courts were to continue admitting Special or Second Appeals from the decisions of Registers and Sadr Amins. By Regulation XXIV of the same year these Courts were authorised to receive Summary Appeals from the orders and Decrees of District Courts in cases in which the latter might have refused to admit an original suit or appeal regularly cognizable by them, or after having admitted it, dismissed the same, for default, without investigation into the merits of the case. In such cases, if the Provincial Court was convinced of the justness of the application by any party, it was to order the District Court concerned to receive the case and make a regular investigation.

The Provincial Courts were vested with original jurisdiction for the first time in 1808. By Regulation XIII of that year all suits of Rs. 5000.00 or above were made triable in the first instance by those Courts. So far all suits irrespective of the amount or value had been triable in the first instance by the District Judge. The following were the motives behind the enactment of this provision.[1]

In the first place it was designed to relieve the District Judges of a portion of the Civil business to enable them to devote more time to their Magisterial duties. An all-round effort was being made at that time to improve the administration of Criminal justice and Police.

The second reason was that this would reduce the expenses to the suitors in cases of higher denomination by allowing them only one chance of appeal instead of two as before. As a corollary to this, the trial and final settlement of claims would be expedited.

[1] Govt. to S.D.A., 2nd Dec. 1808, Civ. Judl. Cons., 2nd Dec. 1808, No. 9.

This argument was justified because the causes of higher denomination were mostly litigated to the end. This provision meant, in effect, that there was to be only one appeal in causes between Rs. 5,000.00 and Rs. 50,000.00 (if above Rs. 50,000.00 a further appeal would lie to the Privy Council), while in causes of less than Rs. 5,000.00 (i.e, of lesser consequence), two appeals were permitted. The apparent anomaly could be justified by pointing out that in cases of Rs. 5,000.00 and above, the original decision was already passed by a superior tribunal which gave a reasonable guarantee of correctness. If, at all, there was an error, the single chance of its correction by the supreme tribunal (the S.D.A.) could be an adequate security for justice.

Thirdly, there being three Judges in the Provincial Courts, the investigation of important causes involving large amounts or value would not be liable to interruption or delay, as they would be from the absence or indisposition of the District Judge, if the causes were tried in his tribunal.

The fourth argument offered was that in view of the general inclination to corruption of the Indian officers of the Courts, it was advisable to remove causes of importance away from their local influences or connections. If such cases were tried by the Provincial Court any pre-existing connections of the local Indian officers of the Zillah Court with the parties could not have a chance of influencing the conduct of the trial.

The last justification was that suits of material importance would under the new arrangement be tried in the first instance by Judges of recognised superior ability and experience.

In 1814, there was a strong move to make all suits of more than Rs. 1,000.00 triable in the first instance by the Provincial Courts. The idea was to provide relief to the District Judges as well as to obtain a greater uniformity of decisions in respect of causes of higher denomination by reducing the number of tribunals dealing with them. It was only on consideration of the inconveniences that many parties might have to suffer in repairing to the Provincial Courts, as also on account of the prospect of these Courts being flooded with small causes, that the idea was dropped. Causes between Rs. 1,000.00 and Rs. 5,000.00 were allowed to be instituted as before in the Zilla Courts but they were made removable to the Provincial Courts for trial in the first instance at the discretion of the latter or on application of the parties.[1]

Already the number of causes triable, in the first instance by the Courts was considerably increased by the enhanced valuation of landed estates. By Regulation I of 1814 (S. 14) the value of rent-paying lands was increased from twice to thrice the amount of annual rent payable on the land. The value of rent-free lands was increased from twelve to eighteen times the expected annual produce.

In 1817 parties were given the option of instituting even suits between Rs. 5,000.00 and 10,000.00 in amount or value in the local District Judge's Court.[2] This was done apparently for the facility of the parties who found it difficult to repair to the Provincial Court for the settlement of their dispute. Practical convenience of suitors was allowed to take precedence over the theoretical justifications (stated in 1808) for making all suits of Rs. 5,000.00 and above cognizable in the first instance by the Provincial Courts.

It has been said earlier that the Provincial Courts were only intended to be a sort of buffer between the District Courts and the S.D.A. They were hardly entrusted with any supervisory function over the District Judiciary beyond the power of hearing and deciding appeals coming up from the Zilla and City Courts. However, in 1814 a portion of the "Miscellaneous Business"* of the S.D.A. was transferred to them on the latter's recommendation.[3] The purpose had been to relieve the S.D.A. of a portion of that branch of its duties. The Provincial Courts were given control over the appointment and removal of Indian Judges and the Pleaders in the District Courts.

Mode of Conducting Business

According to Regulation V of 1793, the Provincial Courts were to hold sittings at least three days in the week or more often if necessary. In actual practice the Judges of these Courts found it necessary to sit on appeals six days in the week whenever they

1 By Regulation XXV of 1814.
2 By Regn. XIX of 1817.
3 Civil Judl. Cons., 19th July 1814, No. 6.
* This was in respect of appointment and removal of Indian Judges.

were at the station. By Regulation XLVII of 1793, at least two Judges were to hold a Court of Appeal and no Decrees of these Courts could be valid unless they had been passed by two Judges present in the Court. But later, on account of the accumulation of arrears of Appeals, and on account of the vesting of original jurisdiction with these Courts in 1808, it became necessary to increase the number of their sittings. Regulation XIII of 1810; which was designed to prevent the business of the Court from coming to a standstill when two Judges were away on Circuit,[1] was also intended to enable the Court to split into two benches at the same time. But a Judge sitting alone could only confirm the decisions of the lower Court. In case he disagreed with the verdict of the Court below and wanted to reverse or modify it, he had to wait until one or more of his colleagues could join him to hear the case. Regulation XIII of 1810 does not specifically state whether single Judges were permitted to sit on original causes instituted before the Provincial Courts under Regulation XIII of 1808. But this practice had already been adopted.[2] The silence of the enactment on the point assumed its continuance. By Regulation I of 1807, single Judges had been authorised to execute Decrees of S.D.A. or those of their own Courts, to receive and admit petitions for Regular Appeals, to summon and examine witnesses under requisition from the combined bench of the Court, to receive miscellaneous petitions, and to conduct correspondence with the S.D.A. or the lower Courts. These functions of the single Judge were continued under Regulation XIII of 1810 as well.

But trial of appeals by single Judges was often found to be inconvenient. In case of disagreement with the verdict of the lower Court another Judge had to sit who found it necessary to go through all the records again. This involved more time in the disposal of the case than if it had been brought at once before a joint sitting. Hence in 1819 Harington, the Chief Justice of S.D.A., issued a Circular Order to the Provincial Courts instructing

[1] See above.

[2] Thus in 1809 the case of *Parsan Lal* vs *Baijnath Sahu* (which had been transferred to the Patna Provincial Court from the Shahabad Court because the value of the suit was more than Rs. 5,000.00 was decided by Judge Hawkins sitting alone. See Chapter VI.

them to bring all the appeals at once before joint sittings,[1] It was, however, suggested to the Courts that whenever the accumulation of arrears made it advisable, the original suits should be brought before the Senior Judge sitting alone and the appeals were to go before the other two. If a fourth Judge was present (it may be recalled that in 1814 the strength of the Provincial Courts had been raised to four Judges), he might hold a second single bench for the trial of original causes.[2]

James Stuart, Member of Supreme Council (and ex-Judge of S.D.A.), attacked the latter part of the above order.[3] He argued that the arrangement of allowing single Judges to sit over appeals and original causes had been adopted when there were only three Judges in those Courts and because the weight of the Criminal business rarely left two Judges at the Headquarters for any considerable length of time. But after 1814 there were four Judges in all the Courts. The weight of Criminal business had also been reduced because the Circuits now became more regular. Hence in the existing circumstances the presence of at least two Judges at the station all the time could be confidently expected. The frequent presence of three Judges and occasionally even that of four could be hoped for. This not only rendered the arrangement of single Judges sitting over original causes unnecessary but added powerfully to the objections against it, which, according to Stuart, were serious. There would be a great practical inconvenience to the officers and Pleaders of the Court if they were split into two or three benches. The most important objection was that all the separate benches would be disposing causes with great haste, and to a great extent without any coordination between them. It was quite likely that separate benches would decide on opposite views or principles, which would be fatal to uniformity and consistency of decisions.

Stuart's reasonings against making single Judges sit on original trials are not convincing. At the District level all suits were being tried by a single Judge. His decision could be rectified by a combined Bench of the Provincial Court. A similar scope for the

[1] Circular Order of S.D.A. to Provincial Courts, 14th Jan. 1819, para I, Civ. Judl. Cons., 11th Jan. 1820, No. 8.

[2] Circular Order of S.D.A. to Provincial Courts, 14th Jan. 1819, para II, Civ. Judl. Cons., 11th Jan. 1820, No. 8.

[3] Stuart's Minute, 14th Dec. 1819, Civ. Judl. Cons., 11th Jan. 1820, No. 9.

correction of the decision of a single Judge of the Provincial Court, by a joint bench, lay in the Regular Appeal allowed to the S.D.A. If single Judges of forty-five Districts were trying and deciding original causes and appeals, why couldn't single Judges of the Provincial Courts who were supposed to be more experienced and mature do the same ?

But Governor-General Hastings agreed with Stuart's opinion and ordered Harington to modify his instructions to the Provincial Courts accordingly.[1] Thus the Regulation permitting single Judges to constitute benches became inoperative in respect of the Provincial Courts.

One of the basic principles of modern legal systems is that no person should be allowed to sit on an appeal from his own decision. Following this, an interesting situation developed in 1824 before the Patna Provincial Court.[2] On the Special Appeals (Nos. 4245 and 4431) before the Court, the First and the Second Judges held different opinions. In the normal course the cases would have been referred for the opinion of one of the remaining two Judges. But it so happened that Elliot and Flemming, the remaining third and forth Judges respectively, had both been concerned with the earlier decisions on the cases. The original decisions in both had been passed by Flemming, as Register of Tirhoot, and both decisions had been reversed on First Appeal by Elliot, while he was the District Judge of Tirhoot. Hence both of them were now disqualified from giving their opinion on the case.

Finally, on S.D.A.'s recommendation, Tippet, the Judge of Patna City, was temporarily commissioned to act as a Judge of Patna Provincial Court for the specific purpose of disposing of those two appeals.[3] The S.D.A. also informed the Patna Court that the same course of commissioning an acting Judge was to be followed in case all the four Judges of the Court might disagree on a particular suit, as they actually did on a Miscellaneous suit.[4] Although Regulation XIV of 1814 (S. 9.) had given to the Senior

[1] Minute of Hastings, 22nd Dec. 1819, Civ. Judl. Cons., 11th Jan. 1820. Nos. 10 & 11.

[2] Patna Provincial Court to S.D.A., 1st April 1824, Civ. Judl. Cons. 6th May 1824, No. 2.

[3] Civ. Judl. Cons., 6th May 1824, No. 3.

[4] *Ibid.*, No. 4.

Judge a casting vote, in case of disagreement among the other three Judges over any case, the S.D.A. held, nevertheless, that for passing a valid decision the Senior Judge must concur with any one of the other Judges. If he did not, an acting Judge was to be commissioned, to obtain a fifth opinion which could be reasonably expected to concur with one of the previous four.

In 1829 the number of Judges of Patna, Dacca, Murshidabad and Barailly Courts had been reduced to two and that of Calcutta and Benares Courts to three.[1] In the Courts left with the Judges only, the problem of a third opinion would arise in case of a disagreement between the two. It was provided that in such cases the Government was to be informed, and it would designate a third Judge to try the suit.[2] In 1830 six cases were reported from the Dacca Division on which the two existing Judges had differed in opinion.[3] The Government nominated Patton, a Judge of Murshidabad Provincial Court, to dispose of those cases.[4] In 1831 the two Judges of Murshidabad Provincial Court (Steer and Patton) having differed over a case the same was referred to Cracoft, a Judge of the Dacca Provincial Court.[5] But Cracoft's opinion differed from those of both the Judges of the Murshidabad Court. A fourth opinion now being necessary, Smith, a Judge of the Dacca Court, was deputed to decide the case.[6]

Working of the Courts

Until 1815 the gap between the number of suits instituted in the Provincial Courts and that disposed of was very wide. For example, during the year 1805, 1,878 suits had been instituted while the number decided was only 757 or nearly two-thirds; during 1810, the number instituted was 1779 and the number decided was 804, i.e. less than half the number instituted; during 1815, the number instituted was 1608, the number decided 594 only—almost one-third.[7] This naturally caused a mounting of arrears. On last January 1803, when the Baraillly Court had not

1 See above.

2 Civ. Judl. Cons., 28th April 1829, Nos. 3 & 4.

3 Civ. Judl. Cons., 20th June 1830, No. 6.

4 *Ibid* No. 8.

5 Civ. Judl. Cons., 7th June 1831, Nos. 5 & 6.

6 *Ibid.*

7 Parl. Branch Colls., 1832, Vol. 77 Appx. V, No. 16

yet begun functioning, the total number of pending causes before the five existing Provincial Courts was 1,107.[1] On lst January 1806, when the Baraiily Court had been in operation for nearly three years, the arrears had increased to 1,283.[2] This figure climbed to 2,909 on lst January 1811 and finally to 3,705 on lst January 1816.[3]

Occupation of the Judges with the duties of Circuit was the general cause of the accumulation of arrears of Civil causes.[4] At times, in some Courts, absence of a Judge on leave, or the deputation of another for conducting enquiries, were added to it. For example, not a single appeal could be decided in the Patna Provincial Court during the first six months of 1809.[5] The reasons were that the first Judge had been away on Circuit and the third Judge during the same period had been on deputation to Saran to enquire into the charges against the local District Judge, which occupied him for nine months.[6] Two of the three Judges being away for those six months, not a single appeal could be taken up for trial because single Judges were not yet authorised to constitute a Court of Appeal.

In 1808, these Courts were given original jurisdiction over causes of Rs. 5,000.00 and above.[7] It is not indicated in the half-yearly reports of the S.D.A. how many original suits were instituted before the Courts in the post-1808 period. But it is hardly likely that any substantial extra load could be caused by them. In fact the aggregate of suits instituted before these Courts seems to be declining after 1808. Thus 1878 suits had been instituted before them during 1805; during 1810 the number instituted was 1,779, and during 1815, 1,608.[8] Actually, no significant increase in the aggregate of causes instituted before the Courts could be anticipated from a mere transfer of more original suits to their cognizance. The reason was that the increase of original suits was balanced by a corresponding decrease

[1] Civ. Judl. Cons., 22nd Sept. 1803, No.7.

[2] Parl. Branch Colls., 1832, Vol. 77, Appx. V, No. 16.

[3] *Ibid.*

[4] See above.

[5] Judl. Despatch, 2nd June 1812, para 7.

[6] *Ibid.*

[7] See above.

[8] parl. Branch Colls., 1832, Vol. 77, Appx. V.

of appeals, which the Provincial Courts would receive if those causes had been originally tried by the District Judges, Hence, even the provisions of 1814,[1] which certainly brought many more original suits before the Provincial Courts, could have little effect on the total number of suits coming before them.

After the strength of the Courts was raised to four Judges in 1814, their disposal capacity was automatically improved. As a result, between 1815 and 1819, disposals led over institutions by an annual average of nearly 225.[2] To take particular examples, in the Calcutta Court, 906 suits were instituted in the period of five years between 1815 and 1819, while the total decided during the same period was 1,238.[3] In the Patna Court the total number instituted had been 1,027 and that decided 1,262.[4]

But this phase was short-lived. As with the Zilla and City Courts,[5] arreas before the Provincial Courts started increasing after 1820. The number of causes disposed of started lagging behind the number instituted. The reason was that the disposals remaining almost constant, there was an increase in the number of suits coming before the Courts. Between 1815 and 1819, 5,499 suits had been instituted and 6,626 causes had been disposed of.[6] This had given a total lead of 1,127 over institutions during that period. Between 1819 and 1824, 6,573 were decided (a little less than in the preceding period), but the number instituted had increased to 7,518.[7] As a result the arrears of pending causes before the Courts rose from 2,449 at the end of 1819 to 3,394 at the end of 1824.[8] The same trend continued after 1824 with the result that by the end of 1829 the arrears before these Courts increased further to 3,603.[9]

[1] See above.

[2] On 1st Jan. 1815, the arrears before all these Courts stood at 3,830; on 1st Jan. 1819, the figure was reduced to 2,703. Minute of Dowdswell (Member of Supreme Council), 22nd Sept. 1819, Civ. Judl. Cons., 5th Nov. 1819, No. 15 'A'.

[3] Parl. Branch Colls., 1832, Vol. 77, Appx. V.

[4] *Ibid.*

[5] See Chapter III.

[6] Figures compiled from the 8 Half-yearly Reports of 1815, 1816, 1817 & 1818, and the 2 Annual Reports of 1818 and 1819.

[7] Figures calculated from Annual Reports of those years.

[8] Annual Report for 1824, Civ. Judl. Cons., 19th Jan. 1826, No. 6.

[9] Annual Report for 1829, Civ. Judl. Cons., 31st May 1831, No.7.

* Causes of higher denomination were mostly appealed at least once.

The factors that could have contributed most to the increase of business before the Courts after 1819 were Special Appeals and separation of Magistracy from the District Judges.

The provision of admission of Second of Special appeals by the Provincial Courts was made by Regulation XIX of 1803. The Courts were authorised by that Regulation to admit a Special Appeal, if from the perusal of the Decree and papers of the lower Court, the Judges considered a further investigation desirable. Under the discretion allowed by the Regulation the number of Special Appeals admitted must have been considerable. It has not been possible to ascertain from the Half-yearly Reports the proportion of Special Appeals admitted because the figures for Special Appeals, Regular Appeals and original suits admitted arc all combined under the heading of "Suits Instituted". Nevertheless some particular instances are found which support the above presumption. For example, in 1814, the Judges of Patna and Murshidabad Provincial Courts wrote to the Government that admission of "Second Appeals" in petty cases retarded the decision of causes of greater value or importance.[1] It was stated by the Murshidabad Court that of 100 appeals filed during the first 6 months of 1814, thirty-six or more than one-third had been "Special Appeals" for petty amounts.[2]

By allowing a second chance for the correction of a decision by a higher tribunal, it was expected to eliminate, to a greater degree, the errors or injustices committed by two successive tribunals. The system of Special Appeals was created on this liberal principle.

But a wide application of this principle having contributed to the accumulation of arrears the admission of Second Appeals was considerably restricted in 1814. By Regulation XXVI of 1814 (which became operative from lst Feb. 1815) the Provincial Courts and the S.D.A. were allowed to admit such appeals only when the judgment of the last Court appeared, on its face, to be inconsistent with any of the laws and Regulations in force, or with any established judicial precedent. This greatly narrowed down the discretion cf the Judges in admitting those appeals.

Between 1815 and 1819, there had been an all round reduction

[1] Home Misc. Series, Vol. 775, ff. 4-5, paras. 5 & 8; f. 12, para 2.
[2] *Ibid.*, f. 4.

of arrears.[1] A feeling of confidence in the ability of the existing judicial machinery to cope with available business was growing as a result. This led to the liberalisation of the admission of Special Appeals, which had always been accepted as a desirable system. By Regulation XIX of 1819 the Provincial Courts and the S.D.A. were allowed a general discretion of admitting a Special Appeal whenever on a perusal of a Decree of the lower Court there might appear a "strong or probable" ground for presuming a failure of justice. The Judges were thus given a very wide discretion.

Under the lattitude allowed by the above Regulation the Special Appeals before the Provincial Courts must have increased. Between 1821 and 1825 the proportion of Special Appeals in relation to the total number of causes admitted in all the Courts annually fluctuated between 23 and 30 percent.[2] On this account and in view of the fact that the arrears before the Provincial Courts and and the S.D.A. had started accumulating again after 1819, it was once again sought to limit the admission of Special Appeals. By Regulation II of 1825, the enactment of 1819, (which had liberalised the admission of such appeals), was rescinded, and the rules (restricting the admission of Special Appeals to cases accompanied with certain specific circumstances) prescribed by Regulation XXVI of 1814, were reimposed. But the Judges of the superior Court, who had become used to exercising a very wide discretion in the admission of those appeals after 1819, did not apparently pay much attention to the latest enactment. During 1825, 298 Special Appeals were admitted in the Provincial Courts; during 1826-283; and during 1827-289.[3] Their proportion to the total number of causes admitted remained nearly the same'* as that of the pre-1825 period above noticed. This drew a comment from the Government that the Judges had not been paying heed to the provisions of Regulation II of 1825 which was

[1] Arrears in the Provincial Courts as well as the S.D.A. had been considerably reduced in that period because more cases were being disposed of than were instituted. See above and Chapter VI.

[2] A table of Special Appeals admitted between 1821 and 1826 is enclosed in the Annual Report for 1826 (recorded in Civ. Judl. Cons. 28th Feb. 1828. No. 8. Vol. 39). The percentage has been calculated from the same.

[3] G.G.-in-C. to S.D.A., 28th Feb. 1828, Civ. Judl. Cons., 28th Feb. 1828, No. 9.

* Between 25% and 28%

designed to restrict the admission of such appeals.[1] They also strongly suggested the abolition & the system of Special Appeals altogether as they were sceptical about its utility.[2] They justified their opinion by a statement marked 'R' submitted with the Annual Report for 1826, which showed that, out of 188 Special Appeals decided by the Provincial Courts during 1826, not a single decision appealed from had been reversed. The S.D.A., however, emphatically opposed the Government's suggestion about the abolition of the system.[3] They informed the Governor General-in-Council that the Statement 'R' on which the latter had based their opinion, had subsequently been discovered to be erroneous. A corrected statement was now submitted which showed that, during 1825 out of 230 decisions on Special Appeals the verdict of the lower Court had been reversed or altered in 60, and during 1826 out of 188 decisions the Decrees of the District Court had been changed in 49. The Government were finally convinced of the arguments of the S.D.A., and Special Appeals continued to form a sizeable portion of the business before the superior Courts.

From 1823 onwards a policy of gradually separating the Magistracy from the District Judges was pursued.[4] Those Judges who were relieved of the change of Magistracy became free to devote thesr entire attention to the disposal of Civil causes. The increased disposal of Civil cases by that officer occasioned, in turn, greater influx of appeals before the Provincial Courts. This tendency was most noticeable in the case of the Calcutta Provincial Court. In most of the Districts under the Calcutta Division, the Magistracy had been separated from the Judgeship. In 1823 the separation was carried out in eight Districts.[5] Five of them, Hooghly, Jessore, Huddea, Rungpur and Junglemahal, were under the Calcutta Provincial Court. This must have been the factor causing the increase of business before that Court after 1823.[6] During 1823, 217 causes had been admitted before

[1] G.G.-in C. to S.D.A., 28th Feb. 1828, Civ. Judl. Cons., 28th Feb. 1828, No. 9.

[2] *Ibid.*

[3] S.A.D. to Govt., 15th Aug. 1828, Civ. Judl Cons., 2nd Oct. 1828, No. 4 B.

[4] See Chapter IV.

[5] See Chapter IV.

[6] Parl. Branch Colls. 1832, Vol. 77, Appx. V.

that Court. In the following three years the number of suits instituted increased as follows:[1]

During 1824—261
,, 1825—317
,, 1826—361

The arrears of pending causes at the beginning of 1823 had been 725. At the end of 1826 they had risen to 1,163, which forced the appointment of a fifth Judge to that Court.[2] A similar result could be anticipated from the separation subsequently made[3] in the Districts under the other Provincial Courts.

Abolition of Provincial Courts

In 1829 the size and functions of the Provincial Courts had been curtailed.[4] In 1831 Bentinck decided to abolish them altogether.[5] An immediate abolition would, however, have been impracticable as a problem of disposing of the causes already on their file would arise. Hence it was decided to retain the Courts until the pending suits were cleared and the alternative arrangements (to be described later) were implemented in all the Districts. Henceforth, the Courts were not to receive any fresh appeals and the vacancies (of Judges) occurring in the Courts by removal or retirement were not to be filled.

The abolition had originally been advocated by W. B. Bayley in 1829.[6] But his proposal had been shelved for the time, on account of the opposition of the majority of Judges of S.D.A., who apprehended an overflooding of appeals in the Sadar Court if the Provincial Courts were to be abolished.[7] But the proposal was revived by the Civil Finance

[1] Parl, Branch Colls. 1832, Vol, 77, Appx.V.

[2] See above.

[3] See Chapter VI.

[4] See above.

[5] Secy to Govn. Gen. to Vice-President-in-Council. 31st May 1831, Civ. Judl. Cons., 19th July 1831, No. 17.

[6] Minute of W.B. Bayley, 5th Nov. 1828, Civ. Judl. Cons., 12th Oct. 1830, No. 69.

[7] Minutes of Js. of S.D.A. On Bayley's proposal, Parl. Branch Colls., 1832. Vol. 77. Appx. V. No. 2.

Committee* in 1830.[1] They advocated that the Provincial Courts would be rendered unnecessary, if the scheme of enhancing the original jurisdiction of Indian Judges and of relieving the Judges of the Charge of Magistracy in all the Districts was adopted. Mackenzie, the Chairman of the Committee, considered the Provincial Courts useless in any case. He observed: "I consider them [Provincial Courts] to be bad Courts at present in general filled by men in no respect superior to the District Judges over whom they are placed, and their decisions are of no value as guides to the District Judges. . . ."[2]

One might agree with the latter part of the above statement, but it would be hard to accept the remark about the non-superiority of the qualifications of the Judges of the Provincial Courts. From the earliest days the Government had endeavoured to fill these Courts with men of ability or experience in the judicial line. In 1794, Governor-General Shore, considering the qualification of the members of those Courts to be of vital importance, had resolved that in future no person was to be appointed a Judge of that Court unless he had served for a sufficient number of years as a District Judge and Magistrate.[3] It was laid down by Regulation XXV of 1814 that no person could be made a Judge of the Provincial Court unless he had previously worked as a District Judge for at least three years or in any other situation in the Judicial Department for at least six years. In actual practice, however, an officer normally had to serve at least six years as District Judge before being promoted to the Provincial Court. In a service cadre qualification is measured by experience. Hence it is absurd to say that the Judges of the Provincial Court were "in no respect superior to the District Judges."

The most valid reason behind the abolition of those Courts was that under the reformed structure of Civil Judiciary adopted in 1831 their existence as a buffer of appeals between the District

[1] Finance Committee to Govt., 12th July 1830, Civ. Judl. Cons., 12th Oct. 1830, No. 1.

[2] Evidence of Mackenzie before Select Committee of House of Lords, 16th March 1832. Parl. Branch Colls. 1832. Vol. 77.

[3] Civ. & Criminal Judl. Cons., 24th June 1794, No. 6.

* The Civil Finance Committee had been constituted in 1829 by Bentinck for recommending administrative reforms for economising the expenditures in all the Presidencies.

Courts and the S.D.A. became superfluous. Under the new scheme, primarily based upon economy, the Indian Judges were vested with almost the entire original jurisdiction.[1] The District Judges by becoming a Court of Appeal from all the decisions of the Indian Judges, and a Court of original jurisdiction for causes of Rs. 5,000.00 and above, took over the entire role of the Provincial Courts. Hence the Provincial Courts could now be conveniently dispensed with. Their abolition was also to affect a good saving in the cost of judicial administration.

Position of Provincial Courts in Company's Judiciary

There is a good deal of truth in Mackenzie's remark about the uselessness of the Provincial Courts in furnishing guidance to the lower Courts.[2] These Courts could, of course, reverse or alter the decisions of the District Courts. But that was about all. They had no authority to control or guide those Courts. On all doubtful questions concerning the laws or regulations, and on all administrative matters, the District Judges were instructed directly by the S.D.A. The Judges of the Provincial Courts were authorised to issue orders or processes to the District Courts in connection with the cases before them. But if the District Judges neglected or disobeyed the precept, the Provincial Court could not punish the defaulters themselves. They were to report the matter to the S.D.A., who alone were entitled to take any action against the officer concerned.[3]

Cornwallis's intention had been to create a very strong institution of Distt. Judge,[4] which might have been incompatible with the latter's subordination to any other authority except the highest—the S.D.A. This is indicated by his remarks on the provisions made in 1793 for enquiry into the charges against District Judges. According to the rules enacted then, if a charge against any District Judge was preferred before any Provincial Court, the latter was not to proceed on it *suo moto* but had to pass the complaint on to the S.D.A. It was to make only such investigations into the charges which the S.D.A. might subsequently commission them to do. Cornwallis thought that if the Provincial Courts were

[1] See Chapter II.
[2] See above.
[3] By Regn. V. of 1793. S. 15.
[4] See Chapter III.

authorised to proceed with the investigation of the charges on their own "... they might from prejudice, misrepresentation or other motives, be induced to give a ready ear to them ..."[1]

He observed further, that:

"To delegate to the Provincial Courts ... such power would, in fact, be making the Judges of the Zillah and City Courts personally subject to their authority. This would soon deprive the Zillah and City Judges of all weight and consequence in the eyes of the people and lessen that respect which is necessary ... the Judges of Provincial Courts of Appeal should possess no authority over the Zillah and City Judges personally. Their control over them should be only that of a superior Court empowered to revise their decrees when regularly brought before them."[2]

Constituted upon the above principles the Provincial Courts did not naturally have much consequence. The chief reason was a lack of adequate authority over the judicial administration in the Districts. The Courts were, as stated earlier, merely to be a buffer between the District Courts and the S.D.A. Their prestige was reduced further when their function of Criminal Justice was withdrawn in 1829.

It was not without valid grounds that Galloway, a contemporary observer; complained in the 1830s:

"At present the Provincial Courts are held in very little esteem, either by the Natives or by the Judicial branch of the service generally. The reason seems plain: they are vested with very little power ...; *quoad these*, therefore, the Courts of appeal are little better than offices for the transmission of causes to higher authorities ..."[3]

[1] Minute Cornwallis, 8th Feb. 1793, paras 65 & 66. Bengal Revenue Cons., 11th Feb. 1793, No. 1.

[2] *Ibid.* para 66.

[3] Galloway, *Observation on Law & Constitution etc.*, 1832, p. 368.

Chapter VI

THE SADR DIWANI ADALAT

Origin and Constitutional Development.

AS THE COMPANY took over the direct administration of the Provinces in 1772 a Diwani (Civil) and a Faujdari (Criminal) Court were established in each District. Two corresponding superior Courts of appeal were created in Calcutta at the same time. They were known as the Sadr Diwani Adalat and the Sadr Nizamat Adalat. The District Criminal Courts as well as the S.N.A. were left in the hands of the Nawab and his officers. This arrangement for Criminal justice continued until 1790 when the administration of Criminal justice was also taken over by the Company. The S.D.A. was to be constituted by the President and two other members of the Supreme Council at Fort William. In the absence of the President, a third member was to sit in the Court so that not less than three members were to decide upon appeals.

The Court started functioning in March 1773.[1] But it was abolished soon after in November 1775 by the Governor-General -in-Council for fear of a clash of jurisdiction with the Supreme Court. It was revived in 1780 after the culmination of the historic controversy between the Supreme Court and the Company.

In 1781 Hastings offered the post of Chief Justice of S.D.A. to Sir Elijah Impey who was to hold it in addition to his assignment in the Supreme Court. Impey produced a plan for judicial reform which was adopted by the Governor-General-in-Council in 1781. According to it certain changes were made in the S.D.A.

The Court, though remaining primarily a Court of Appeal, was

[1] Revn. letter from Bengal, 25th March 1775, p.2.

given a discretion to try any particular cause in the first instance if the Judges considered it to be of special importance. The Judges or Superintendents of the eighteen District Adalats (created in accordance with Impey's scheme) were put under the control of the S.D.A. Henceforth the Judges of the subordinate Courts were to be required to take an oath of loyalty and uprightness before the S.D.A. The S.D.A. were also authorised to frame rules of practice, and issue standing orders for administration of justice for their own conduct, as well as that of the Mofussil Courts. Thus the S.D.A. was given a new and very significant role—that of the coordinator of the judicial system. With the expansion of the judicial administration, this function of the Court became increasingly vital and extensive.

Impey also proposed some changes in the constitution of the Court. He wanted the Court to be constituted by the Governor-General-in-Council and the Chief Justice and the four Puisne Judges of the Supreme Court. But this proposal met with a stiff opposition from the members of Hasting's Council, probably because of their general dislike for Hastings and his association with Impey. Hence it could not be implemented. Impey himself was condemned in Parliament for his acceptance of an office under the Company's Government. He was removed both from the S.D.A. and from the Supreme Court in 1782. After Impey's recall the S.D.A. reverted to its original constitution (i.e. by the Governor-General and his Council).

In 1790, after Cornwallis decided to take over the direct management of the Criminal judiciary, the S.N.A. (which had so far functioned at Murshidabad under the Nazim*) was transferred to Calcutta and joined with the S.D.A.

The arrangements of 1793 did not modify the constitution of the Court. As before it was to be formed by the Governor-General and members of the Supreme Council. Although Cornwallis and his admirers claimed that the system established in 1793 was based upon the principle of separation of powers, the retention of the supreme judicial office in the hands of the supreme executive was an obvious contradiction. The "Glorious Revolution" had completely freed the English judiciary from the executive's domination, by the beginning of the 18th century. Hence this

* Reza Khan.

arrangement was not the transmission of a British idea but the continuation of despotic tradition inherited from the Moghul rule.

A combination of the supreme judiciary with the executive was assailable in theory and inconvenient in practice. It was left to the succeeding Governors-General, Shore, Wellesley, Barlow and Minto, to work towards the separation of the Court from the Governor-General and his Council.

Cornwallis's successor, Shore, first pointed out the risk of the abuse by the Governor-General-in-Council, of the uncontrolled exercise of ultimate judicial authority.[1]

In 1781, when the S.D.A. had been reconstituted, the number of judicial tribunals it was called upon to superintend was only eighteen. In 1790 the S.N.A. was also joined to it. In 1793 four provincial Courts of Appeal and Circuit had been established. Another was added in 1795. The number of District Courts had been increased from eighteen to twentysix in 1793. The management and superintendence of all these inferior Courts was S.D.A.'s job. Sitting as the Nizamat Adalat, it had to hear appeals direct, in all serious crimes, from the decisions of the Judges of Circuit (who administered Criminal justice in the Mofussil). Besides, it had to supervise the management of Police. In Civil cases the Court found great relief from the Provincial Courts which buffered the appeals from the District Courts. Still, the number of first and second or Special Appeals filtering through the Provincial Courts to the S.D.A. was found to be considerable. In spite of the limitations put on the appeals to the S.D.A. by Regulations XII of 1797 and V of 1798, one hundred and twenty four Criminal and forty Civil trials were received by the Courts during 1800.[2] At the end of 1801 one hundred and ten Civil and one hundred and twenty-two Criminal trials were pending before them.[3]

The volume of the forthcoming business required the attention of full-time Judges. The Court's functions could not be performed

[1] Minute of Sir John Shore, 29th May 1795, Civ. Judl. Cons. , 29th May 1795, No.10.

[2] Appx. to Minute of Stuart, 15th Nov. 1815, Papers on the Judl. System of Bengal, I.O. Reg. (71) 197.

[3] Civ. Judl. Cons. , 19th July 1814, No. 6.

efficiently by the ruling authority who were distracted by so many other problems. This reasoning was particularly valid in the case of Wellesley, who was so occupied with political and military affairs. It is no wonder that the first initiative for the separation of the Court from the Council came from him. Wellesley made out a very strong case for divesting the Governor-General-in-Council of their judicial functions in the S.D.A. He pointed out the theoretical objections first.

Justice in an open Court has been recognised as one of the basic guarantees of its proper dispensation. Following this principle the S.D.A. (like the other tribunals) was required to be an open Court.[1] But on account of the Governor-General-in-Council constituting the Court, this provision could not be adhered to. The Court's sittings had so far been held in the Council Chamber.[2] Neither the parties nor their Pleaders used to be present at any of the trials. The proceedings (i.e. the plaints, the written statements, the pleadings, the evidences and the judgments of the lower Courts) were all translated into English and then read to the members present, who then passed the decision. The reasons given for the Governor-General-in-Council not sitting in an open Court were, first, that it would be incompatible with dignity of the ruling authority to do so.[3] Secondly, their presence in the open Court would prevent the pleading of the causes with due freedom. "No Native Pleader would venture to contest his [Governor-General's] opinions, and the will of the Governor-General and not the law would be considered [by the Pleaders and the Suitors] as the rule for decision."[4] The Governor-General's ignorance of the local languages also made it impracticable for him to preside at the trials in an open Court, unless it was decided to conduct the proceedings in English and by English Pleaders.[5]

Talking about the dangers of the abuse of judicial power in the hands of the supreme legislative and executive authority, Wellesley stated :

"The honour and interests of the British nation and the sacred moral obligations which it has contracted by extending its dominions over the

1 By Regulation VI of 1793, S.6.

2 General Despatch from Bengal, 9th July 1800.

3 *Ibid.*

4 *Ibid.* 5 *Ibid.*

numerous inhabitants, . . . demand that every practicable precaution should be adopted to preclude the ruinous consequences of the abuse of power . . ."[1]

According to him the ideal state of affairs would be when.

" . . . the Governor-General-in-Council would be divested of the power of interfering in the immediate administration of the laws, and when his own acts in his executive capacity together with those of the officers of the Government in all questions relating to private rights of property, will be subjected to the cognizance of Courts of judicature."[2]

Wellesley wrote to Dundas that a few things were still lacking to secure the noble objects contemplated by Cornwallis. The first and the most important of them was the institution of a Court of S.D.A. and S.N.A. distinct from the Council.[3]

On the practical difficulties in the existing system, Wellesley observed :

"The extent and importance of the causes to be determined in these Courts furnished sufficient occupation to require from the Governor-General and Members of the Council the entire sacrifice of every other duty. and the Governor-General and the Members, therefore, had to keep content with either an incomplete and tardy administration of the highest judicial function, or the neglect of the arduous charge of the executive and legislative Government of this extensive Empire."[4]

But instead of making any abrupt change, Wellesley proceeded step by step. In 1801 the constitution of the Court was modified to the extent that it was to be constituted by only one Member of the Council, not being the Governor-General or the Commander-in-Chief, and two covenanted civil servants.[5] The Council Member was naturally (on account of his superior status) to be the Chief Justice. G.H. Barlow, Member of Wellesley's Council who presided over the Board of Revenue, was nominated to act as the Chief Justice. H. T. Colebrooke J.'H. Harington, both covenanted servants, were appointed as Puisne Judges. All these persons had borne a principal share in the framing of the system adopted by Cornwallis in 1793. This was advanced as

[1] Proceedings of G-G.-in-Council, 12th March 1801, Civ. Judl. Con, 14th March 1801, No. 2.

[2] *Ibid*

[3] Wellesley to Dundas, 5th March 1800. *Wellesley Papers*, Vol. II. p. 231.

[4] Proceedings of G-G. - in-Council, 12th March 1801, Civ. Judl. Cons., 14th March 1801, No. 2.

[5] *Ibid*

the reason for their selection.[1]

In 1805 Wellesley took the final step by providing that the Chief Justice too, like the other two members of the Court, was to be selected from amongst the covenanted servants of the Company.[2] Colebrooke was now appointed Chief Judge and Harington and Fombelle as Puisne Judges. The Chief Judge was to receive a salary of Rs. 60,000.00 per annum. The two Puisne Judges were to be paid Rs. 55,000.00 each.

But the Directors disapproved the complete separation of the Court from the Council. In 1807 they directed the Bengal Government to revert to the arrangement of 1801 by which a member of the Council was to be the Chief Justice of the Court.[3] They rejected the plea of principles and ideology. "We refuse to accept that the endeavour to secure the blessings of just law duly administered shall in any way be affected by the vesting of the supreme judicial power in the executive."[4] Earlier they had criticised the Bengal Government for having made such an important change without consulting them :

"... nor can we approve of the manner in which you have taken upon yourself to alter the constitution of the S.D.A. . . . We expect that no changes of importance shall actually be made till our opinion shall have been taken. . . ."[5]

One of the considerations which impelled the Directors was economic. Wellesley's wars had been very expensive. The surplus revenues from the newly acquired territories was not equal to the large loans contracted in India. During 1806-7 the deficit of the three Presidencies was more than £3 million sterling.[6]

[1] Wellesley acknowledged their contribution in his letter to Dundas dated 5th March 1800. *Wellesly Papers*, Mont. Martin. Vol. II, p. 231. Earlier he had referred to Harington (while the latter was acting as the Registerar of the Court) as the "ablest officer in the Court of S. D. A. . . . a person who possesses just pretensions to an eminent situation in the judicial dept . . . " Wellesley to Lord Clive, 29th July 1798. *Ibid.*, Vol. I, p. 327.

[2] Minute of G.-G.-in-C, 25th July 1805, Civ. Judl. Cons., 25th July 1805 No.14.

[3] Judi, Despatch, 7th Jan. 1807, I. O. Vol. I.

[4] *Ibid.*

[5] Judl. Despatch 17th Dec. 1806, para 39, I.O. Vol. I.

[6] 2nd Report of Select Committee of House of Commons, Parl. Paper, 1810. Vol. 5.

Hence the Directors had a natural reluctance to sanction any judicial reform involving increased expenditure. This economic consideration was common in their extreme reluctance to sanction the appointment of Assistant Judges,[1] and in their opposition to the establishment of the College at Fort William for training the officers of the Company. Besides, Wellesley's pursuance of an independent policy, in which he had Dundas on his side, had been consistently irritating the Directors.[2] A general apathy towards his reforms could naturally be expected from the Direction.

Barlow, who succeeded Wellesley in August 1805, completely agreed with latter's views. Though he carried out the instruction of the Directors by enacting Regulation XV of 1807, which provided for a Council Member to be the Chief Justice, he strongly championed separation. He justified the preceding Government's action, without prior sanction of the Directors, on the ground of the urgency of preventing an accumulation of arrears.[3] The number of Provincial and District Courts had risen from thirty-four in 1801 to fifty-one in 1807. Adverting to that and to the consequent increase in the number of Civil and Criminal appeals to the Court, Barlow asserted the necessity of maintaining at least three full-time Judges.[4] He therefore resolved to employ three Judges from the covenanted servants of the Company besides the Chief Justice, who was to be a member of the Council.[5] At the same time he urged the Directors to reconsider their instruction on the issue.[6] In the meantime Minto took over the Governor-Generalship from Barlow on 31st July 1807. He carried out the resolution of his predecessor. Barlow, who, after Minto's arrival, had reverted to his place in the Council as the President of the Board of Revenue, was appointed the Chief Justice. Colebrooke, Harington and Fombelle were to continue

[1] See Chapter III.

[2] Wellesley's policy over the issues of private trade and the establishment of the College at Fort William had annoyed the Directors most.

[3] Barlow's Minute, 23rd July 1807, paras 1 and 6, Civ. Judl. Cons., 23rd July 1807. No. 1.

[4] *Ibid. para 7.*

[5] *Ibid.*

[6] Judl. letter, 31st July 1807, paras 29-43.

as Puisne Judges of the Court.[1] In fact, the idea of having three Puisne Judges instead of two was a convenient arrangement in another respect too. The Government would otherwise have been faced with the immediate problem of finding an alternative employment for one of the three covenanted servants who had been sitting in the Court since 1805.

Shortly afterwards Barlow was appointed Governor of Madras. Colebrooke, was then allowed to succeed him both in the Council and in the Court.[2] Burnish Crisp was appointed the new fourth Judge. He was succeeded by James Stuart in 1810.

Meanwhile the pressure of business before the Courts continued to rise. The number of Criminal trials pending before the Nizamat Adalat increased from 170 at the end of 1809 to 234 by the close of 1810.[3] Civil trials before the S.D.A. swelled from 104 on 1st January 1809, to 224 on 1st January 1810.[4] The anti-dacoity campaign launched in 1808 meant a new load for the S.N.A. By Section 2 of Regulation VIII of 1808, all cases of robbery with violence were required to be brought before the S.N.A. for confirmation of sentences of the Circuit Judges. The number of such references alone was 346 in 1809. In 1810 it increased to 492 and during the first six months of 1811 a still larger proportion of 303 references had already been received.[5] The attention of the Court had been further occupied in the last few years with inquiries into the charges preferred against certain public officers.[6] On account of above factors and on the ground of his being unable to devote adequate attention to the business of the Court (due to his responsibilities in the Board of Revenue) Colebrooke made a plea for an increase in the number of Judges of the Court.[7] The Minto Government responded by passing a Regulation which provided that henceforth the Court was to consist of "a Chief Judge and of as many Puisne Judges as the Governor-General-in-Council may from time to time deem necessary for the despatch of the

[1] Minute of G.-G., 14th Aug. 1807, Civ. Judl. Cons., 14th Aug. 1807, No. 1.
[2] Civ. Judl. Cons., 27th August 1811. No. 1.
[3] *Ibid*
[4] *Ibid.* [5] *Ibid.*
[6] The most tedious and prolonged inquiries over those years had been in the cases of C. Boddam, Judge-Magt. of Saran, and that of W. Broddie, ex-Collector of Purnea.
[7] Minute of Colebrooke (n.d.). Civ. Judl. Cons., 27th Aug. 1811, No. 1.

business of those Courts."[1] The idea was to make the strength of the Court elastic. Under the above provision J.M. Rees, a Judge of the Calcutta Court of Appeal, was appointed officiating additional Judge of the S.D.A. This arrangement was stipulated to be temporary, to be discontinued after the arrears had been reduced. Still the Minto Administration informed the authorities in London that it was very doubtful that the existing number of permanent Judges could ever be equal to the business before the Courts.[2]

It was Colebrooke, once again, who initiated the final separattion of the Court from the Government.[3] He argued that being a member of the Government such as he was incompatible with being the Chief Justice of the Court. The former occupation hardly allowed any leisure which could be employed in the Courts. He informed the Governor-General-in-Council that his predecessor, Sir G.K. Barlow, had never been able to attend either of the Courts while ostensibly the Chief Justice of them. And whatever time he himself had been able to devote to the Adalats had been at the cost of neglect of his duties in the Government.[4]

In 1810 Charles Reed, an European settler of Purnea, had made some libellous remarks against Colebrooke and other Judges of the Court.[5] Those remarks had been made in a complaint to the Governor-General-in-Council. The conduct of the Judges in the investigation of charges against Broddie, the ex-Collector of Purnea, had been the main issue of the complaint. Although the imputations of dishonesty and collusion made by Reed against the Judges were found to be baseless and Reed was subsequently found guilty of libel by the Supreme Court, the fact of Colebrooke being a member of the Supreme Council caused considerable embarrassment to the Government. Colebrooke made this another justification for the separation of the Court from the Government.[6] He stated that if a Member of the Council was not nominally the Chief Justice of the Court there would be no excuse for mixing up the Government with the proceedings or decisions of the Court.

[1] S. 2 of Regulation XII of 1811.

[2] Judl. letter, 29th Oct. 1811, paras 17-19.

[3] *Ibid.*

[4] Minute of Colebrooke, 7th Dec. 1811, Civ. Judl. Cons., 17th Dec. 1811. Nos. 1 & 2.

[5] The case has been referred to in Colebrooke's above Minute, *Ibid.*

[6] *Ibid.*

Nor would there be any opening for venting libels against a member of the Government, under the cover of complaints to a competent authority, and with consequent impunity. If the Judges of the S.D.A. were answerable to the Supreme Court, as they would all be if no Member of the Council was nominally its head,* there would be no scope of preferring such charges before the Government and thereby creating an awkward situation for them.[1]

The other reason advanced by Colebrooke for the separation was the theoretical one that had been stated earlier by Wellesley.[2]

On the above grounds Colebrooke proposed that he should be allowed to quit his situation in the Court and the senior sitting Puisne Judge be allowed to succeed to it. Colebrooke was an influential Member of the Council. The Governor-General, Lord Minto, was an ardent believer in the ideal of separation of powers.[3] The proposal, therefore, easily got through the Supreme Council.[4]

J.H. Harington was appointed the new Chief Justice.[5] He was the second person to hold this situation without having a seat in the Council (the first had been Colebrooke, between 1805 and 1807). His salary was fixed at Rs. 60,000.00 per annum, the same that had been allowed to Colebrooke in 1805.

Until 1812 the Directors remained unconvinced of the need for having an independent Chief Justice. Replying to the Judicial letter of 31st July 1807,[6] they said: "Your statements of the expediency of completely separating the judicial power from executive are no doubt theoretically just, though hardly practicable ever . . . We see no inconvenience in placing one of the members of the Council at the head of the department [Courts] . . ."[7]

But in 1814, they sanctioned the separation made by the Minto Government, " . . . in view of the difficulties in the continuation

[1] Colebrooke's Minute, 7th Dec. 1811, Civ. Judl. Cons., 17th Dec. 1811, No. 1.

[2] *Ibid.*

[3] See Chapter III.

[4] Secy. to Govt. to S.D.A., 17th Dec. 1811, Civ. Judl. Cons., 17th Dec. 1811. No. 2.

[5] Civ. Judl. Cons., 17th Dec. 1811. No. 2.

[6] See above.

[7] Judl. Despath, 14th Feb. 1812, para 33.

* By St. 21 Geo. III. C. 70, the G.G. and Members of the Council had been made immune from the jurisdiction of the Supreme Court for acts done in official capacity.

of the earlier system of the Chief Justice being a member of the Council . . ."[1]

Like Wellesley, Minto had made this change without waiting for the approval of the Directors. But while Wellesley had been snubbed for having carried out such an "important change" without having obtained sanction from London, Minto's identical action got through without exciting any comment of that nature. Obviously the personal relations of Wellesley with the Directors was also responsible for the disapproval of his reforms.

It was enacted by Regulation XXV of 1814 that from 1st February 1815 onwards no person could be considered qualified to be appointed as a Judge of S.D.A. and S.N.A., unless he should have previously officiated as a Judge of a Provincial Court for at least three years, or have been employed in any other judicial capacity for at least nine years. By implication this further insured the separation of the Courts' personnel from the executive or revenue branches of service.[2]

Except for a short break during 1813-14, while he was away on leave, Harington remained Chief Justice of the Courts until 1820. After him, William Leyester was appointed to that situation in 1821. Leycester remained Chief Justice until 1829, when the distinction between the Senior and Junior or Puisne Judges of the Court was abolished.[3]

Although the permanent sanctioned strength of the Court in 1811 was only three, the services of an additional acting Judge were constantly retained. In 1816 the number of permanent Judges was increased to four. An acting fifth Judge was added besides. In 1823 two of the Judges were required to act part-time (two days in the week) on the Sadr Special Commission.[3] In view of that the permanent establishment of the Court was increased to five Judges. In 1828 the Court requested the Government to increase the permanent strength of the Court to six Judges.[4] But the Bentinck administration bent upon economy

[1] Judl. Despatch, 28th Oct. 1814.

[2] By Regulation III of 1829.

[3] The Sadr Special Commission had been established by Regulation I of 1821, to settle disputes arising out of settlements in the Western Provinces.

[4] S.D.A. to Govt. 5th Aug. 1828, Civ. Judl. Cons., 2nd October 1828, No. 4A.

was reluctant to make new appointments. Instead the services of two part-time Judges was made available to the Court. They were C.R. Barwell and N.J. Halhead, who held the offices of Special Commissioners for Calcutta and Murshidabad, constituted under Regulation III of 1828. They had their office at the Presidency. The work of their commissions did not engage them fully. Hence Bentinck resolved to make use of their spare time to provide assistance to the Courts by making them act as Judges of the S.D.A.[1]

In 1814 the Directors suggested the separation of the S.D.A. from the S.N.A.[2] They thought that the S.D.A. and the S.N.A. with two Judges, a Register and an Assistant each, would ensure a more convenient despatch of business by the Courts then under the existing set-up. Substantial objections were raised against this proposal by the S.D.A.[3] In the first place, a superior Court of appeal could not be constituted by only two Judges wiihout giving a casting voice to a third in the event of a difference of opinion. Thus if the Courts were separated they would at least require three Judges each, i.e. a total of six instead of five existing. This, coupled with the necessity of maintaining two separate establishments with a Register and an Assistant for each, would entail a considerable financial burden. Secondly, so long as offices of District Judges and Magistrates were united and the Judges of Circuit were also the Judges of the Provincial Courts of Appeal, a convenience of reference from, and a facility of control over, the subordinate judicial officers was insured by the union of Civil and Criminal Courts at the top. This advantage was to be lost if the Courts were to be separated. Besides, the S.D.A. found the proposed separation entirely unnecessary. Under the existing arrangement for distribution of business among the five Judges the Courts had been functioning very successfully. The arrears of Criminal business had been wiped out and that of Civil cases had been much reduced.

The proposal was therefore shelved at least for the time being.

[1] Judl. letter, 9th Sept. 1833.

[2] Judl. despatch, 9th Nov. 1814, para 66.

[3] S.D.A. to Govt. (n.d.) para 56, Papers relating to the Judl. System of Bengal, Reg. (71) 197, p. 56.

By 1826 the arrears of Civil causes before the Court had accumulated to 425, in spite of all efforts to keep them down. The Amherst Government, finding the situation hopeless, sought the sanction of Directors either for establishing a separate Court in the Western Provinces, or else for separating the S.D.A., from the S.N.A. The Directors reserved their opinion on the question of establishment of another Court in the Western Provinces, but permitted the Bengal Government to separate the Court if they expected that to be beneficial.

The proposal for establishing a separate Court in the Western Provinces was, however, getting more popular in the meantime. Hence the idea of bifurcation was not considered any more.

The establishment of the Courts at Calcutta meant great inconvenience to the suitors of the outlying Districts of the Benares and Barailly Divisions. Some of the Districts of Western Provinces, like Saharanpur and Meerut, were 900 miles away from Calcutta. The hardship that this distance implied to the suitors and the witnesses in those days of primitive transport can well be imagined. The Bengal Government rightly remarked that in the absence of a separate Court in the Western Provinces, justice was being virtually denied to the inhabitants of that territory.[1]

In 1820 Harington, the Chief Justice, had proposed the transfer of the seat of the Court to a more central place, so as to make it more accessible to the inhabitants of the distant regions.[2] But nothing came out. The Government appears to have ignored the proposal completely.

In 1829 W.B. Bayley, then a Member of Council, advocated the creation of separate Court in the Western Provinces.[3]

The Judges of the Court, particularly Ross, strongly objected to the suggestion on the ground that the existence of two Supreme Courts would destroy the consistency of decisions.[4] But both

[1] Judl. letter; 15th September 1831, para 15.

[2] Minutes of Harington (n.d.) para 22, Civ. Judl. Cons., 11th Jan. 1820, No. 8

[3] Minutes of W.B. Bayley, 5th Nov. 1829, Civ. Judl. Cons., 12th Oct. 1830, No. 69.

[4] Minutes of Js. of S.D.A. on Bayley's proposals, Parl. Branch Colls., 1832, Vol. 77. No. 2.

Bentinck and Metcalfe favoured the proposal. They were convinced that a single Court was absolutely inadequate to dispose of the business arising out of the two provinces.[1] The establishment of a second Court in the Western Provinces was considered necessary for "affording efficient protection to those living in the distant provinces", as well as for maintaining "an adequate control over the inferior tribunals".[2] But considerations of economy made the Government hesitant. The Finance Committee advised against the creation of another Court.[3]

In the meantime, however, the sanction of the Directors for the creation of another Court for Western Provinces was received.[4] The necessary arrangements were made at once.[5] The Sadr Diwani and Nizamat Adalat for Western Provinces began functioning at Allahabad in 1833. At first it started with only two Judges, Turnbull and Colvin.[6] By 1835 the number of Judges of the Allahabad Court was raised to six.[7]

The S.D.As., functioned until 1861. On account of the inconvenience of maintaining two different systems of Courts, the S.D.As., and the Supreme Courts were abolished and their jurisdictions were merged into the High Courts, established under the Indian High Courts Act of 1861.[8]

Powers and Functions

The S.D.A. had been instituted as a Court of Appeal.[9] Under Regulation VI of 1793 it was authorised to receive appeals from the decisions of Provincial Courts in cases in which the amount or value exceeded Rs. 1,000./00 Due to a heavy influx of appeals this limit had to be raised from Rs. 1,000./00 to Rs. 5,000./00.

The jurisdiction of the Court was redefined in 1814.[10] The Court

[1] Judl. letter, 6th Sept. 1831, para 20.

[2] *Ibid.*, para 18.

[3] Civil Finance Committee to Govt, 12th July 1830, Civ. Judl. Cons., 12th Oct. 1830, No. 1.

[4] Judl. despatch, 26th Jan. 1831, para 10.

[5] Judl. letter, 15th Sept. 1831, para 15.

[6] *India Register.*

[7] *Ibid.*

[8] For full discussion see Chapter VII.

[9] By Regulations XII of 1797 and V of 1798.

[10] By Section 5 of Regulation XXV of 1814.

was authorised to receive an appeal from all judgments passed by the Provincial Courts on cases tried and determined by them in the first instance.[1] A Second or special Appeal also lay to the Court, in certain circumstances, from the decisions of the Provincial Courts over regular or first appeals from the District Courts.[2]

The system of Special Appeals had been originally instituted by Regulations XIX of 1803, and VIII of 1805. By these the Provincial Courts and the S.D.A. were allowed to admit a Special Appeal in all cases not open to a Regular Appeal if the original decision seemed to be unjust or erroneous or if from any other cause a further investigation seemed desirable. The discretion allowed on admission of Special Appeals was restricted by Regulation XXVI of 1814. Under it no Special Appeal could be admitted by any Court unless the previous judgment appeared to be inconsistent with some established precedent or with some law, regulation or usages, or unless the case involved some point of general interest not previously decided by a superior Court. To discourage litigants from seeking a second appeal it was further provided that petitions for Special Appeals were to be presented on Stamp Paper. But the restrictions on the admission of Special Appeals were considerably relaxed by Regulation XIX of 1819.[3] By it the S.D.A., and the Provincial Courts were given a general discretion to admit such an appeal whenever—on a perusal of the Decree of the Lower Court--there might appear strong and probable ground for presuming a failure of justice. Besides, the District Courts were authorised to certify to the Provincial Courts, and the latter to the S.D.A., that a particular case in which no regular appeal lay to the higher Court involved some point of general importance hitherto unsettled. If a Provincial Court rejected a petition so certified by the District Court their order was not to be final. The party seeking a Second Appeal was at liberty to file a petition before the S.D.A., for admission. The S.D.A., if after the perusal of the application it thought it proper, was to direct the Provincial Court to admit the Special Appeal in question. Petitions of Special Appeals were, however, to be considered by at least two Judges. This was

[1] *Ibid.*, Cl. 2.
[2] *Ibid.*, Cl. 3.
[3] For reasons see Chap. V.

intended to introduce a greater circumspection in the admission of those appeals.

But the above relaxation having caused considerable increase in the influx of such appeals, particularly in the Provincial Courts, Regulation XIX of 1819 was rescinded, and the limitations provided under Regulation XXVI of 1814 were brought back into force.

In addition to the Regular and Special Appeals, the S.D.A., was made competent to receive Summary Appeals from the orders and decrees of the Provincial Courts "in all cases in which the latter may have refused to admit a regular suit or appeal regularly cognizable by them, or having admitted such suit or appeal, may have dismissed it on the ground of delay, informality or other default, without investigation into the merits of the case"[1] These appeals were, however, not to be tried by the S.D.A., itself. The Court, after a perusal of the application, was either to reject it or order the Lower Court refusing or rejecting the original suit or appeal, to admit the same and make a regular investigation. This process was also commonly termed 'Review'.

The Court was also authorised to exercise original jurisdiction. It was empowered to remove causes above the amount or value of £5,000 from the Provincial Courts and try those itself in the first instance. The justification offered was,

"... We conceive that substantial advantage would arise from the trial, in the first instance, by the S.D.A., of some of those causes of primary magnitude and importance in which not only the interests of the individual but those of the Government may be involved, and which may in their operation, possibly affect the general .... interests of the country."[2]

It was, however, not intended to burden the already overworked S.D.A., by making an extensive operation of this provision. The idea only was that should the Court find enough leisure in future the rule might be extensively employed.[3] The Court, however, never, found enough respite from the appeals and other business to be able to devote any time to trial of original causes.

[1] Regulation XXVI of 1814, Section 3, Cl. 2.

[2] Judl. Letter 29th Nov. 1814.

[3] Chief Secretary Dowdswell's Report on Judicial Reforms, 17th Oct. 1814, Civ. Judl. Cons., 29th Nov. 1814, No. 27.

As Nizamat Adalat the Court had to deal with all matters relating to the administration of criminal justice[1] and the management of Police and Jails.

It has been noticed earlier that the Court had been established in the role of the controller and coordinator of the entire machinery of judicial administration. Its function in that capacity came to be classified under the head of "Miscellaneous and English" business. These functions of the Court were summarised by Stuart in the following words:

". . . to watch over the whole vast organisation by which laws are dispensed . . . , to see that the Courts and judicial officers are in constant motion; that as far as may be practicable, justice is not denied or improperly delayed, . . . to attend to the state of Jails, the health, treatment and disposal of prisoners and convicts; to issue instructions to the Courts and officers below, in various cases requiring reference to the Court, or in which those officers needed advice, and finally to check all irregularities, abuses and misconduct. In the same Miscellaneous Department the Court conduct their correspondence with the Government, in which they have to report on numerous matters of difficulty, frequently to discuss plans for the improvement of the systems, and to frame regulations accordingly . . . . "[2]

This branch further involved all questions (excepting the trials of cases) relating to the S.D.A.'s own proceedings or those of the subordinate Courts, over fifty in number. A portion of the above business, like correspondence with Government or with the subordinate Courts concerning administrative matters, was carried out in English. This was often more specifically termed English business, as distinguished from the Miscellaneous which was generally conducted in Persian.

To aid them in their supervisory functions, the S.D.As., were given authority to suspend any Judge or officer of a Provincial or District Court, for disobedience or neglect of any process, rule or order issued by the Court, or for making a false return to it.[3] The

[1] All sentences of transportation for life, or of death, passed by the Judges of Circuit, and all convictions in cases of Robbery with violence by the Circuit Judges, were required to be referred to the S.N.A. for confirmation. Besides, all those cases in which the Futwa (opinion) of the Mufti (Law Officer) differed from the opinion of the Circuit J. were to be sent to the S.N.A. for final decision.

[2] Minute of J. Stuart, 3rd J. of S.D.A. , 15th Nov. 1815, paras 6-8, Papers relating to judicial system of Bengal, I.O. Reg. (71) 197.

[3] By Regulations II of 1801 and VIII of 1803.

S.D.A., could also suspend any District Judge for a neglect or disobedience of any order of a Provincial Court.

According to Statute 21 Geo. III, Cap. 70 (Section 21) of 1781, the jurisdiction of the Company's highest tribunal was to be final and conclusive in all cases (under its cognizance) up to the amount or value of £5,000 or Sicca Rupees 50,000./00. In cases of above that amount or value an appeal was to lie from the S.D.A.'s decision to the King-in-Council. In the case of Parsan Lal vs. Baijnath Sahu, however, the Court thought that their jurisdiction had been threatened by the Supreme Court and hence they made a loud protest to the Governor General-in-Council.[1]

The case in brief was as follows: In 1806 one Parsan Lal filed a suit against Baijnath Sahu for the recovery of certain property and sums of money. The case was originally instituted in the Shahabad Zillah Court where the pleadings were completed. The value of the claimed property and money exceeded Rs. 5,000/-. Hence, after the passing of Regulation XIII of 1808 which made all such cases triable in the first instance by the Provincial Courts, it was transferred to the Patna Provincial Court. Hawkins, the second Judge of the latter Court, sat singly on its trial. He decreed the case in favour of the Defendant Baijnath Sahu in 1812, both on the merits of the case as well as on the ground of the Plaintiff's suit being time-barred. From the Patna Court's decision Parsan Lal appealed as Pauper to the S.D.A. in 1814. The S.D.A. thereupon affirmed the decree of the Provincial Court on 23rd August 1816. Subsequently the plaintiff filed a petition for review before the S.D.A. This again was rejected on the 14th May 1819.

After this, in December 1819 Parsan Lal filed a Bill of Complaint before the Equity jurisdiction of the Supreme Court. In that he set forth the whole matter of his suit and charged that the Defendant had heretofore obtained the decision in his favour in the Company's Courts by fraud and collusion. He particularly alleged that the Patna Court's decree in favour of Baijnath Sahu had been obtained by corrupt bribes of money given to Hawkins, the second Judge, and to the officers of his Court. In May 1820 the

[1] S.D.A.'s report on the case of Parsan Lal *vs*. B. Sahu has been recorded under Civ. Judl. Cons., 30th Oct. 1822, No. 5.

Defendant filed his answer before the Supreme Court denying those allegations.

The Supreme Court at first issued a commission to the Judge and Register of Shahabad Court to investigate and report on the allegations of bribe against Hawkins. But this order was subsequently countermanded and another issued. As per the last order, the Bill of Complaint of Parsan Lal was to be retained in Equity till the following October to allow him (Parsan Lal) to prosecute Hawkins for bribery before the next session of Oyer and Terminer (The Criminal bench of the Supreme Court).

The S.D.A. regarded the Supreme Court's admission of a Bill pertaining to a matter already decided by them, as a direct infringement upon their jurisdiction.[1] They asserted that according to the sense of the existing Parliamentary enactments, any interference, direct or indirect, by the Supreme Court, to alter, modify, rescind or in any way discredit or invalidate any decision of that Court was illegal.[2] Such a pretension of the Supreme Court, as in Parsan Lal's case, they claimed, "must render the decisions of the Court [S.D.A.] uncertain and inconclusive, though the Parliament has declared it to be final and conclusive against every jurisdiction except that of His Majesty-in-Council."[3]

The Court also criticised the Supreme Court's nomination of the Judge and Register of the Shahabad Zillah Court, on a commission to examine the witnesses in respect of the charge of bribery against Hawkins. They considered the investigation into charges against a superior officer, by persons directly subordinate to him (such as the Judge and Register of Shahabad had been to Hawkins), as an extremely objectionable procedure.

Though the above objectionable course had been happily abandoned, yet the resolution of the Supreme Court to allow the suit of Parsan Lal to be retained in Equity to give him an opportunity of proceeding against Hawkins in the Sessions, had, according to S.D.A. , some serious implications.[4] If Parsan Lal's complaint was found valid by the Sessions and Hawkins was

[1] No. 6. S.D.A. to Govt., 27th Aug., 1823, Civ. Judl. Cons., 30th October 1822, No. 6.

[2] S.D.A. to Govt., 27th Aug. 1822, Civ. Judl. Cons., 30th Oct. 1822, No. 6.

[3] *Ibid.*

[4] S.D.A. to Govt., 27th Aug. 1822, Civ, Judl. Cons., 30th August, 1822, No. 6.

accordingly convicted by the Jury, the Supreme Court would continue the suit in Equity. They would regard the decree of the Patna Court and that of the S.D.A. confirming it, as nullities. The Supreme Court would then enter into the merits of the case and, if their view of the evidence were otherwise, they would award to Parsan Lal the estate which the S.D.A. had determined to be the rightful property of Baijnath Sahu.

The S.D.A. did not deny that Hawkins or any other judicial officer was amenable to the Supreme Court. But they asserted that if such corruption were proved, it should rest solely with the S.D.A. to make that a ground for a fresh trial or not. It would in no case have given that discretion to the Supreme Court.[1]

The Advocate General, Fergusson, considered that so far the Supreme Court had not invaded the jurisdiction of the S.D.A.[2] It would do so only if, after the trial of the original equity suit still pending, the Supreme Court gave a judgment which in any way affected the decision of the S.D.A.[3]

The Advocate General's opinion promised only the actual outcome of the Supreme Court's action and not its possible implications. It completely ignored the constitutional contention that the very fact of the Supreme Court having admitted a Civil action in Equity against a decision of Company's highest tribunal threatened latter's privilege. The S.D.A. was right to raise this important question of principle. But the Government seemed to be in no mood to pick a quarrel with the Supreme Court.[4] They kept silent, presumably in view of Fergusson's opinion.

By St. 53 Geo. III. Cap. 155, Cl. 113 of 1813, the S.D.A. was empowered to issue processes against individuals or property in Calcutta. The provision was intended to give the Company Courts a means of completing their investigation in cases when a person becoming subject to their jurisdiction resided

[1] S.D.A. to Govt., 27th Aug. 1822, Civ. Judl. Cons., 30th Aug. 1822, No. 6.

[2] R.C. Fergusson to Govt., 7th Oct. 1822, Civ. Judl. Cons., 30th Oct. 1822.

[3] The indictment against Hawkins failed before the Sessions. Consequently the Equity suit was also dismissed on 5th Nov. 1823.

[4] This point has been elaborated in Chapter VII.

in Calcutta or had his property there.* The question arose whether the S.D.A. could issue such a process only in cases actually before it or also in aid of the jurisdiction of the subordinate Courts. For the fulfilment of the intention of the above Act it was only logical that the latter course should be adopted. But the Clause did not clearly state that. The matter was thus left to legal interpretation.

In 1815 Advocate-General Strettel held that if an inhabitant of Calcutta who sued in one of the Zilla or Provincial Courts was cast with costs, the S.D.A. could not issue a process against him in Calcutta in aid of the Lower Court.[1]

He gave a similar opinion later in the case of *Dr. Smet* vs. *Native Resident.*[2] From the last opinion it could be deduced that if 'A' sued 'B' in the Provincial Court of Barailly and a decree was passed in A's favour, B not having sufficient property at Barailly to satisfy the decree but having some goods at Calcutta, the S. D. A. could not issue a process for the seizure of those goods.

In 1817, in a Criminal case against certain residents of Calcutta who were accused of being "accessory before fact" to a serious assault committed within the jurisdiction of the Magistrate of twenty-four Parganas, Advocate-General Fergusson gave a different opinion.[3] He viewed that the Court could in its Criminal jurisdiction issue a process of arrest against a resident of Calcutta, for a Criminal offence committed beyond the limits of Calcutta and consequently cognizable by the local Magistrate.

But in 1819 Advocate-General Spankie leaned back on Strettel's opinion[4]. When, in a case (*Bheemkhan vs Bhuwan Mohan Gosain)* an inhabitant of Calcutta refused to abide by the orders of the

[1] Strettel to S.D.A., 19th July 1815, Civ. Judl. Cons., 12th March 1819, No. 8. Encl. 'A'.

[2] Strettel to S.D.A., 13th Nov. 1815, Civ. Judl. Cons., 12th March 1819, No. 8, Encl. 'B'.

[3] Fergusson to S.D.A., 26th Feb. 1819, para 9. *Ibid.*

[4] S.D.A. to Govt., 6th March 1819, Civ. Judl. Cons., 12th March 1819. No. 7.

* Before the enactment of this provision the Courts of the Company found themselves absolutely crippled, once a person subject to their jurisdiction entered the limits of Calcutta or held or transferred his property there.

Provincial Court for payment of certain fees to Pleaders, Spankie held that the S.D.A. had no authority to issue a process within Calcutta except upon persons directly subject to their jurisdiction. In other words the S.D.A. could issue a process against a resident of Calcutta only in connection with matters before it and not in the aid of the jurisdiction of another Court where the case may be pending.

Referring to the opinion earlier given by Fergusson in 1817, the S.D.A. pointed out that unless a distinction was to be drawn between Civil and Criminal processes, Fergusson's opinion was at variance with those of Strettel's and Spankie.[1]

The Court decided to request the Government to approach the Directors for obtaining a clearer declaration by the Parliament of the powers intended to be given by the Act.* They rightly held that the powers as they now stood and had been interpreted, had to a great extent been defeated.[2]

The existence of the S.D.A. in Calcutta where the Supreme Court functioned affected its authority in some more ways.

The Judges of the Companies' Courts were authorised, by the Regulations in force to prosecute and punish any witness for the Crime of perjury. But while the Judges of the Provincial and District Courts could exercise this power without any hindrance, the highest tribunal, the S.D.A., was unable to exercise this authority. In 1807 Smith, the Advocate-General, ruled in the case of Maya Ram, who was alleged to have impersonated another person and given false evidence before the S.D.A., that the Court could not take cognizance of his crime. As the crime had been committed within the limits of Calcutta it could be tried only by the Supreme Court.[3]

The Court also found itself impotent to punish Europeans for contempt. Parties often employed the English Attorneys of the

[1] S.D.A. to Govt., 6th March 1819, Civ. Judl. Cons., 12th March 1819, No. 7.

[2] *Ibid.*

[3] Opinion of Advocate-General Smith on *Maya Ram's* case, vide letter to Govt. dtd. 16th March 1807, Civ. Judl. Cons., 19th March 1807, No. 5.

* The entire problem of obtaining Parliamentary enactments for legal reform in India was resolved in 1833 by St. 3 & 4 Will. IV., Cap. 85. which transferred full legislative authority to the G.G.-in-C. See Chap. VII.

Supreme Court for pleading their cases before the S.D.A. which functioned at the same place. These Attorneys who had a professional background and legal training naturally felt little regard for the Judges of the S.D.A., who, in spite of their judicial experience, could boast of neither. In 1828 one of the Attorneys, Allan Cameroon, grossly misbehaved before the Court and libelled the Judges in a case in which he had been employed by his client Fateh Yab Khan.[1] The Judges naturally wanted to punish Cameroon for contempt. But the Advocate-General held the view that the S.D.A. possessed no power to punish a British European subject for contempt.[2] He stated that the only punishment that the S.D.A. could inflict on Cameroon was to forbid him from appearing before the Court in future. The Court considered such a punishment to be totally inadequate. They therefore urged upon the Governor-General-in-Council to take steps to secure an enactment by which the Court could be empowered to punish a British European subject for contempt.[3] Such a power, they said, was essential for maintaining the dignity of the Court.[4]

Mode of Conducting Business

As described earlier the duties of the Court were divided into three branches—Civil, Criminal and Miscellaneous. Under the arrangements of 1793, the members of the Council used to sit three days in the S.D.A. The number of sittings of the Nizamat Adalat was not fixed. It varied from one day to three days in the week, according to the pending business. The Courts normally devoted one day in the week to the disposal of English and Miscellaneous business.

After 1801, when the Court was partially separated from the Governor-General-in-Council, the following routine of business was being followed :[5]

[1] S.D.A. to Govt., 30th Dec. 1828, Civ. Judl. Cons., 17th Feb. 1829, No. 15.

[2] S.D.A. to Govt., 5th June 1829, Civ. Judl. Cons., 14th July 1829, No. 3.

[3] *Ibid.*

[4] *Ibid.*

[5] Judl. letter, 30th Jan. 1808, para 31.

Day	Court Sitting as	Business transacted	Number of Js. sitting
Monday	S.D.A.	Trial of Appeals	2
Tuesday	S.N.A.	Criminal trials	2
Wednesday	S.D.A.	Hearing petitions and deciding on motions etc.	2
Thursday	S.N.A.	Criminal trials	2
Friday	S.D.A.	Trial of Appeals	2
Saturday	Joint Sitting	Miscellaneous and English Proceedings	3

As would be apparent from above there were three sittings of S.D.A. and two for the S.N.A. One day in the week was devoted to Miscellaneous business. On most days only two Judges sat in the Court. The third by rotation had to keep busy with preparation of decrees and other routine administrative matters.

After 1807 the assistance of four Judges was sought to be made available to the Courts. But so long as the Chief Justice continued to be a member of the Council his assistance to the Court was not very effective.[1] The actual working strength of the Court virtually remained at three Judges. In 1811 the Chief Justice also became a full-time member of the Court and the actual working strength was raised to four whole-time Judges. Even then the same weekly routine of business seems to have been continued. The extra assistance of a fourth Judge was utilised for the creation of an additional Criminal bench of one Judge.[2]

In 1816 five Judges were provided—four permanent and one acting. Simultaneously, a new arrangement for the distribution of business was adopted for the Courts.[3] Under it the day to day

[1] See above.

[2] Under Regulation XIII of 1810.

[3] The arrangement had been suggested by the G.G.-in-C. Vide Minute of G.G.-in-C. 16th June 1816, Civ. Judl. Cons. 26th June 1816, No. 4. the S.D.A. resolved to adopt it from 18th March 1816. Vide Civ. Judl. Cons,, 13th April 1816, Nos. 3 & 4.

routine English correspondence and Miscellaneous business was to be conducted by the Chief Justice, Harington, and in his absence, by the second Judge. The Chief Justice, when not occupied in the English Department, was to assist the other Judges in the disposal of Civil and Criminal cases. He was also to sit on trial of cases over which two Judges had differed in opinion.

The ordinary sittings of the S.N.A. and the other Criminal business not pertaining to the Miscellaneous department were to be held by the second Judge and the officiating third Judge. Both were to sit singly, except on cases which according to the Regulations required the decision of more than one Judge. They were also given the discretion to sit together on any other case which they considered important enough. This arrangement was, however, not to preclude the two Judges above mentioned (the second and the third) or either of them from sitting in the Civil Court, whenever they might not be engaged with the Criminal benches.

The ordinary sittings of the S.D.A. were likewise to be held by the two remaining Puisne Judges, the fourth and the additional fifth Judge. They too were to sit singly but had the discretion of sitting together on all important causes. When not occupied with Civil causes they were to sit on Criminal trials.

As mentioned earlier the Chief Justice was to conduct the day-to-day English correspondence and Miscellaneous business. But for dealing with matters of importance in that department, the Court was to hold one sitting every week. At least two Judges were to hold the Miscellaneous Bench with the occasional assistance of a third. The Chief Justice, being primarily concerned with this duty, was naturally to be one of them.

The above distribution had been primarily devised to expand the disposal capacity of the Courts. This had been found necessary on account of the increasing pressure of business, particularly Criminal, after 1810.

According to this arrangement, there could now be a simultaneous sitting of the Civil and Criminal benches. Following its adoption, the S.D.A. began sitting all six days in the week. The S.N.A. sat on five, while two Judges used to constitute a Miscellaneous bench on one day.[1] If single Judges were to sit all along over Civil and Criminal trials, it could be possible in theory to have $6\times2=12$ sittings per week of S.D.A. and $5\times2=10$ of the Criminal benches.

The arrangement was also designed to make individual Judges particularly versed in the Civil or the Criminal side. At the same time the scheme was based upon mobility. The services of all the Judges could be canalised to either department according to need.

This system was carried on through the rest of period under consideration. The increase in the number of the Judges after 1823 further facilitated its working. After a sixth acting Judge was added to the Court in 1826, the Courts could split themselves into three, four or even five benches at a time. But the system of 1816 was altered in one respect after 1820. That was in the mode of conducting English and Miscellaneous business by the Court.

Under Leycester's Chief Justiceship the Court reverted to the old system of conducting Miscellaneous business which ensured the participation of all the Judges in the perusal of that part of the Court's duty. After 1820 all the Judges of the Court started sitting together on Fridays for the disposal of Miscellaneous and English business. This was probably done in deference to the sentiments of the Judges who used to be left out of it. The business in this department often concerned matters of delicacy and importance. It involved control over the Provincial and District Courts, drafting of Regulations and other measures of general importance, like deciding doubtful questions arising out of the Regulations. On such issues the Judges often held different opinions. Hence they all liked to be consulted.

This, however, cut down the sittings of the Civil Court by one day because of all the Judges being required to assemble for Miscellaneous business on Friday. The existing arrears of business did not recommend this. Besides promptness and despatch could not be expected when five persons sat to take decisions on urgent administrative matters.

[1] Harington's minute, 5th February 1827, Civ. Judl. Cons., 15th Feb. 1827, No. 13.

In 1826 the Governor-General-in-Council pointed out the impropriety of this measure.[1] They suggested that only three Judges should conduct the Miscellaneous business on Friday so that the remaining two could constitute a Civil bench on that day.[2] But all the Judges except the fifth, Ahmuty opposed the proposal of the Government. On that account the matter had to be dropped.[3]

By Regulations XIII of 1810 and XXV of 1814 single Judges of Provincial Courts and S.D.A. and S.N.A. were authorised to hold sittings whenever considered necessary by them. According to the above Regulations the Judge sitting alone on appeals was empowered to confirm the judgment of the lower Court, whose judgment had been appealed against. His judgment confirming the decree of the Court below was to have the same effect as the one passed by the joint benches. But single Judges were not empowered to reverse or alter the judgment of the lower Courts. In such cases the opinion of a second Judge was also to be taken before a judgment could be passed. A single Judge could, however, determine the admission or rejection of regular appeals and his decision in that respect was to be final.

It has been noticed that under the arrangement for distribution of business adopted by the Courts in 1816, four of the Judges were authorised to constitute single benches.[4] But the provision of single Judges sitting over Civil Appeals was not much utilised because it was found to be inconvenient. The S.D.A. reported to the Government in 1817 that :

"... in the trial of appeals the S.D.A. have found it preferable to bring the case at once before a sitting of two Judges if practicable. By doing so not only the matter in appeal must necessarily be examined and determined by at least two Judges but if there appears to be reason for altering the original Judgement, a final decision to that effect can be immediately passed, instead of waiting for the investigation of another Judge ..."[5]

Harington, who was the Chief Justice during these years, remained a consistent advocate of the system of two Judges sitting on appeals. In 1820 he stated that "It appears to me

1 Govt. to S.D.A., 14th Sept. 1826, Civ. Judl. Cons., 14th Sept. 1826, No. 1

2 Civ. Judl. Cons., 14th Sept. 1826, Nos. 2 & 3.

3 *Ibid.*

4 See above.

5 Half Yearly Report of S. D. A., Civ. Judl. 4,. Cons., July 1817, No. 20

essential that the sitting upon appeals should be held before two Judges."[1] In 1826, as Member of the Council, he proposed an enactment for modifying the existing rules regarding trial of appeals by single Judges.[2]

The Government felt strongly inclined to enact the draft proposed by Harington.[3] But the majority of the Judges of the Court (Smith, Sealey and Ross) opposed this proposal on the ground that it would greatly reduce the disposal of appeals by the Court. The idea had, therefore, to be abandoned. All the same the Vice-President-in-Council directed the Court that the practice of two Judges sitting together on appeals was to be pursued as far as feasible.[4]

Ross was the strongest advocate of the system of single benches because that would insure a greater disposal of suits. Later, he even went to the extent of suggesting that the decisions of single Judges, when reversing or modifying the Judgment of the Court below, should be made final.[5] The Directors seemed to favour this idea.[6] They had perhaps also been influenced by James Mill who had suggested that all the Judges of the S.D.A. should sit separately, each deciding as many appeals as possible.[7] Apparently on account of these influences as the powers of single Judges of S.D.A. were enhanced, though not to the extent advocated by Ross and Mill. By Regulation IX of 1831, a Judge sitting alone on an appeal was authorised to refer the same back for retrial to the Court whose decision was appealed against, if there was an apparent fault in the latter's judgment. Single Judges were also authorised to admit Special Appeals.

Working of the Court

It has been attempted to make an appreciation of the working of the S.D.A. by analysing the data from four selected periods

[1] Minute of Harington, 4th Jan. 1820, Civ. Judl. Cons., 11th Jan. 1820, No. 8.

[2] Minute of Harington, 16th Dec. 1826, Civ. Judl. Cons., 21st Dec. 1826, No. 11.

[3] Judl. letter, 30th Aug. 1827, para 195.

[4] *Ibid.*

[5] Judl. despatch 11th Jan. 1832, para 4.

[6] *Ibid.*

[7] Evidence of James Mill before Select Committee of House of Lords, 29th June 1832, Parl. Branch Colls. 1832, Vol. 77, pp. 119-28.

of seven years each. The periods considered are :

1) 1801- 7;
2) 1808-14;
3) 1815-21;
and 4) 1822-28.

The above division has been deemed convenient because it enables the influences of policies and other factors on the working of the Court to be traced best.

The following table shows the working of the S.D.A. over those four periods:[1]

Period	Total number of suits Instituted	Total number decided	Average number Instituted annually	Average number decided annually	Lead of average annual disposal over Institution
1801- 7	367	373	52.4	53.2	+.8
1808-14	589	328	84	47	—37
1815-21	844	953	120.6	136.1	+15.5
1822-28	937	762	134	109	–25

It is clear from the above figures that in the first period disposals managed to keep just abreast of institutions. Very few appeals were received in this period from the newly acquired territories of the Western Provinces. The Provincial Court of Barailly had started functioning only from 1804. Appeals from the decision of that Court only started coming from the end of 1805 or the beginning of 1806. Besides, Wellesley's reforms in

[1] This table has been compiled on the basis of data collected from the Half-yearly and Annual Reports of S. D. A., Judicial despatches and some Parliamentary Papers. Those data have been condensed by arithmetical calculation to arrive at the figures presented in the table. Therefore it is not possible to quote individual references.

the Constitution of the Court[1] must have contributed to its efficiency. Both these factors combined to keep the S.D.A. equal to the incoming business. At the end of 1801, 110 appeals had been pending before the Court. After seven years, at the end of 1807 the number of pending appeals was reduced to 106.

Until 1807 the Court had only three Judges. The second period (1808-14) saw further reforms in the constitution of the Court.[2] This certainly did improve the capacity of the Court. Still we notice that the aggregate disposal of appeals over this period lagged behind the institutions. The plausible explanation is that the additional efficiency of the Court was more than absorbed by the heavy influx of Criminal references. This had been caused by Regulation VIII of 1808 which made all convictions for Robbery with violence referable to the S.N.A. for confirmation of sentence. In the seven years preceding 1808 the total number of Criminal trials received by the Court had been 1,225 of which the Court decided 1,178. In the seven years following 1808, both the number of institutions as well as decisions almost trebled. Thus during 1808-14, the Court received 3,356 Criminal trials and decided 3,307. Besides, during this period, a good deal of the time of the Judges had been occupied by the inquiries into the charges against two public officers, Boddam and Broddie. Hence the diminished disposal of Civil appeals in spite of the increase of the Court's Capacity is not surprising.

In the next period we notice that the number of appeals instituted greatly increased over the figure of the preceding period. But the number of decisions increased in a still greater proportion.

The factors influencing increased institution must have been, first, the extended capacity of the Provincial Courts. From 1815 the strength of all the Provincial Courts had been raised to four Judges. More causes were now disposed of by those Courts which in turn meant a greater number of appeals to the S.D.A. In the second place, due to the enhancement of the value of landed property in 1814, the number of causes triable by the Provincial Courts, in the first instance, and conversely those directly

[1] See above.
[2] See above.

appealable to the S.D.A., increased.[1] Harington rightly anticipated an increase in the business before the S.D.A. on account of the above two factors affecting the Provincial Courts.[2]

The increased disposal by the Court was achieved by the efforts of the Government to keep the services of a fifth Judge available from 1816 onwards. But the element contributing most to the Court's efficiency was the new arrangement for distribution of business adopted in 1816.[3] The arrears of pending Suits before the S.D.A. on lst January 1815 had been 415. By 1st January 1819 the figure had been brought down to 302.[4]

In the last period (1822-28) the lead of institutions over disposals was again established. There was an increase in the total number of causes instituted and an appreciable decline in the number decided.

The reason for reduced disposal was the occupation of two Judges of the Court with the Sadar Special Commission* from 1821 onwards. Between 1821-25, two Judges were sitting three days in the week on the Commission. This instantaneously affected the disposal of Civil causes. While 485 appeals had been decided by the Court in three years (1820-22) only 295 could be disposed of during the next three years (1823-25).[5] In 1826 Colebrooke was appointed as the permanent President of the Sadar Commission. This freed one of the two Judges who reverted to his full time duties in the Court. Colebrooke was also required to act as a part time Judge of the S.D.A.[6] This made the working strength of the Court—four full-time Judges and two part-time. The capacity of the Court naturally improved. Still the Court was unequal to the heavy accumulation of arrears.

From the above review it in apparent that the capacity of the Court was only equal to the incoming business during the first and

[1] For details see Chap. V.

[2] Harington's minute, 15th Oct. 1815, Civ. Judl. Cons., 24th Oct. 1815, No. 18.

[3] See above.

[4] Dowdswell's (Member of Council) Minute, 22nd Sept. 1819, Civ. Judl. Cons., 5th Nov. 1819, No. 15A.

[5] Harington's minute, 16th Dec. 1826, para 8, Civ. Judl. Cons., 21st Dec. 1826, No. 11.

[6] Civ. Judl. Cons., 4th Jan. 1827, Nos. 27-28.

* See above.

the third periods. The gap between institutions and disposals led to a gradual mounting of arrears. The total number of pending causes at the end of the periods and the expected delays in their clearance, calculated on the basis of the average disposals of preceding three years, is presented in the table below:[1]

At the end of the year	Number of pending Civil Appeals	Expected delays in their clearance
1801	110	2 yrs 1½ months
1808	104	1 yr 2½ ,,
1815	467	*6 yrs 2¾ ,,
1822	320	1 yr 11¾ ,,
1828	492	4 yrs 1½ ,,
1830	444	3 yrs

The disposal of Civil appeals by the Court was seriously handicapped by its occupation with the other duties—Criminal and Miscellaneous.

James Stuart, who had been associated with the Courts for nearly thirteen years as Register and Judge successively, analysed this problem very lucidly.[2] Between 1799 and 1803 inclusive, the total number of Criminal trials decided by the Court was 627, an annual average of 125 over those five years. After 1804, due to the improvements in Police, annexation of new territory and the anti-Dacoity measures, there was a sharp increase in the number of Criminal trials.[3]

[1] This table has also been computed from the same data from which the preceding table on p. 145 has been compiled.

[2] Minute of Stuart, 15th Nov, paras 17-19, Papers relating to the Judl. system of Bengal, Reg. (71) 197.

[3] See above.

* This figure might not be realistic. After 1808 the Court's attention had been heavily occupied with Criminal causes. The disposal of Civil causes was naturally slowed down. The average annual decisions of Civil appeals of 1813, 1814 & 1815 amounted to 70 only. Hence the calculated delay for

(contd.

Superintendence over Police also pressed heavily on the Court's time. It was the arduous and delicate duty of the Court to guide and restrain the ardour of the Magistrates and Police officers. The duties of the Court in the Miscellaneous and English Departments have been noticed earlier.[1] Stuart estimated that each of the above three branches engaged a third portion of the Court's time.[2] The complexity of Civil causes also slowed down their disposal. They frequently comprehended transactions of long standing, of numerous parties and of complicated interests. Stuart talked about some more difficulties :

"They [the Civil Appeals] are appeals upon written evidences of facts and the tediousness which attends such proceedings is well known. The Courts are, further, without any fixed system of jurisprudence to direct their investigation and govern their decision."[3]

Second or Special Appeals formed another major part of the Court's duties. By 1815, three days in the month had to be devoted to Special Appeals.[4]

Status of S.D.A.

Under Cornwallis's scheme of establishing a rule of law, the Judicial authority was intended to function independently of the Executive. Although, like the Revenue Department, Judiciary was to be one of the organs of administration, the degree of interference which the Government was to exercise in the functioning of the two differed. Theoretically, the control of the Government, or the Executive, over the judicial administration was to be restricted to the appointment, transfer and removal of its functionaries and to the framing of the laws in its legislative capacity. The Government had nothing to do with the individual decisions of the Judges given in discharge of their office.

* (*Contd.*) clearance of the 467 causes pending at the end of 1815 became enormous. But in the light of the increased efficiency of the Court from 1816 onwards this figure (of 6 yrs $2^3/_4$ months) was unrealistic.

[1] See above.

[2] Stuart's Minute, 15th Nov. 1815, para 17. Papers on the Judl. system of Bengal, Reg. (71) 197.

[3] Stuart's minute, 15th Nov. 1815, para 19. Papers on the Judl. system of Bengal, Reg. (71) 197.

[4] *Ibid.*, para 27.

The S.D.A. was the nucleus of the judicial system. It would be interesting to analyse the degree of independence that this highest tribunal of justice enjoyed, or, putting it conversely, the amount of interference and control that the Government exercised over the activities of this Court.

There was an apparent contradiction between Cornwallis's philosophy of "Separation of Powers" and the constitution of the S.D.A. as established in 1793. Until 1801 the Court was constituted by the Governor-General-in-Council, the same body which formed the executive authority. It was, however, stipulated that while performing the functions of the Court the Governor-General-in-Council were to consider themselves dissociated from the "Executive." Still the position was untenable. Hence it is only after 1801, when the Court became separated from the Council, that an analysis of its position and status in relation to the ruling power, can be made with propriety.

Wellesley held very liberal sentiments about the Court. He wanted to establish it on a very respectable footing. This is apparent from his intention to ask London for a Parliamentary enactment which might put the Chief Justice of the S.D.A. and S.N.A. "...as nearly as possible, on the same level with the Chief Justice of the Supreme Court..."[1]

In 1831 Metcalfe, the Vice-President of Bentinck's Council, lamented the reform of 1801 by which the control previously maintained by the Governor-General-in-Council over the Court had been abandoned. He said :

"The Natives of India are accustomed to look upon their rulers, as the Supreme power to which they can appeal for justice, and our Government, in depriving itself of that character, committed. I fear, a great error, calculated to lower it in the estimation of its subjects. The utter helplessness of Government which cannot redress the grossest injury to individuals, if they have been judicially committed, seems to me, likely to excite any feeling but that of respect or attachment, while the State struggling in vain for justice before tribunals composed of its servants, who decide according to their own whims and fancies, can only be an object of ridicule."[2]

Metcalfe was in fact expressing his concurrence with the views of

[1] Wellesley to Dundas, 5th March 1800. *Wallesley Papers.* Montgomery Martin, Vol. II, p. 231.

[2] Metcalfe's Minute, 11th April, 1831, Civ. Judl. Cons., 19th April 1831, No. 20,

Mackenzie but in much stronger terms.[1]

The contemptuous opinion expressed above, on the subject of independence of the S.D.A., stands at the opposite extreme to the ideals entertained by Wellesley.

In reality, however the S.D.A. never acquired the status visualised by Wellesley. Nor did it become a mere branch of the Executive as Mackenzie and Metcalfe desired it to be. There was nothing like the concept of an independent judiciary as the guardian of the constitution emerging. The Court all along functioned under the thumb of the Governor-General-in-Council. Still, within its own sphere it enjoyed a certain degree of non-interference from the Executive.

This independence of S.D.A. as of the other Courts, was primarily in respect of freedom of judicial decisions according to the laws and regulations or in accordance with justice, equity and good conscience. As the coordinator of the judicial system, the Court was to regulate the conduct of the subordinate judicial officers and as the ultimate Court of Appeal it was to rectify the errors committed by them. All questions relating to the interpretation of the Regulations of Government, arising in course of trials, were to be referred by the subordinate Courts to the S.D.A. for clarification. The Court enjoyed autonomy in such matters.

Constitutionally, the Government was to exercise only a general control over the judiciary through the power of appointment and removal of its personnel and through the framing of the laws in its legislative capacity.

In actual practice, however, the interference of Executive extended much further. The Court had to submit to the Government periodical reports containing a statement of the business transacted and pending in all the Courts and of the problems concerning the different aspects of judicial administration. It was the practice of the Supreme Council to issue such orders, instructions or remarks to the Court as they deemed necessary after a perusal of the periodical reports. These orders or remarks did not pertain to individual cases. They mostly related to the mode of disposal of judicial business. The idea was to keep Government's supervision over the conduct and management of judicial business.

[1] Holt Mackenzie (then Chairman Finance Committee), had expressed an identical opinion in, Letter from Civil Finance Committee to Govt., 12th June 1830. Civ. Judl. Cons., 12th Oct. 1830, No. 1.

But this, strictly speaking, was the exclusive province of the Court.

All cases of doubts regarding the meaning of the Regulations were to be referred to the S.D.A. for interpretation or explanation under Regulations X of 1796 and XXII of 1803. The Court, if itself in doubt, was to refer the matter to the legislative authority —the Governor-General-in-Council. Otherwise the Court was to give the interpretation of the law as it understood it and direct the Court seeking clarification accordingly. It also adopted the practice of directing, on its own initiative, the construction to be put on specific Regulations. The Court's interpretation was issued for the guidance of the subordinate tribunals in the Circular orders that it sent to the Provincial and District Courts from time to time.

The Directors found this practice objectionable. In 1820 they directed the Bengal Government that henceforth all such Circular orders were to be submitted for the approval of the Government before they were issued.[1] They thought that the authority which enacted the Regulation in question could alone be certain of the intentions in framing it. They stated their conviction that:

"A certain latitude of power to interpret must necessarily be conceded to every judicial tribunal but a power to enact its own interpretations and to distribute such enactments under the name of Circular Orders, with authority equal to that of the original Regulation, without sanction or knowledge of the original legislative power, can not be delegated to any subordinate authority."[2]

Technically, the Directors were right. The function of interpretation of the law in relation to a specific case was of course within the competence of the Judges. By this activity judicial precedents and Judge-made laws were created. But making a general interpretation on its own initiative and then circulating it to all the Courts for observance was not merely establishing a judicial precedent. It was tantamount to explanatory legislative enactment.

Whatever the justification; the authority enjoyed by the Court in this respect was made subject to the Government's approval after 1821, in obedience to the instructions of the Directors. The Directors also advised the Bengal Government that it would be better to repeal such Regulations as were of a doubtful meaning and promulgate new ones, rather than attempt to amend the existing ones by supplementary explanations.

[1] Judl. Despatch, 26th April 1820, para 62.

[2] *Ibid.*, paras 60-61.

Although the mode of regulating its own proceedings as well as those of the lower Courts was in theory, the sole concern of the S. D. A., there were occasional interferences from the Government in that direction too. For example, the system of distribution of business adopted by the Court in 1816 had been suggested by the Government.[1]

It has been mentioned earlier that the Government had made a suggestion to the Court in 1826 for altering the system of conducting the Miscellaneous business by all five Judges.[2]

In 1819, on the advice of Stuart. Hastings disapproved Harington's instruction to the Provincial Courts for conducting original trials in those Courts before single benches.[3]

In the month of July 1826 only three causes had been decided by the S.D.A. After perusing the Court's report for that month, the Governor-General-in-Council issued an order to the Court directing them to attach an explanation with their monthly reports whenever they might decide less than ten causes in any particular month.[4] This order was indeed humiliating for the highest tribunal of justice. All five Judges of the Court protested unanimously against it.[5] Smith, the second Judge, was most critical of the order. He said : "Its only effect can be to raise an idea that in the Government's opinion the highest of their Courts of justice requires watching and stimulating, because it has proved itself deficient in diligence or energy."[6] The Government, however, dismissed the objections raised by the Judges and insisted on compliance with the order.[7] The Judges had no choice but to bear with it.

The above order indicates the paternal attitude which the Govt. held towards the S. D. A. and the judiciary. This is borne out

[1] Minute of Governor General-in-Council, 19th Jan. 1816, Civ. Judl. Cons., 26th Jan. 1816, No. 4.

[2] See above.

[3] Minute of Gov. General, 22nd Dec. 1819, Civ. Judl. Cons., 11th Jan. 1820, No. 10.

[4] Govt. to S. D. A., 14th Sept. 1826, Civ. Judl. Cons., 14th Sept. 1826, No. 2.

[5] S. D. A. to Govt., 18th Nov. 1826, Civ. Judl. Cons., 21st Dec. 1826, No. 10.

[6] *Ibid.*, para 6 of Smith's Minute.

[7] V. P.-in-C. to S. D. A., 21st Dec. 1826, *Ibid.*, No. 11.

more clearly by another instance.

In 1826 the S. D. A. had rejected the appeal of *Bibee Asmat* against one *Shah Kabiruddin*, the "Sajjada Nishin" or the "Spiritual Superior" of the Dargah (Shrine) of Sasaram. The matter in issue had been whether certain grants of land for the Dargah of Sasaram was an "endowment" within the meaning of the Mohammedan law and the Regulations in force. Bibee Asmat preferred an appeal against the S. D. A.'s decision to the King-in-Council. According to the current procedure the Respondent in the case, Shah Kabiruddin, was required to tender before the S. D. A. his security for the performance of the decree of the King-in-Council, in case the same was passed against him. The Government offered "security " on behalf of the Respondent through its Remembrancer of Legal Affairs.[1]

On 13th Feb. 1827, the usual motion for admission of the security was made before the Court. Smith, the second Judge, who sat alone to consider it, rejected the security offered by the Government. He took the plea that only a small period remained before the expiration of the Company's Charter. It was not certain whether it was going to be renewed in 1832 and the Company's Government was to continue or not. The appeals to England took a very long time in disposal. Hence the security of the present Government under such circumstances could not be accepted.

Smith's opinion on the inadmissibility of Government's security was, however, immediately overruled by the concurrent opinion of two other Judges. On 15th February the security offered by the Government was finally accepted by the Court.

But the Government were extremely annoyed at Smith's insolence in refusing to accept the credit of the Government to whom he owed his appointment. He was at once asked to explain his conduct in the following stringent note :-

"the only conclusion the Vice-President-in-Council can draw from such proceeding is that it evinces a perversity of judgement or disposition, such

[1] The case has been recorded in detail, in the Proceedings of Vice President-in-Council, in the Territorial Department dtd. 22nd Feb. 1827. Also mentioned in Civ. Judl. Cons., 8th March 1827, No. 6.

as, unless explained by Mr. Smith, proves him unfit to be employed by the Government, in the high station he now fills."[1]

In reply Smith stated that he had not rejected the Government's security on any suspicion of "mala fides" on the part of the Government.[2] "No fear suggested itself to my mind, of Government being displeased at this, nor had it, could I, consistently with the oath of my office . . . have allowed such fear to deter me from acting as I did."[3] He explained further,

"It is true also that it was an order passed against Government, in a Court in which the Government has appointed me to be a Judge [but] such orders are of frequent occurrence, and arise out of the Regulations which have put the Government, in the Courts, upon the same footing with individuals, and out of the terms of the judicial oath which solemnly binds the Judges to discharge the functions of the office without favour or fear."[4]

Smith reminded the Government of the independence of opinion among the Judges "My opinion was overruled by two other Judges. They were free to accept [the security] as I was to reject, nor is it within my province to make any remark upon their judgement.'[5]

As is apparent from the above, Smith at first tried to justify his action. But in view of the stern attitude of the Government he was persuaded to climb down most disgracefully and apologise for his behaviour.[6] He realised that his proceedings of 13th Feb. were calculated to do mischief and he promised that he would refrain from acting similarly in the future. In view of the regret expressed by Smith the Government dropped further proceedings against him.[7]

It is true that Smith's decision of rejecting the security of the Government was absurd. Even if the Crown's Government came to be established after the expiration of the Company's Charter, it could well be presumed that the succeeding Government would have honoured a pledge involving a purely pecuniary responsibility. Even so it was a judicial decision. The action of the

[1] Proceedings of Vice President-in-Council in Territorial Dept. 22nd Feb. 1827. Civ. Judl. Cons. 8th March 1827. No. 7.

[2] Smith to Govt. 5th March 1827, *Ibid.*, No. 8.

[3] *Ibid.*, para 5.

[4] Smith to Govt., 5th March 1827, para 6, Civ. Judl. Cons., 8th March 1827, No. 7.

[5] *Ibid.*

[6] Civ. Judl. Cons., 19th April 1827, No. 1.

[7] *Ibid.*

Government in questioning its legitimacy and threatening the Judge with dismissal, strangled the concept of freedom of judiciary. It was against the ideal and oath-undertaking to act without favour or fear—on which the judicial offices were constituted in 1793. It must have created the impression that the independence of judicial decision which the Judges of the Courts enjoyed was conditioned by the acquiescence and tolerance of the Government.

In 1831 Holt Mackenzie, an officer held in high esteem, complained of an absence of adequate control of the Executive over the judicial organ, which according to him had resulted in much evil.[1] Metcalfe entirely agreed with this view.[2] But Bentinck disagreed with both.[3] He thought that in the selection of proper persons to be the judges of the Court, and in its power of removing them for sloth and misconduct, the Government preserved adequate security against any abuse of authority by the Court. In his opinion, the only interference the ruling power could exercise with propriety in the administration of justice was in its legislative capacity. The power of general control which the Government reserved to itself was, according to Bentinck, enough. He deprecated meddling with individual cases under any circumstances whatsoever.[4] He also rejected a proposal from Mackenzie that all Circular Orders of the S.D.A. to the subordinate Courts should be sent to the Government before transmission.[5]

Bentinck's attitude was that of a practical reformer. He was no blind opponent of Cornwallis's ideology like Metcalfe or Mackenzie were; neither was he its blind follower. He subscribed to the above view more on practical grounds. He stated that he "was at a loss to understand what degree of interference [beyond that being already exercised] the Executive could possibly exercise, consistently with a prompt and efficient award of justice and with-

[1] Civil Finance Committee to. Govt., 13th Dec. 1829, Civ. Judl. Cons., 12th Oct. 1830, No.1.

[2] See above.

[3] Secy. to Govn. General to Territorial Dept., 26th Jan. 1831, Parl. Papers 1831-32, Vol. 12, pp. 490-95.

[4] Secy. to Govn. General to Territorial Dept., 26th Jan. 1831, para 8. Parl. Papers 1831-32, Vol. 12, pp. 490-95.

[5] *Ibid.*, para 27.

out sacrifice of other important duties."[1]

Though Bentinck refused to put a curb on any of the powers exercised by the S.D.A. he did not show much respect for the Court's opinion on matters of judicial reform. Hitherto all important changes in the judicial system had been either on the Court's suggestion or with their concurrence. The Regulations incorporating the reforms of 1814 had been framed under the supervision of S.D.A. The Court's objections, to a great extent, prevented the reestablishment of the Nal Adalats in 1816.[2] In 1824 the Regulation empowering Collectors to decide Summary suits had been enacted on the initiative of the Court.[3] It was again on account of the Court's opinion that the general transfer of Magistracy to the Collectors had been held up by the Bengal Government.[4]

But the S.D.A. was given no such voice or initiative in the reforms of Bentinck era. In 1829 Commissioners of Revenue were given jurisdiction over Criminal cases without consulting the S.D.A. at all. The general transfer of Magistracy to the Collectors was accepted in opposition to their views. Collectors were given original jurisdiction over Summary suits in face of a strong opposition to that measure by the S.D.A.[5]

The above discussion leads to the conclusion that the status of the Court was not in reality founded on the basis of the Regulations. The extent of its independence depended on the discretion of the Executive.

[1] Secy. to Govn. Gen. to Territorial Dept., 13th Dec. 1829, para 7. Civ. Judl, Cons., 12th Oct. 1830, No. 1.

[2] See Chapter IV.

[3] See Chapter IV.

[4] See Chapter IV.

[5] See Chapter IV.

Chapter VII

THE SUPREME COURT AND THE BENGAL ADMINISTRATION

THE SUPREME COURT was established in Calcutta (under the provision of the Regulating Act of 1773) by a Charter of George III issued on 26th March 1744. It was to consist of a Chief Justice and three Puisne Judges, all of whom were to be appointed by the Crown. Sir Elijah Impey was nominated as its first Chief Justice.

This Court superseded the Mayor's Court, which had been functioning in Calcutta under the Royal Charter of 1753. It was thought that the Judges of the Mayor's Court, thr Mayor and Aldermen of the Calcutta Corporation, could not take an independent or impartial stand when the Company's interests were at stake. William Bolts, who had personally served as an Alderman of the Calcutta Mayor's Court. He wrote that Justice was everywhere defeated by the overriding power of control, appointment and interference which the Governor-General held over the Courts in Calcutta.[1]

The main idea behind the establishment of the Supreme Court in Calcutta had been to purify the administration of justice (according to English law) in the British settlement of Calcutta by creating a Court which could function independently of the influence of the Company's Executive. It was to be constituted by persons who had been professional lawyers for at least five years and the appointments and removals were vested with the Crown. As such the Court was better equipped to secure a fair and impartial administration of justice than its predecessor. Though the Supreme Court was primarily designed to administer

[1] Bolts, *Considerations on India Affairs*, etc. p. 86.

justice according to English law to the British persons in Bengal, it was also intended to afford protection to the Indians against any oppression by the Company's servants.

To achieve this object, the Court was given a wide jurisdiction in both Civil and Criminal matters. Certain specified categories of persons were made amenable to them. They were all British subjects,[1] persons employed by, or being directly or indirectly in the service of the Company, or by any of His Majesty's subjects; and any Indian living outside Calcutta, if he submitted himself voluntarily to the jurisdiction of the Court, in a suit instituted against him by a British subject when the cause of action exceeded Rs. 500/-.

The Charter of 1774 defining the jurisdiction of the Court was, however, not clear on certain questions. In the first place, it was not stated whether the Company in its Diwani capacity was to be subject to the jurisdiction of the Court. The Company's Government asserted that the Court had no right to question any of its activities and that its servants were immune from the jurisdiction of the Court for acts done in their official capacity. The Supreme Court refused to accept this claim and they were probably right in doing so. There were many provisions in the Regulating Act which indicated that it was intended to establish an impartial control over the vagaries and excesses of the servants of the Company. The Charter had expressly provided that the Court was authorised to take cognizance of all Civil and Criminal cases in which the servants of the Company were involved without drawing a distinction between acts done in their private or public capacity. On these grounds the Court proceeded to regard not only the Collectors of Revenue but all servants of the Company, whether British or Indian, as within their jurisdiction for any acts, public or private. The Kazis and Pandits, or the Indian Law Officers of the Company's Courts, were therefore considered by the Supreme Court to be answerable to them for

[1] It may be recalled that the territory forming the city of Calcutta was regarded as British territory ever since the purchase by the Company of the villages of Kalikata, Sutanti and Govindpur, from the Nawab, towards the end of the 17th century. The Indians living within the limits of the city of Calcutta were regarded as British subjects. They had therefore been amenable to the Mayor's Court and became automatically so to the Supreme Court.

acts done in the discharge of their office. Thus in 1778 in the case of Nadrah Begum (regarding partition of certain property at Patna), the Kazi and Mufti of the Adalat (Court) of Patna Council were summoned by the Supreme Court to answer for the acts done in their official capacity and in obedience to the order of the Patna Council. The Company described the Court's exercise of jurisdiction in the above case (popularly known as the Patna Case) as being completely illegal.

The amenability of the zamindars to the court's authority formed another bone of contention between it and the government. The supreme court had been allowed jurisdiction over persons either "directly or indirectly" in the service of the Company. Having contracted to secure revenue for the Company's government, the zamindars were considered by the court as fitting the category of persons "indirectly employed" by the Company. On this issue matters reached an ugly climax in the *Kashijura* case in 1779, in which the government resisted with its own force the court's process against the zamindar of Kashijura and generally instructed all the zamindars not to submit to the jurisdiction of the Supreme Court.

The Supreme Court had failed. It had been unpopular with the administration as well as with the Indian population. The Company's servants detested it because it faced them with the prospect of being prosecuted for acts done in their public capacity. The Government hated it because it sought to restrict their freedom. Its interference in the revenue affairs threatened the collection which was the Company's chief concern. The Court was dreaded by most Indians. The examples of Bahadur Beg and the Law Officers of the Patna Adalat who were dragged all the way to Calcutta (the old Maulvi having expired on the way), and those of Raja Nandkumar*, who was executed for an ordinary crime of forgery, and of the Zamindar of Kashijura, who was humiliated by its processes, were enough to terrorise the Indians. It was more horrifying to them because the procedure, the law and the language used in the Court were completely foreign to them.

Matters having reached a crisis, Parliament was obliged to

* Raja Nandkumar had been sentenced to death in 1776 for the crime of forgery which was then a capital offence under English law.

intervene through the Act of Settlement in 1781[1]. The preamble and the provisions of the Act show that in the preceding contest between the Court and the Company the Parliament had given its verdict in favour of the latter. The jurisdiction of the Court was curtailed so as to remove the areas of dispute.

In the first place, the Governor-General and his Council were guaranteed absolute immunity from the Court's jurisdiction for acts done in their official capacity.

Except British subjects, all other persons were exempted from the jurisdiction of the Court, for acts done in pursuance of an order of the Governor-General-in-Council.

Section 8 of the Act provided that the Court was not to have, or exercise, any jurisdiction in matters concerning revenue. They were also prohibited from interfering with any acts or orders of the Government, relating to the collection of revenue.

Section 9 of the Act declared that no person was to be subject to the jurisdiction of the Court on account of his being a Landholder or Farmer. This directly reversed the assumptions of the Supreme Court in the Kashijura case.

It was specifically declared by Section 17 that the Court was to have full authority over British subjects and over all inhabitants of Calcutta whether British, European or Indian. This was no new provision. The town of Calcutta had already been regarded as British territory.[2] All its inhabitants were therefore legally subjects of the Crown. The juristic position of the rest of the territory administered by the Company was, however, different. Over these areas the Moghul Emperor was still considered to be the legal sovereign. The Company was carrying on the administration as his Diwan or Agent.

The most significant part of the Act of Settlement was that for the first time it gave Parliamentary recognition to the judicial system organised and maintained by the Company. By Section 21, the Sadr Diwani Adalat was recognised as the highest Court of the Company, competent to hear and determine appeals and references from the Country Courts. Its judgment was to be

[1] Act 21, Geo. III, Cap. 63.

[2] See above, Ch. VII.

final except on causes of Rs. 50,000/-00 and above, when a further appeal lay to the King-in-Council (commonly referred to as Privy Council).

By Section 24, Magistrates and Judicial Officers (both Indian and British) were made immune from any action in the Supreme Court for any act done in their official capacity. The exemption also extended to persons acting under the orders of any such Judicial Officer. Apparently this provision was directly suggested by the Patna Cause. It was intended to make the local Judicial Officers and functionaries more secure in the exercise of their duties. All the same, the European officers were made liable to prosecution in the Supreme Court for any acts of corruption. Section 25 laid down the process by which an action could be instituted before the Court.

The jurisdiction of the Court thus curtailed and defined, it was expected to function smoothly along with the machinery of Company's administration. At the same time it was anticipated that the Company's administration in the Provinces would now function without any interference from the Court. But such hopes were not fulfilled. Although such scenes of open conflict between the Government and the Court as those of the pre-1781 period did not recur, instances were not lacking in the post-1781 period when the actions of the one irritated or inconvenienced the functioning of the other. The Government protested that the Court had exceeded their jurisdiction; the Court complained that the Government had refused cooperation. A number of such instances are to be found in the period 1793-1800, and then in the period after 1828 when the powers of the Supreme Court became a matter of controversy between the Court and the Government.

The first incident occurred in 1793.[1] In that year a certain Mirza Mohammad, a resident of Dacca City, had filed a Civil suit for possession of certain property against one Agha Asee, an Armenian Christian resident of Dacca. The case was filed before Patterson, the Judge of Dacca City. Agha Asee refused to abide by the jurisdiction of the local Court, claiming

1 Case of *Mirza Mohammad* vs. *Agha Asee* recorded in Revenue & Judl. Cons., 26th April 1793, Nos. 39-43.

that being a foreigner he could only be subject to the Supreme Court. On a petition being presented by the Agha to the Supreme Court, the latter issued a writ declaring that the petitioner being an Armenian Christian was subject to the jurisdiction of the Supreme Court. They further directed the plaintiff Mirza Mohammad, to cease all proceedings against the Agha in the Dacca Court. The above order was served through Patterson, who had earlier, on Agha's petition to him, decided that Agha Asee, not being an European British subject or a French subject, could not be amenable to the jurisdiction of the Supreme Court. Patterson sought instruction from the Government. After consulting the Company's Attorney, Simon, on the case, the Governor-General-in-Council directed Patterson to take no cognizance of the Supreme Court's order to the Plaintiff and proceed with the case.[1]

Under the terms of the Charter of 1774, the Supreme Court's jurisdiction outside Calcutta extended only over British subjects, over persons in the service of the Company or of a servant of His Majesty, or over Indians voluntarily submitting to its jurisdiction in a case against a British subject.[2] It is apparent that Agha Asee did not fit into either of the above classifications. The Government's defiance to the ordre of the Supreme Court was justified.

On several occasions the Bengal Government was persuaded to resist the processes of attachment or sale issued by the Supreme Court against properties in the Mofussil.

Indians residing outside Calcutta could make themselves subject to the jurisdiction of the Supreme Court by election. From this permissive clause parties losing or expecting to lose an action in one of the Company's Courts found an easy way of defeating the execution of Decrees of the latter Courts.[3] A Defendant in the District Adalat, when anticipating a Decree against him, transferred the whole of his property to one of his

[1]Revn. & Judl. Cons., 26th April 1793, No. 43.

[2]This jurisdiction was defined more restrictively by the Act of 1780 (to the extent that zamindars were specifically declared exempt from the jurisdiction of the Supreme Court).

[3]Letter from Thompson, Burdwan J., to Govt., 5th June 1794, Criminal & Judl. Cons., 13th June 1794, No. 7.

friends or relatives residing in Calcutta. The transferee at once in collusion with the transferor, applied to the Supreme Court for an attachment of the said property on the basis of the Deed of transfer. The imposter transferor then made himself amenable to the jurisdiction of the Supreme Court by executing a bond. On his admitting the transfer, his collaborator, the fictitious Plaintiff, found no difficulty in procuring the attachment which was granted by the Supreme Court as a matter of course. When the real creditor obtained a Decree in his favour from the Mofussil Court he found the whole property of the Defendant, from which the Decree could be satisfied, in the hands of the Sheriff. The Decree could not, therefore, be carried into effect.

This practice became prevalent in the Districts adjoining Calcutta, like Burdwan, Hooghly, and the twenty-four Parganas because the Supreme Court was more easily accessible to their inhabitants and because it was not difficult for them to find a relative or connection in Calcutta to collaborate with them in the fraud.

In the case of *Gaya Ram Bose* vs. *Ramjai Baral,* in the Burdwan District Court, the Judge had attached the crops standing on the lands belonging to the Defendant and had the same sold under his orders.[1] The defendant had since proceeded to Calcutta and manipulated to procure from the Supreme Court an attachment in favour of a local resident, for the whole land (including the standing crop already sold) in dispute. An officer from the Supreme Court arrived at the spot and executed the attachment. Thompson, the Judge of Burdwan referred the case to the Government for instructions.

After consulting the Advocate General, Burroughs,[2] on the case, the Governor-General-in-Council directed Thompson to give notice to the Sheriff of the said property already being subject to a suit in the Mofussil Court and require him to vacate the attachment. In case the Sheriff did not comply with his requisition, the Judge was to proceed with the trial and execute his Decree without taking cognizance of the Sheriff's attachment.[3]

[1] Criminal & Civil Judl. Cons., 13th June 1794, No. 6.

[2] Burrough's opinion has been recorded in Criminal & Civil Judl. Cons., 24th Oct. 1794, No. 10.

[3] Criminal & Civil Judl. Cons., 24th Oct. 1794, No. 11.

The Governor-General-in-Council issued an identical order in a similar case of Gour Mohan Chaudhry vs. Harchandra Chaudhry when certain property litigated in the District Court of Burdwan had been attached and sold by the Sheriff.[1] The Judge of Burdwan was directed to inform the Sheriff that any application from the purchaser at the Sheriff's sale for being put into the possession of the property purchased, could not be complied with until the contested right (to the property) was finally determined by the Burdwan Court.

In the case of *Banarsi Ghosh* vs. *Radha Mohan Ghosh* the execution of a process of the Supreme Court was resisted again by the Government.[2] In the year 1793 the Judge of Zilla Hooghly had attached certain lands in connection with the above cause. The case had since been decreed in favour of the Plaintiff. Subsequently, the Defendant, Radha Mohan, manipulated to secure an attachment from the Supreme Court in favour of a party in Calcutta of the disputed lands which had already been decreed by the Hooghly Judge in Banarsi Ghosh's favour. The Sheriff then planned to put the lands on sale.

The Advocate General considered in the case that the Sheriff's sale did not create a new title but merely conveyed the existing one to the purchaser.[3] As such, only the title which had been declared valid by a competent Court (of the Company) could be conveyed at the Sheriff's sale. The title of Radha Mohan Ghosh to the lands in question had been declared invalid by the Hooghly Judge. Hence there was no question of the property being conveyed to any purchaser at the Sheriff's sale. The Governor-General-in-Council accordingly decided to withhold the conveyance of the lands to any prospective purchaser at the Sheriff's sale.[4]

The Governments of Cornwallis and Shore thus denied the assertion of the Supreme Court in one case (that of Agha Asee) and resisted the execution of their processes in others when they tended to interfere with the Company's judicial and revenue administration.

But the Supreme Court had lost the earlier bite after their

[1] Civ. Judl. Cons., 11th Nov. 1796, No. 5.
[2] Civ. Judl. Cons., 18th Nov. 1796, No.14.
[3] *Ibid.*
[4] *Ibid.*

recent defeat of 1781 in their contest with the Government. Hence, instead of raking up another quarrel they decided to appeal to the Government for their cooperation in the functioning of the Court. Governor-General Wellesley (who assumed office on 18th May 1798) was very responsive to the new approach. On a request from the Supreme Court, Wellesley and his Council pledged to bind the Judicial Officers of the Company to assist in the execution of the processes of that Court.[1] Wellesley did, in fact, inaugurate an era of amity and cooperation between the Government and the Court, which was to last through the subsequent Governor-Generalships until the advent of Bentinck. Wellesley's attitude towards the Supreme Court must have been conditioned by his liberal approach towards the judiciary in general, which is apparent from his views on the independence of the S.D.A.[2] He was very friendly with Anstruther, the contemporary Chief Justice of the Supreme Court.[3] He even tried to revive to an extent the Hastings-Impey tradition of the head of the Government seeking the personal advice of the head of the King's Court on judicial affairs.[4]

The Government of Wellesley, and those following, lived up to the assurances given to the Court in 1798. The preceding Governments of Shore and Cornwallis had denied a jurisdiction claimed by the Court and had resisted their processes when found inconvenient to the administration. But from 1800 onward there was a striking change. Henceforth the Bengal Government toed the line that the Supreme Court was the only competent body to decide whether a particular person was subject to their jurisdiction or not and that the local officers were not to interfere with the execution of their processes on any grounds whatsoever. The following instances demonstrate the zeal of the Government to assist, and cooperate with the Court.

In 1800 Osborne, a British resident of Calcutta, obtained from the Supreme Court a letter of Administration to the Estate of a

[1] Civ. Judl. Cons., 24th Aug. 1798, Nos. 1 & 2.

[2] See Chapter VI.

[3] This can be inferred from his private correspondence with Anstruther on all kinds of affairs including even political and military.

[4] This view is supported by a letter from Ansgruther to Wellesley, 27th March 1799. *Wellesley Papers*, Vol. 1, p. 508.

certain Werber, deceased. The latter's property and effects had been in deposit with the City Court of Dacca. Since Werber had been a foreigner (not being a subject of the Crown) residing in Dacca for some time past, the Dacca Court asserted that he was subject to its jurisdiction and not to that of the Supreme Court.[1] The assertion seems to be reasonable. All the same the Government ordered the Dacca Court to honour the writ of the Supreme Court and deliver the property in question to Osborne.[2]

In the 1802 the Governor-General-in-Council readily agreed to a suggestion of the Chief Justice of the Supreme Court for stationing one of the Sheriff's officers at Benares. This was to facilitate the execution of the Court's processes against persons resident in that area.[3] They also directed the Judge and Magistrate and the Officer Commanding the Battalion at Chunar to afford every protection and assistance to the officers of the Sheriff.[4]

In 1805 the Sheriff sent an officer with a writ to Murshidabad to seize a local resident, Srikanta by name. Srikanta sought the Murshidabad Judge's protection, stating on oath, that he had never executed any bond, or made himself amenable to the Supreme Court otherwise (i.e. by residence in Calcutta). On the basis of the above statement the Judge, Becher, deferred his permission to the Sheriff's officer for seizing the person of Srikanta and wrote to the Government for instruction.[5] The Governor-General-in-Council remarked that whenever any question arose regarding any person being subject to the jurisdiction of the Court or not, the Judges of Supreme Court alone were competent to decide the issue.[6] Becher was told that his resistance to the Sheriff's writ was unjustified and he was bound to render every possible assistance to the Sheriff's officer.[7]

In the same year, Massie, the Judge of Nuddea, refused to assist

1 Letter from Register, Dacca Court to Govt., 1st July 1800. Criminal Judl. Cons., 20th Nov. 1800, No. 4.

2 *Ibid.*, No. 5. (Resolution of G.-G.-in-C., 20th Nov. 1800).

3 Civ. Judl. Cons., 26th Aug. 1802, No. 17.

4 *Ibid.*, No. 20.

5 Letter from Becher to Govt., 2nd Jan. 1805, Civ. Judl. Cons., 10th Jan. 1805, No. 15.

6 Letter from Secy. to Govt. to Murshidabad J., 10th Jan. 1805, Civ. Judl. Cons., 10th Jan. 1805, No. 17.

7 *Ibid.*

the Sheriff's officer in seizing an estate in satisfaction of a process of the Supreme Court issued in the case of *William Marshall* vs. *Raja Shambhu Chandra.*[1] The reason for the Judge's refusal was that the said estate (which had been assumed by the Supreme Court to be the property of the Raja) had been mortgaged to a third party who had already obtained its possession, under an order of the Nuddea Court. Massie referred the case to the Government.

After consulting Advocate General Smith on the case, the Government reiterated their earlier stand. The Nuddea Judge was informed that his resistance to the Supreme Court's order had been absolutely unjustified.[2] A Circular Order was also issued to all the Judges and Magistrates in the Provinces forbidding them to resist the processes of Supreme Court on any plea whatsoever and requiring them to assist the officers of the Supreme Court in every possible way.[3]

The above decision of the Government stands in exact contrast to their attitude in the case of *Banarsi Ghosh* vs. *Radha Mohan Ghosh* in 1796.[4] This indicates that the Bengal Government were now determined to extend maximum cooperation for a smoother functioning of the Court.

In 1818 the Government of Bombay solicited instructions from the Bengal Government in a case in which the Judge of District Salsette (under the Bombay Presidency) had protested against the operation of a writ of the Supreme Court of Bombay on property situated within his jurisdiction.[5] Spankie, the Advocate General of Bengal justified the action of the Bombay Supreme Court saying that it was the constant practice of the Supreme Court of Calcutta to issue writs against properties situated in the mofussil if their owners happened to come within the jurisdiction of the Court.[6] "The jurisdiction of the Supreme Court," he commented "was confined only by the description of persons, and I have never heard of resistance or remonstrance against the legality of such

[1] Civ. Judl. Cons., 14th Nov. 1805; No. 3.
[2] Civ. Judl. Cons., 14th Nov, 1805, No. 5.
[3] *Ibid.*, No. 6. (Circular Order, 7th Nov. 1805).
[4] See ante p. 165.
[5] Civ. Judl. Cons., 16th Oct. 1818. No. 20.
[6] *Ibid.*, No. 22.

writs by any Judge and Magistrate [of Bengal], or by any other person, for which, indeed, there could be no column or foundation."[1]

The Bombay administration was instructed accordingly by the Governor-General-in-Council.[2]

In 1820 the Sheriff requested the assistance of the Government for delivering the possession of certain Taluks (Estates) in the District of Midnapore to a particular person, in the execution of an order of the Supreme Court.[3] The Government responded enthusiastically. They drew the attention of the Magistrate of Midnapur to the Circular Order of 7th November 1805[4] and ordered : "You will of course give such assistance as may be necessary to the Sheriff's Officers. . .in the legal execution of the process. . ."[5]

In 1822 the Government kept silent over a very strong protest made by the S.D.A. against an alleged invasion of their jurisdiction by the Supreme Court.[6]

So far the Supreme Court had functioned smoothly. Their writs against the persons or properties of individuals (both British and Indian) had been running freely throughout Bengal without any hindrance. Whether an Indian or any other person living outside Calcutta was subject to its jurisdiction or not, was left to the determination of the Judges themselves. And their decisions were never disputed or doubted.

But with the arrival of Bentinck in 1828, the earlier passiveness of the Bengal Government towards the Supreme Court vanished and an attitude of criticism and hostility towards the Court started developing. Several factors might have caused this change.

The Government of Bombay and the Supreme Court there had been locked in bitter dispute over the past few years.[7] As a result,

[1] Civ. Judl. Cons., 16th Oct. 1818, No. 22.

[2] *Ibid.*, No. 23.

[3] Civ. Judl. Cons., 13th Oct. 1820, No. 17.

[4] See ante p. 168.

[5] Civ. Judl. Cons., 13th Oct. 1820, No. 20.

[6] In the case of *Parsan Lal* vs. *Baijnath Sahu*, see Chapter VI.

[7] The origin of the Bombay dispute had been the Supreme Court's assertion of a right to issue writs of *habeas corpus* for the release of Indians detained by the Government, and the Government's firms denial of it.

a general reaction against the King's Courts may have been growing at the controlling Presidency.

With the appointment of Metcalfe as the Vice-President of the Supreme Council, in 1828, a very strong authoritarian element was introduced in the Bengal administration. This was irreconcilable with any degree of passivity or acquiescence on the part of the ruling power, towards the exercise of any authority by the Court which had not been explicitly sanctioned by the Statutes. Metcalfe's ideal was an all-pervading Executive. In the Districts he desired the Collectors to be vested with the powers of Judgeship as well as Magistracy.[1] He lamented the fact that the Executive (Governor-General-in-Council) had dissociated themselves from the functions of the Company's highest tribunal of justice—the S.D.A.[2] And he wanted the Supreme Court to function in complete subordination to the ruling power. He observed :

"To me, it seems quite clear that the supreme power ought to rest with the Government, and that in any case in which the exercise of the powers of the Court might be deemed injurious to the safety or welfare of the State, the Government ought to possess authority to suspend the function of the Court as regarding that particular case, and the Court be bound to acknowledge and abide by the restrictive powers of the Government pending a reference to a superior authority in England."[3]

Metcalfe's influence was another factor shaping the attitude of the Administration towards the Court.

Lastly, the Governor-General, Bentinck, himself was not very happily disposed towards the Court. The conflict between the Judges of Madras Supreme Court and the Government during his administration of that Presidency was most likely to have prejudiced his mind with a feeling of apprehension towards the exercise of unauthorised powers by the Judges of the King's Court. He actually apprehended great injury to the Government and the people of Bengal from the powers assumed by the Supreme Court, and he rejoiced at the assurances given by Ellenborough (President, Board of Control) to support the Government against the Court. He wrote : "I shall hail as a great public benefit the communication of your determination to support the authority of the

[1] See Chapter IV.

[2] See Chapter VI.

[3] Minute of Metcalfe (Vice-President-in-Council in Secret Dept., 15th April 1829, Parl. Papers, 1831, Vol. 6, Appx V. Encl. 8, pp. 13-14.

Government, and to protect the feelings and interests of the Natives against the ever-extending jurisdiction and the ruinous processes of the Supreme Court . . . "[1]

With this composition the Bengal Administration became determined to dispute some of the powers which the Court had assumed, not from any specific provision, but by an interpretation of the Statutes. The Governor-General wrote to the Supreme Court:

"On several important points the jurisdiction of the Supreme Court appears to be doubtful, productive of alarm to our native subjects, of embarrassment to the local Governments and discreditable to our country. In some instances it seems that those Courts have been compelled by a construction of law, contrary to the probable intention of the Legislature, to extend their jurisdiction in [*Sic*] a degree inconsistent with the public convenience..."[2]

In 1829 the Vice-President-in-Council specifically alleged that the Supreme Court had exceeded their jurisdiction in four cases over the recent years.[3] Those were :

(1) Case of *Morton* vs. *Mehdi Ali Khan* ;
(2) Case between two British partnership firms of Calcutta;
(3) Case of *Khudabaksh and 'C'* vs. *Government*, and
(4) Case of *Umesh Chandra Pal Chaudhry* and *Rattan Chandra Pal Chaudhry* vs. *Prem Chandra Pal Chaudhry* and others.

It may be worth narrating briefly the issues in each of the above cases, the allegations of the Government about the Court having exceeded their jurisdictions, and the replies of the Supreme Court to such charges.[4]

In the first case the Plaintiff, Morton, was a British resident of Calcutta. He had commenced an action in the Supreme Court against one Mehdi Ali Khan, for the recovery of certain debts. Though the Defendant, a resident of Oudh, had never lived in Calcutta he was carrying on some trade there, through his servants. The debt was alleged to have been contracted by the

1 Bentinck to Ellenborough, 6th July 1829, Colchester Papers.

2 Letter from Govn. Gen. to Supreme Court, 14th July 1829, para 4, Parl. Papers 1831, Vol. 6, Appx. V, p. 2.

3 Metcalfe's Minute, 15th April 1829, Parl. Papers 1831, Vol. 6, Appx V, pp. 20-28.

4 The issues in three of the above cases (Nos. 1, 2 & 4) and the Court's answer to the allegation of the Govt. (vide Bentinck's and Metcalfe's minutes on the preceding pages) have been stated in the Letter from C. Crey, C.J. of Supreme Court to G.-G.-in-C., 22nd Oct. 1829, Parl. Papers 1831, Vol. 6, Appx V, Encl. 19.

servants on behalf of their master Mehdi Ali Khan. The Supreme Court considered the Defendant as amenable to their jurisdiction, took cognizance of the Plaint and had the goods and properties of Khan seized.

The Government contended that Mehdi Ali Khan could not be subject to the jurisdiction of the King's Court because he was not only an Indian living outside Calcutta, but he was not even a resident of any part of Company territory.[1] And without his having voluntarily submitted to their jurisdiction, the Court's assumption of jurisdiction over him was entirely illegal. Besides, the Government asserted that the allegation of the debt on which the action against Khan was based was false.

As to the ground of action being a fake, the Chief Justice stated that no Court could be so constituted as to be "exempt from the evil consequences of perjury". But in fact there had been nothing to warrant the assertion of false testimony on the part of the Plaintiff. About the Government's claim of Mehdi Ali Khan being without the jurisdiction of the Court, the Chief Justice gave the following reply.

He accepted that no specific provision had been made in the Statutes for the Supreme Court exercising jurisdiction in such cases. Statute 21 Geo. III. Cap. 70, S. 28 (of 1781) had prohibited a British subject from proceeding beyond the radius of ten miles of Calcutta without obtaining a special license from the Government. The Chief Justice asserted "with confidence" that even the above provision did not intend to place those established at Calcutta without a legal remedy there, against an Indian trader or banker of Calcutta, who might choose to live away from that city. Besides, argued the Chief Justice, the meaning of the word "inhabitants" could not be confined to include only residents. This had been established long before by Coke.* St. 22 Hen. VIII. Cap. 5, regarding repair of bridges had made the inhabitants of the Shire or Riding liable to contribute towards the repair and

[1] Oudh was Nawab's territory directly administered by him.

* Sir Edward Coke was Attorney General of England at the beginning of the 17th century. He later became the Chief Justice of Common Pleas and Chief Justice of King's Bench during the early Stuart period. He is famous for his '*Reports and Institutes*' which form an important contribution to the evolution of the English legal system.

maintenance of the bridges in the locality. From this Coke had construed that although a man may be dwelling in a foreign country, yet if he had lands or tenements in his possession or management in the country (England) he was an "inhabitant both where his person dwelleth and where he hath lands or tenements in possession . . ."[1] Hence to regard Mehdi Ali Khan as being beyond the Court's jurisdiction, just on the ground of being a resident of Oudh, without considering the fact of his having trading establishments in Calcutta, would have been establishing a precedent contract to the principle established by Coke. It would also, argued the Chief Justice, have been at variance with the principles of justice and against the ordinary course of Law of Merchants of most civilised nations of the world. He also emphasised the practical inconveniences to the settlers in Calcutta if the word "inhabitants" was interpreted to include physical residents only. It was common for Indians to carry on extensive trade and dealings in money and securities at Calcutta by means of servants, while they themselves resided at Murshidabad, Patna, Dacca, Benares or elsewhere. Besides, it would follow from the above construction that any Indian resident of Calcutta, having all his transactions and property in Calcutta, might cease to be an inhabitant of Calcutta the moment he chose to remove his physical presence from the city. There being no court at Calcutta which had any means of providing for the trial in the Provinces, the net result of the above construction would be that the mercantile parties of Calcutta might have to ask for licences to go to half the Zilla Courts of Bengal, if they had to sue those with whom they dealt only in the vicinity of their own dwelling places.

The second case in which the Supreme Court was alleged to have exceeded its jurisdiction was one between two British partnership firms of Calcutta. One had made some advances of money to the other, who subsequently became insolvent. The Creditors obtained a Decree from the Supreme Court and the entire property of the insolvent Partnership, including some stock in trade, indigo factories and properties lying in Barailly, were seized by the Sheriff in satisfaction of the Decree.

[1] Coke's II Instr. 697, p. 702. Quoted by Sir J. Frank, Judge of Supreme Court. Minute of J. Frank, 23rd Sept. 1829, Parl. Papers 1831, Vol. 6, p. 83.

The Government charged that the Court had no authority to seize the properties in Barailly, particularly when there were local Indian Creditors of the insolvent firm.

The Chief Justice answered that, since no law of Bankruptcy or Insolvency had yet been introduced into India, each Creditor had to take care of himself. As for the Court's right to seize property situated outside Calcutta, he stated that the same was absolutely necessary under particular circumstances, for the fulfilment of its task. The Court was empowered to decide suits. He enquired, "... what sort of determination would it be if the Defendant, by removing himself and his goods and chattels, during the progress of the suit, beyond the limits of Calcutta, might make execution impossible and judgment nugatory ?"

The third was a Criminal case in which four Indian inhabitants of Calcutta were involved.[1] They were Khudabaksh, Sadatullah, Shallaroo and Asgar Khansama. The first three were charged with burglary committed just outside the limits of Calcutta, and the fourth with having been in possession of stolen goods. They were all tried by the Judge of Circuit of Calcutta Division. Khudabaksh, Sadatullah and Shallaroo were acquitted by the Company's Court because their guilt could not be proved. Asgar Khansama was released because the Company's Court could not take cognizance of his case since he was found in possession of the stolen goods at Kalinga, which was within the defined limits of the city of Calcutta. The Magistrate of the Suburbs of Calcutta, after releasing all the above prisoners from his custody (as per the above order) referred those persons to the Calcutta Police for investigation into their characters because they were inhabitants of Calcutta. The Calcutta Justice of the peace (i. e. Magistrate) took them in his custody and committed them for trial before the Supreme Court. The latter took up their trial and convicted all four.

The Government charged the Supreme Court for not only having exceeded their jurisdiction by trying Indians for crimes committed outside Calcutta, but also of having violated the privilege of the Company's judiciary by retrying three of the prisoners

[1] This case has been described in detail, and the allegations of the Government answered in Letter from Supreme Court to Board of Control (n.d.), Parl. Papers 1831, Vol. 6, Appx V, Encls. 16-18, pp. 44-48.

already tried and acquitted by the Calcutta Provincial Court.

As to the first part of the allegation, the Chief Justice claimed that the natives of Calcutta were to be considered British subjects, under the meaning of Act 13, Geo. III, Cap. 63, S. 14 (of 1773) and the Charter establishing the Supreme Court, and hence were amenable to that Court for all acts done within or without Calcutta, in the same manner as an European born British subject. The Chief Justice's reply to the second part of the charge (i.e. about taking up the trial of a case already decided by Company's Court) was that, in the first place, the Supreme Court had no judicial information about the parties having been already tried and arraigned by the Company's Court. His impression had been that the Calcutta Provincial Court had merely disclaimed the cognizance of the case on the ground of the parties being residents of Calcutta. Even if the Supreme Court had the information, that, in the opinion of the Chief Justice, would not have formed any legal ground for the acquittal of the prisoners.

In the last case (that of *Umesh Chandra Pal Chaudhry* and *Rattan Chandra Pal Chaudhry* vs. *Prem Chandra Pal Chaudhry and 'C'*) both parties were residents of Calcutta. The case had been for the partition of an estate in Nuddea District which had been jointly owned by the Plaintiffs and the Defendants. In 1829 the Supreme Court decreed the partition, adjudging to the Plaintiffs a certain fraction of the joint estate. They also assigned the specific villages and lands constituting the Plaintiff's share. As the public assessment of revenue had so far been on the whole estate, the Court after assigning the shares also distributed the public assessment on each. And to compel the performance of the Decree, the rents and profits of the joint estate were sequestered and an officer of the Court was appointed as Receiver to collect the Revenue on the spot.

The last action drew the strongest objection from the Administration. The Revenue Board protested that great inconvenience was likely to be caused by the appointment of an European officer of the Court to collect the public revenue because that officer would not be amenable to the Mofussil Courts or liable to the penalties prescribed for the undue exaction of rent.[1]

[1] Letter from Board of Revenue to Vice-President-in-Council, 6th March 1829, para 3, Parl. Papers, 1831, Vol. 6, Appx V, Encl. 7.

Holt Mackensie apprehended that the appointment of Receivers by the Supreme Court would prejudice the revenue collection.[1] Metcalfe stated that such an action was calculated to set the Regulations of the Government at nought.[2]

The Government also contended that the Supreme Court had no authority to partition or transfer property in the Mofussil. Though Advocate General Pearson admitted that such a power had been exercised by the Court from the earliest times, he doubted whether it had any legal basis at all.[3]

The Chief Justice's reply to all this was that under the Charter constituting the Court, full and exclusive powers had been given to them to decide suits between inhabitants of Calcutta. By Statute 21 Geog, III, Cap. 70, S. 17, the Court was given full authority to decide disputes concerning their succession and inheritance. There could be no other way of securing the adjudged shares in the Mofussil except by appointing a Receiver. He argued :

> "It can not be seriously meant as a more easy proceeding that a suit should be instituted against an inhabitant of Calcutta in each Zilla in which any of the Taluks [Estates] may be; or even that this Court, after having declared the rights of the parties to a partition, should direct them to bring a second suit against the Defendant in any other Court [of the Company] and take the chance of having the same thing decreed all over again . . ."

In 1831 the Bengal Government reported another series of cases to London in which the Supreme Court had exceeded their powers by exercising jurisdiction over succession to, and transfer of, property in the Mofussil.[4] On one of such cases (*Kistonand Biswas* vs. *Pran Khrishna Biswas),* Advocate General Pearson repeated his earlier opinion[5] that the Supreme Court had been exercising this power without the sanction of the Legislature.[6] He admitted at the same time that this authority had been exercised by the Court from the earliest times without being challenged. Cases in which this issue had appeared upon the pleadings had

[1] Quoted in the Note by Macnaghten (Register of S.D.A.), 9th April 1829, Parl. Papers 1831, Vol. 6, Appx V, Encl. 11.

[2] Minute of Metcalfe, 15th April 1829, Parl. Papers 1831, Vol. 6, Appx V, pp. 20-28.

[3] This opinion was given by Pearson in the case of *Hurruck Chandra Ghosh* vs. *Bundichand Datta,* Civ. Judl. Cons., 24th July 1828. Nos. 1-5.

[4] Judl. letter, 19th April 1831.

[5] See above.

[6] Pearson to Govt., 3rd Feb. 1831, printed in Circular Orders of S. D. A. (ed. T. Jones 1855), pp. 360-61.

gone to England on appeal and the King-in-Council had decided them, without it having struck them that the Supreme Court had exceeded their jurisdiction.

But while the Governments of Wellesley, Barlow, Minto, Hastings and Amherst had acquiesced and assisted in the exercise of such a jurisdiction by the Court, the administration of Bentinck and Metcalfe were bent upon challenging its propriety. Metcalfe informed the Directors that : "In our address to the Judges [of the Supreme Court] as well as in our correspondence with the Governor General, we have specially guarded against the drawing of any inference which might imply an acquiescence, on the part of the Government, in the jurisdiction exercised by the Supreme Court over Estates in the Mofussil..."[1] He then urged the Directors to press the Privy Council to give a clarification or to obtain an explanatory enactment from the Parliament itself.[2]

It may be noticed from the preceding narrative that all the disputes between the Court and the Government originated from the issue of the former's processes against persons or properties in the Mofussil. Metcalfe alleged that the Judges were always inclined to take advantage of the vagueness of the Statutes and extend their jurisdiction beyond the actual provisions. He said that the Barristers and Attorneys of the Court also had the strongest inducement to urge such extensions as their income improved with the increase of business brought before the Court.[3]

The Judges of the Court on the other hand complained of a lack of cooperation from the Government. They regretted that instead of trying to bring about a synthesis between the Company's judiciary and the Supreme Court, the Government had been inclined to erect their judicial structure separately and in a form of opposition to the King's Court.[4]

Both were extreme views. In fact the incidents of conflict between the Court and the Government, either during the pre-1800 period, or during the post-1828 period, were neither the outcome of a passion on the part of the Judges to enlarge their powers,

[1] Judl. Letter, 19th April 1831.

[2] *Ibid.*

[3] Minute of Metcalfe-in-Council, in Secret Dept., 15th April 1829, Parl. Papers 1831, Vol. 6, Appx. V. Encl. 8.

[4] Letter from Supreme Court to Board of Control, Sept. 1830, Parl. Papers 1831, Vol. 6, Appx. V, No. 26, Encl. 4.

nor the result of an attempt by the Government to obstruct the functioning of the Court. The occasions for friction arose out of the inadequacy of provisions with regard to the jurisdiction of the Court and the consequent uncertainty in the exercise of their powers. Neither St. 13 Geo. III, Cap. 63 (of 1773), by which the Court had been created, nor St. 21 Geo. III, Cap. 70, by which its jurisdiction was redefined, specifically provided for the contingencies in which the Court might have to issue processes against persons or properties outside Calcutta. As it came to be, persons or properties coming directly under the jurisdiction of the Supreme Court often involved persons or properties lying in the Mofussil under the exclusive jurisdiction of the Company's administration. The Supreme Court when called upon to decide such cases were faced with the choice of either issuing their processes in the Mofussil or abandoning their legitimate jurisdiction over persons or properties within Calcutta. The Government on the other hand found the sanctity of its own administration threatened when the writs of the Supreme Court started running into the Districts. Very often estates attached or sequestered by the Supreme Court were found subject to another litigation in the Company's Court, or even already adjudged to a particular party by the latter.

Persons directly subject to the Court's jurisdiction often held lands which contributed their share of revenue to the administration. In the suits against them the Court frequently found it necessary to seize, divide or sell such lands. Yet by St. 21 Geo. III, Cap. 70, S. 8, they were forbidden to exercise jurisdiction in any matter which concerned public revenue. This was another ambiguous provision the Court had to deal with.

Even the definition of persons who were to be subject to the Court's jurisdiction was left vague in the Statutes. This gave rise to many doubtful cases. Under the Charter of 1774 the jurisdiction of the Court was prescribed over certain classes of persons. Among them were all "British" subjects and all inhabitants of Calcutta, whether Indians or Europeans. The question was—who were the British subjects ? In St. 21 Geo. III and other Acts, the term "British subject" is never used in a sense to include any category of Indians. But even in 1773, Calcutta was Crown's territory and the Indians living there must have been regarded as subjects of the Crown. That is why they were made amenable to the King's Court. A distinction had therefore to be maintained between the "British subjects" and the "Subjects of the Crown."[1] This distinction was never specifically provided for by any of the enactments. It rested upon the inference drawn from the term "British subjects" in the several Statutes, particularly St. 21, Geo. III, Cap. 70. It was generally agreed that the term "British subjects" included all persons born in Great Britain, or whose fathers or paternal grand fathers were born there, so as to exclude the Hindu and Muslim inhabitants within or without the Presidency towns.[2]

The liabilities of the "British subject" were fully defined by the Statutes. He was to be amenable to the Supreme Court for any Criminal act committed in any part of the Presidency.[3] In Civil causes too he was liable to the same Court so long as he resided in Calcutta. But if he went out of Calcutta as a private citizen, he was required to obtain a licence from the Company's Government.[4] If he wanted to live anywhere beyond a radius of ten miles from Calcutta for personal reasons, he was required to execute a bond making himself amenable to the local Company's Court for Civil actions against him.[5] By St. 53 Geo. III, Cap. 155, of 1813, British subjects residing in the interior were generally made amenable to the local Courts of the Company in all Civil actions against Indians. No bond was to be required now. But the British subject was allowed the choice of appealing from the local Court's decision to the Supreme Court, instead of the S.D.A.

But the position of an Indian inhabitant of Calcutta who was only "Subject of the King" was not as certain once he left Calcutta. He was required neither to take a licence for going out of

[1] Letter from Supreme Court to Board of Control, Sept. 1830. Parl. Papers 1831, Vol. 6, Appx. V, No. 26, Encl. 4.

[2] Letter from Supreme Court to Board of Control. Sept. 1830, Parl. Papers 1831, Vol. 6. Appx. V, No. 26, Encl. 4.

[3] An exception was made to this rule by St. 53. Geo. III, Cap. 155 passed in 1813. By Cl. 105 of the Act British subjects residing outside the Presidency towns were for petty crimes made amenable to punishment by fine up to Rs. 500.00 by the local Magistrate.

[4] By Section 28 of St. 21 Geo. III, Cap. 70.

[5] By Regulation XXVIII of 1793.

Calcutta into the Provinces, nor to execute a bond when he transferred his residence from Calcutta to some place in the interior. What would be his position if he decided to go out of Calcutta or to live in the interior? To whom would he be amenable if he committed a crime outside Calcutta? In the absence of any statutory declaration the answers to such questions had to be supplied by interpretation. From the practice followed by the Supreme Court it is apparent that they tended to place the Indians of Calcutta in the same position as the British subjects in respect of their liabilities to the Court. Thus Indians living out of Calcutta were allowed to sue, or be sued by, the Indians of Calcutta.[1] This was obviously done under the sanction of that clause of the Charter which permitted Indians not amenable to the Court to submit voluntarily to their jurisdiction, in suits instituted against them by British subjects.[2] Likewise the Supreme Court regarded the Indians of Calcutta as liable, in the same manner as the British subjects, to them for crimes committed in any part of the Presidency.[3] The Court was willing to go even a step further. They claimed that the existing legal status of even the Indians living out of Calcutta was the same as that of the Calcutta Indians. They were now equally subjects of the Crown and there was no constitutional justification why even they should not be liable to the Supreme Court for crimes committed anywhere.[4] Their reasoning was as follows: In the Charter of 1774 the term "British subjects" had been used generally to exclude the Indians living outside Calcutta who, though being governed by the Company, were still nominally regarded as the Subjects of the Moghul Emperor. But since then the situation had materially altered. Though it can not be precisely stated when the dominion of the Moghul Emperor formally terminated and that of the Crown began over the whole of the Presidency, it was at least clear that the sovereignty of the British Crown over all the territorial acquisitions in India was indirectly asserted in 1813 by Act 53 Geo. III, Cap. 155. In that Statute the territories under Company's

[1] See above.

[2] See above.

[3] Particular reference: case of Khudabaksh and 'C'. See above.

[4] Letter from Supreme Court to Board of Control (n.d.), Parl. Papers 1831, Vol. 6, Appx. V, Encls. 16-18.

administration lying outside the limits of the Presidency towns of Calcutta, Madras and Bombay are referred to throughout as "British Territories". And from this it followed that all those residing there were King's subjects.

The Judges even argued that so far the Supreme Court was the only tribunal in Bengal which was legally (under the Parliamentary Statutes) competent to try charges of crimes and misdemeanours, other than abuses in collection of revenue.[1] They claimed that the entire establishment of the Sadr-nizamat Adalat and the subordinate Courts of Criminal justice created and maintained by the Company had been made without any authority of the Crown or Parliament. St. 21 Geo. III, Cap. 70 had recognised the existence of the Courts maintained by the Company. But the only Courts maintained by the Company then were the S.D.A. and the subordinate Courts of Civil judicature. The Sadr Nizamat Adalat and the entire machinery of Criminal judicial administration was then under the management of the Nawab. The Company took over the Sadr Nizamat Adalat and the administration of Criminal justice from him in 1790. The arrangement was incorporated in the Regulations passed by the Government in 1793. But in 1793, the Judges argued, no power had been created by the Crown or Parliament, under which, except for revenue offences, the Bengal Government could establish Courts of Criminal justice. In other words St. 21 Geo. III, Cap 70, had only given retrospective recognition to the judicial Courts existing in 1781. It had extended no prospective sanction for tribunals to be erected by them in future.

The legal analysis of the Judges might not have been wrong though it would have been impracticable and impossible to put that into practice. The Judges never did, in practice, regard the Indians living out of Calcutta as amenable to their Court for crimes committed by them. Nor did they ever challenge the existence of the S.N.A. or the subordinate Criminal Courts. Their arguments were only meant to prove that the jurisdiction already being exercised by them was well within their permitted authority.

The stand taken by the Government boiled down to this.

1 Letter from Supreme Court to Board of Control (n.d.), Parl. Papers 1831, Vol. 6, Appx. V, No. 26, Encl. 4. pp. 117-140.

Indians were subject to the Supreme Court's jurisdiction only so long as they lived in Calcutta. Once they moved out of Calcutta they moved out of the Court's jurisdiction, both in Civil and Criminal matters. After leaving Calcutta they could be liable to the Supreme Court's jurisdiction only for crimes committed during their residence there, but for any crimes committed outside that city they were to be subject to the ordinary jurisdiction of the local Company's Court.[1]

So long as the Parliament did not declare its actual intention on the above issues both the Court and the Government could assert with equal justification that their own interpretation was correct. Here lay the seed of contention. Metcalfe rightly observed that after 1780,

"Either from a better understanding of the intentions of the legislature, or from a mutual moderation between the Government and the Judges, or from a submission of the Government to gradual or quiet encroachments [by the Supreme Court]. . . there has not been the same degree of misunderstanding or dispute regarding the powers of the King's Courts ; but it is evident from what is now passing on at this Presidency and from what has happened before, both at Madras and Bombay, that seeds of dissension still exist in the undefined condition of the jurisdiction of the Supreme Courts."[2]

Following the recent disputes several suggestions were made for working out an arrangement that would reduce the chances of friction between the Court and the Government.

Bentinck carried on some discussions with the Court for exploring ways and means by which the Court and the Government might arrive at a smoother working arrangement. But there could be no agreement between him and the Judges.[3]

The merger of the Supreme Court with the Company's judicial system was the answer to all the difficulties. Several authorities, including Bentinck and Metcalfe, subscribed to this idea.[4]

But the amalgamation of the Supreme Court with the Company's judiciary would not have been practicable without the creation of a common law giving authority for all persons and the formation of common codes applicable to Indians and Britons alike.

[1] The views of the Government are deducible from Metcalfe's Minute in Secret Deptt., 15th April 1829, Parl. Papers 1831, Vol. 6, Appx. V. Encl. 8.

[2] *Ibid.*

[3] Bentinck to Ellenborough, 23rd Feb. 1830, Colchester Papers.

[4] Metcalfe to Bentinck, 11th Oct. 1829, Colchester Papers.

Meanwhile, the existing rivalry between the Government and the Supreme Court had been engaging the attention of the authorities in London. A strong opinion was building up at the Board for an intervention in favour of the Government. Already in 1829, Ellenborough, President of Board of Control, had privately communicated to Bentinck his determination to support the Government against the Court.[1] His successor, Charles Grant, made a strong plea for putting the jurisdiction of the Supreme Courts under the control of Indian Governments.[2] Two more personalities pushed the campaign against the Courts with great zeal. They were T.B. Macaulay, the Secretary of the Board, and James Mill, the Examiner of Company's correspondence.

Macaulay held a contemptuous opinion of the Court and expressed it most forcefully with his magnificent rhetoric. He regarded the Supreme Courts as unfit to administer justice to any class of Indians because the Judges were not familiar with their customs and usages.[3] He argued that the maintenance of the Supreme Courts (apparently considered to be constituted by better qualified Judges and applying a superior system of laws) for a handful of British subjects in India gave an impression of partiality to the latter. This in effect meant that : "We proclaim to the people that there are two sorts of justice, a coarse one, which we think good enough for them, and another of a superior quality reserved for ourselves."[4]

James Mill questioned the utility of maintaining the Supreme Courts at all.[5] He argued that the Courts applying English laws had been originally established to administer justice to a small number of Englishmen who settled around the factories because it was not considered safe to subject them to the strange Courts and procedures of the Moghul system. But the situation had changed since. A fully fledged structure of judicial tribunals was now organised and maintained in India by an English administration which was under the constant control and supervision of

[1] See above.

[2] Grant's speech in Parliament, Hansard, Series III, Vol. XIX, pp. 512-13.

[3] Macaulay, *Essays*, Vol. III, p. 388.

[4] Minute of Macaulay (n.d.), Parl. Papers, 1837-38, Vol. 41, pp. 218-20.

[5] Evidence of James Mill before Select Committee of House of Lord. 29th June 1832, Parl. Branch Colls., 1832, Vol. 77, pp. 119-21.

Parliament. Hence it had become superfluous to maintain a separate judicial establishment for administering justice to a handful of Englishmen. This argument was quite plausible.

Replying to a notion that the Supreme Courts could act as a bar to the illegal acts of the Government*, Mill stated that the Courts could offer such protection only to an Englishman. This was because the acts of the Indian Government could be judged illegal only in relation to the laws made by a superior authority (King and Parliament) upon which the rights and liberties of the English settlers still depended. The rights of Indian subjects were based solely upon the laws enacted by the Indian Governments. Hence there was no question of an Indian Government committing an illegal act against any Indian subject. This point had been more lucidly analysed by George Norton, the Advocate General of Madras. He observed :

"The duty of the judicial authority is to administer that as a law, and to declare that to be illegal, which the Government has pronounced [to be so]. To bar any acts of a Government as illegal, is to assume to be the Government . . . When the Court would bar any acts as illegal it is precisely because they are not authorised by Government, though they may be under the guise of acts so authorised; when the local Government affects to authorise an act forbidden by the law of a superior paramount Government, the local Government is not, in fact, the Government, but the organ of the Supreme Government [i.e. the British] . . . [when only it] is subjected to be judged of [for legality]."[1]

Even as regards the British subjects, Mill commented that there had been very few instances in which the Government had been charged for injury to an Englishman before the Supreme Court. Besides, he said, an Englishman would have abundant means of making his complaints known, and for urging his claims to redress (in England) if the Supreme Court ceased to exist.

Mill also denied that the Supreme Court on account of their superior legal knowledge and proceedings had any influence in ameliorating the proceedings of the Company's Courts. The reason was that the system followed in the Supreme Court was basically different from that followed in Company Courts. Also,

*The Bombay Supreme Court had made this assertion in effect by issuing a writ of *habeas corpus* for the release of an Indian detained under official orders.

[1] Norton to Malcolm (Governor of Bombay), 1st Jan. 1830, Bentinck MSS.

only a very small section of the population and the Company's judicial officers had the opportunity of becoming acquainted with the working of the Supreme Court. He remarked: "In my opinion the English Courts afford more examples of what is to be avoided than what is to be followed in the tribunals erected in India."[1]

These were the influences that were brought to bear upon the Parliament while they considered their verdict on the issues between the Courts and the Indian Governments. The Charter Act was passed in 1833. One of its main objects was to improve the legislature and reform the conflicting judicatures.

The Act established a central legislative authority for the whole of India. This was to be the Governor-General-in-Council at Calcutta. They were empowered to make or repeal laws for all the three Presidencies and for "all persons whether British or Native, Foreigners or others, and for all the Courts of Justice, whether established by His Majesty's Charters or otherwise, and the jurisdictions thereof . . . "[2]

The long controversy between the Supreme Court and the Government of the Company thus came to an end. The latter had emerged decisively victorious. The jurisdiction of the Court which formed the theme of the dispute was now put completely at the discretion of the Governor-General-in-Council. Only, the Governor-General-in-Council were prohibited from abolishing the Supreme Courts without the sanction of the Home authorities[3].

One might ask why the Supreme Courts were not abolished and merged into a common judicial system in 1833. The reason was that until the common codes suitable for all were framed, it was considered prudent to continue administering justice to the British subjects according to the English procedure. The Judges of the Company who had no professional training, were considered unfit to administer justice according to the English legal system. The Supreme Courts were, therefore, retained pending the formation of the Indian Codes.

A Law Commission had been constituted under the Act of 1833 for the purpose of recommending a common legal system for

[1] Mill, *loc. cit.*, p. 183.

[2] 3 & 4. Will. IV, Cap. 85, S. 47.

[3] St. 3 & 4 Will, IV, Cap. 85, S. 46.

India. For several reasons its deliberations were unduly delayed. It was only after the Civil Procedure Code was passed by the Legislature of India that the existing Supreme Court and the S.D.A., and their jurisdictions, were merged into the High Courts, established under the Indian High Courts Act of 1861.

SOME CONCLUSIONS

THE COMPANY'S JUDICIAL structure marked a great advance over the Moghul system. Uncertain justice according to personal discretion was replaced by a more certain justice according to the 'rule of law', and for the most irregularly distributed judicial tribunals acting without any coordination were substituted a gradation of Courts uniformly distributed, each exercising control over the one below, through the revision of its decisions and inspection of its periodical reports on the amount of business transacted and pending. The former oral proceedings, which left no evidence if the Judge made a faulty assessment of testimony and passed a wrong decision, were now replaced by a system which required every stage of the trial, from institution to termination, to be committed to writing.

But in spite of these revolutionary improvements, the judicial structure established in 1793 was not equal to the pressure of work imposed upon it. The handful of tribunals was unable to cope with the enormous volume of litigation which arose. The progressive increase of litigation had an inherent cause in the laws of inheritance in India. There being no law of primogeniture either among the Hindus or among the Muslims, each son being entitled to an equal share of the family property, there could be no limit to the division of property and to the creation of new titles. Individual property rights could now be easily contested and legally established through the Courts and an increase of litigation naturally resulted. A new element of commercialism which came into operation with the progress of Company's rule created new interests and opened fresh avenues of litigation. Apart from these general causes, a factor responsible for a major portion of the litigation was the "precipitation with which the Permanent Settlement was carried into effect without previously defining the relative rights and interests of the Zamindars . . . and the various other classes of the cultivating population."[1] While the disputes between the Zamindars and the raiyats formed the bulk of the cases, the lack of recorded documents defining their respective positions rendered the settlement of such controversies complicated and dilatory.[2] The result was the growth of a backlog of pending suits and delays in obtaining decisions. In the Courts of European Judges it was impossible to have a decision within two or three years of the institution of the complaint. Even in the Courts of Indian Judges suitors had to wait for five to six months before getting a Decree. The trials, more particularly in the European Judges' Courts, involved a long drawn-out process. Sometimes, parties had to be prepared to be in attendance at the Courts for months at a stretch. But obtaining the Decree was not always the end of the suitor's pursuit of justice. If the judgment "debtor" refused to abide by the Court's decision or order voluntarily the Decree holder had to apply for an "execution" to the District Judge under whose jurisdiction the "debtor" resided or held property. More often than not, the Judge was prevented from taking immediate cognizance of the application on account of his other pressing duties, and also because he already had a waiting list of such applications which deserved prior attention. Lord Hastings rightly observed in 1820 : "To pass decrees is unfortunately no test of diligence or judgment. But to cause them to be fulfilled, to make them effectual to the parties . . . [is the ultimate object] . . . These operations require the most serious sacrifice of time."[3] The Decrees of Munsiffs could be executed by the Judge or the Register only. Hence, a person who obtained a decision from the Munsiff of his locality was likely to lose most of the advantage of having a tribunal near at hand, if to have the decision implemented he had to travel all the way to the District headquarters.

Not only was the Company's judicial system dilatory but it turned out to be intolerably expensive for many. In all suits of less than Rs. 500.00 the expenses of the plaintiffs were calculated

[1] Judl. Letter from Bengal (Western Province), 22nd Feb. 1827, para. 12. Vol. 10.

[2] *Ibid.*

[3] Resolution of Govn. Gen.-in-Council, 14th Feb. 1820, Civ. Judl. Cons., 23rd April 1821, Nos. 8 and 9.

at 22 per cent of the amount or value of the case.[1] For instance, if a raiyat had to sue a Zamindar for an undue exaction of Rs. 120.00 he would have to pay Rs. 8 as the institution fee and another Rs. 32.00 on account of the subsequent charges on the exhibits and on Pleaders, Witnesses and Peons.[2] But this amount includes only the expenses required by the Regulations. It does not take into account the allowances for private agents *(Mokhtears)* whom the suitors invariably retained during the trial of their case.[3]

The delays and expenses of obtaining justice ruined many and often prevented sufferers from seeking redress. Henry Strachey, the Judge of Midnapur, stated : "I have often seen a suitor when stripped of his last rupee and called upon for the fee on a document, produce in the Court a silver ring or a trinket and beg that it might be received as a pledge . . . "[4]

The delay of years before a suit was taken up for trial often complicated the issues. For instance, in the interval between the institution and the trial of a suit concerning the "forcible dispossession" of a piece of land, the landmarks of the property in dispute might disappear, or the area of the land situated on a river bank might increase or decrease as a result of the annual inundation.

Another harmful result of the long gap between institution and trial was the danger of perversion of the testimony. While the recollection of facts might be weakened in the minds of the genuine witnesses due to the lapse of time, it gave the contending parties ample leisure to prepare and tutor fake witnesses as well as to influence the genuine ones to give concocted evidence in their favour. Perjury among Indians was a crime commonly complained of by the contemporary Judges. One might wonder whether the operation of the Company's judicial system was not indirectly responsible for it to a considerable extent.

Delays in justice also affected the peace of the society. Failure

[1] Note of H. Shakespear, Superintendent of Police (n.d.), Bentinck MSS., Pw Jf, 2566.

[2] Evidence of Holt Mackenzie before Parliamentary Committee of enquiry, 3rd April 1832, Parl. Branch Colls., 1832, Vol. 77, pp. 41-43.

[3] *Ibid.*

[4] Civ. Judl. Cons., 8th July 1802, No. 55.

to obtain redress expeditiously through the judicial Courts often induced the aggrieved parties to take the law into their own hands. This was particularly true of cases concerning forcible dispossession of lands and crops, which might be the only source of livelihood for the dispossessed persons. Under such circumstances the dispossessed party tried to recover his property by physical force with the help of friends and relatives. The dispossessor, equally determined to retain the possession, resisted with his own army of supporters. Such affrays, often accompanied with grievous injury and murder, became exceedingly common during the Company's administration.[1]

In 1815, Governor-General Moira assessed the effects of Company's judicial system as follows :

"I am reluctantly compelled to confess that its [judicial system's] operation appears not to correspond with what was to be anticipated from the expectations of those who framed the machinery of our judicial administration, or from the uprightness of those who execute its details : we seem to have accomplished a revolution in society which by an unexpected fatality, proved detrimental to general morals, and by no means conducive to the convenience of our Government."[2]

The cost of obtaining justice could not be minimised without sacrificing the procedure which assured a proper investigation before decision, and without incurring the danger of overflooding the Courts already in heavy arrears of pending litigation. But means must be devised to reduce the delays in securing justice. This was the task to which the attention of the Bengal Government was constantly rivetted throughout the period under reference. After a detailed analysis of the reforms made for the achievement of that object, it would be worth while noticing the general trends influencing their course.

The Bengal Government's approach until the arrival of Bentinck was to find a solution within the fold of Cornwallis's ideals. Wellesley separated the S.D.A. from the Council for the sake of the efficiency of the Court and because the exercise of the highest

[1] For example, in 1804 in the District of Jaunpur alone 5,700 persons had been involved in affrays over dispossession of lands and crops : Vide report of Meguthrie, Jaunpur J., 20th May, 1812, quoted in Judl. Despatch, 9th Nov. 1814, para, 47, Vol. 2.

[2] Moira's Minute, 21st Sept. 1815, para 108, Papers on the judicial system of Bengal, I.O. Reg. (71) 197.

judicial functions by the Executive body seemed highly objectionable in principle. By making this important change and withdrawing the preference in favour of Zamindars and revenue officers for recruitment as Munsiffs, Wellesley had in fact removed the discrepancy that had existed between Cornwallis's philosophy of "separation of powers" and his judicial arrangements of 1793. Wellesley's successor, Minto, further consolidated this principle by providing for a complete separation between the judicial and other services. In fact, the absolute faith in Cornwallis's principles that was held by Shore, Wellesley and Minto, and the advocacy of the S.D.A. after 1812, set up an administrative tradition in Bengal which could be shaken only by the continued pressure from London and the pragmatic approach of that reforming Governor-General, William Bentinck. The inconveniences of the combination of the Judgeship and the Magistracy had been repeatedly pointed out by the judicial officers of Bengal. The fifth report of the Select Committee of House of Commons emphasised its impracticability in 1812, and Governor-General Hastings admitted its incompatibility in 1815. The Directors came out in 1814 with a programme for relieving the District Judges by transferring all revenue suits, along with the Magisterial function, to the Collectors. In 1816 the Directors made their desire imperative on this issue. Hastings himself was amenable to the proposal but he was led to reject it under the influence of the S.D.A. and his chief adviser, George Dowdswell. It was only on the grounds of the absolute necessity of relieving the overburdened District Judges that his successor, John Adam, allowed the transfer of Magistracy to a few Collectors, and that only as a temporary measure. The following Government of Amherst firmly opposed the union of Magistracies with the Collectorships and advocated the appointment of separate officers in each District as the Magistrate. The Amherst Government allowed the Collectors the authority to decide revenue suits but a firm control over their judicial activity was lodged with the District Judges, who still held the discretion of referring such suits to those officers.

Cornwallis's scheme of keeping the association of Indians with the judicial administration at a very low level could not be rigidly maintained because the agency of Indians, unlike that of Europeans could be expanded to any degree demanded by the pressure of business without major financial embarrassment. Still, the prejudice of the "founder" definitely operated to slow down the extension of that side of the judiciary. Until 1821 the jurisdiction of Munsiffs extended to causes up to Rs. 64.00 only (an insignificant increase over the limit of Rs. 50.00 fixed by Cornwallis), and that of Sadr Amins up to Rs. 150.00 In 1821, on account of the shortage of European officers, the Government conceded the extension of the power of Munsiffs to cases up to Rs. 150.00, and that of specially selected Sadr Amins to Rs. 500.00. But when the Directors suggested the transfer of the entire original jurisdiction to the Indian Judges in 1824, the Amherst Government and the S.D.A. both opposed the proposal on the ground of such a sweeping change being beyond the scheme contemplated by Cornwallis.

During his Madras Governorship (1803-07), Bentinck had been impressed by Munro and his advocacy of the *ryotwari* settlement. At the same time he had expressed his faith in Cornwallis's judicial system, which had been introduced into the Madras Presidency in 1802. He condemned the previous system in which the Collectors were also Judges,[1] and stated: "The judicial system has answered the expectation formed by the illustrious founder, our late revered Governor-General."[2] Bentinck's above judgment on Cornwallis's system, which was not completely established in Madras until 1806, was premature. It seems to have been founded on his admiration of the progressive principles behind it rather than on the experience of its practical operation.

Bentinck came to assume the Governor-Generalship of Bengal in 1828, with the memory of his disgraceful recall from Madras following the Vellore mutiny in 1807, and with a keen desire to acquit himself with credit this time and to restore his reputation.[3] He had to erase the deficit of 2½ crores and set the Company's house in order before the question of renewal of its Charter came up before Parliament in 1833. Under these circumstances it was

[1] Bentinck to Sir Thomas Strange, 7th March 1805, Bentinck MSS, (Pw/Jb).

[2] Bentinck to Charles Grant, 11th May 1806, Bentinck MSS (Pw/Jb).

[3] This view was expressed by Prof. C. H. Philips in a Seminar lecture delivered at the School of Oriental and African Studies, London, on 16th March 1965. The present author agrees with it.

natural for him to adopt a pragmatic approach towards administrative problems rather than lean on abstract principles.

The need for making major changes in the existing judicial machinery was immediately appreciated by Bentinck, After completing an extensive tour of the Bengal Presidency shortly after his arrival he wrote to Metcalfe: "Closely connected with the same subject [happiness and welfare of the people] is the administration of justice admitted by all to be greatly defective, to be slow, expensive and unsatisfactory to the people. . ."[1] In his reforms Bentinck showed no hesitation in sacrificing Cornwallis's principles for the sake of practical benefits, but at the same time he avoided the opposite extreme of becoming a slave to Munro's authoritarian paternalism, which was pressed upon him by its champions, Metcalfe and Mackenzie. Bayley's and Mackenzie's proposals for transferring nearly the entire original jurisdiction to the Indian Judges, for abolishing the Provincial Courts and the District Registerships, found ready acceptance from Bentinck because they coincided with the scheme of achieving maximum efficiency with minimum expenses. But the proposal for making the decisions of the highest Court subject to the approval of the Government advocated by Metcalfe and Mackenzie were indignantly rejected by him. Likewise Metcalfe's scheme for uniting the functions of Judge, Magistrate and Collector in one officer at the District level was refused consideration. Bentinck accepted the plan of generally uniting the Magistracy with the Collectorship, which had been originally recommended by the Directors on the advocacy of Munro, and later argued for by Mackenzie and Metcalfe, the leading contemporary exponents of Munro's philosophy in Bengal. In adopting this reform Bentinck admitted to the influence of Munro's doctrines[2] but he hastened to justify that measure on practical grounds as well by saying. "It became necessary to divest the Judges of their Magisterial powers, and there was no alternative consistent with the dictates of financial necessity than to transfer those powers to the Collectors."[3]

Eric Stokes, in his celebrated book named *The English Utilitarians and India*, has made a brilliant effort to trace the impact of the Uti-

1 Bentinck to Metcalfe, 16th Sept. 1829, Bentinck MSS.

2 See Chap. IV.

3 Judl. Letter, 15th Sept. 1831, para 17. Vol. 15.

litarian movement in England, inspired by Jeremy Bentham, upon the administrative developments in India. According to Stokes the Utilitarian influence was projected into India through James Mill, who was appointed Assistant Examiner of the Company's correspondence in 1819 and promoted to the office of Examiner in 1830, where he remained until 1834. In Bengal the Utilitarian banner was carried forward consciously by Alexander Ross and Holt Mackenzie, and unconsciously by W. B. Bayley.* The main features of the Utilitarians programme concerning the reform of the judiciary were as follows:

1. The number of tribunals was to be multiplied to bring justice to the doors of every person.
2. Only one appeal was to be allowed against a decision passed by any Judge.
3. Single Judges were to be allowed complete authority to dispose of appeals. Joint benches were to be dispensed with.
4. Proceedings in the Courts were to be expedited by doing away with the formality of committing the depositions and cross examinations to writing.
5. The jurisdiction of tribunals was not to be divided on a pecuniary basis and original and appellate Courts were to be kept entirely distinct.

The above ideas made little headway in the reforms of the Bentinck era, as Stokes himself seems to agree. The number of tribunals was not multiplied (though Stokes inferred that they were[1] from the implementation of the plan creating a new class of Indian Judges and transferring almost the entire original jurisdiction to the Indian officers). The Principal Sadr Amins (the new class of Indian Judges) merely filled the gap created by the abolition of Registers, and the number of Munsiffs was actually reduced by more than half following the Government's decision to abolish those Munsiffships whose incomes from fees averaged below Rs. 50.00 per month.[2] The system of allowing two appeals,

* This is to be inferred from Dr. Stokes' remark that Bayley's proposal for multiplication of tribunals agreed with the broad outlines of Bentham's teaching but that his inspiration was not Benthamite.—Dr. Eric Stokes, *op. cit.*, p. 156.

[1] Dr. Stokes, *op. cit.*, p. 155-6.

[2] See Chap. II.

one "regular" and one "special", was also continued under the arrangements of 1831. In fact Ross, the most "orthodox in the Utilitarian tradition",[1] had been the strongest advocate for retaining the system of special appeals.[2] James Mill and Ross did combine in making a strong plea for allowing all the Judges of the S.D.A. to sit separately and decide the appeals entirely on their own.[3] But what they achieved was only a slight increase in the powers of "single" Judges. By Regulation IX of 1831, single Judges were permitted to admit special appeals and to refer an appeal back for retrial to the Court whose judgment was appealed against. But no change was made in the previous restriction of single Judges not being allowed to reverse a decision on appeal.

Neither was any change made in the system of recording the depositions and cross examinations. The jurisdiction of Courts was still divided on a pecuniary basis, starting from the limit of Rs. 300.00 for Munsiffs and extending to the limit of Rs. 5,000.00 for the Principal Sadr Amin. Original and appellate jurisdictions were separated but not completely. The District Judges had the appellate authority over the decision of the Indian Judges, but they also had original jurisdiction over cases of more than Rs. 5,000.00. Even the Principal Sadr Amins were allowed to hear appeals from the subordinate Indian Judges under permission from the S.D.A. Here again the Utilitarian doctrines had little success.

On the issue of the combination of executive and judicial powers Bentham's opinion does not appear to be clear. At one stage Stokes states that Bentham's political philosophy was authoritarian in origin and he was critical of the Whigs for their "vaunted principle of separation of powers."[4] At another he declares that the union of Collector and Magistrate brought about by Bentinck commanded no definite support from Bentham's teachings,[5] although he adds that Bentham was not averse to an officer uniting all executive and judicial functions at the

[1] Stokes, *op. cit.*, p. 157.
[2] See Chap. VI.
[3] See Chap. VI.
[4] Stokes, *op. cit.*, p. 73.
[5] Stokes, *op. cit.*, p. 164.

local level, as the powers of the "local Headman" in the *Constitutional Code* indicate.[1]

In Bengal the Utilitarian ranks were divided on this issue. Ross, the "more orthodox in the Utilitarian tradition",[2] vehemently opposed the union of judicial powers with the executive officer of the District, whereas Mackenzie, drawing his inspiration from the authoritarian strain in Bentham's philosophy, strongly championed union of Magistracy with the Collectorships. "James Mill's opinion is unknown apart from his common rejection with Bentham of the division of powers as a constitutional principle."[3] But if James Mill, the Examiner of Company's Correspondence, described by Stokes as the Company's chief "Executive", had any influence on the Judicial Despatch to Bengal of 1st Feb. 1832, which directed the Bengal Government to appoint separate Magistrates in each District instead of combining that office with that of Collectors, it can be assumed that he too stood against the union.

After the above analysis the present author is led to conclude that the Utilitarian doctrines had very little influence on the Civil judicial reforms of the Bentinck era. Theoretical considerations had but very little effect. The reforms were primarily dictated by the practical need of reducing arrears and delays without increasing expenditure.

[1] Stokes, *op. cit.*, p. 165.

[2] *Ibid.*, p. 157.

[3] *Ibid.*, pp. 164-5.

Bibliography

I COLLECTIONS OF PRIVATE MANUSCRIPTS

Bentinck Papers at the Nottingham University Library

PW/JB

Private correspondence of Lord William Bentinck as Governor of Madras (1803-7) particularly his correspondence with Sir George Barlow, Lord Minto, Sir Thomas Strange and Charles Grant :

Letter Books, 722-727

PW/JF

Private correspondence of Lord William Bentinck as Governor-General, 1828-35. Folders Nos. 2566, 2571, 2634, 2653 and 2715, which include some official Minutes and Papers and some letters not directly concerning Bentinck. In addition Bentinck's correspondence during the period of his Governor-Generalship, with the following persons has been consulted :

Sir Charles T. Metcalfe	PW/JF	1510-1698
Holt Mackenzie	,,	1340-51
W. B. Bayley	,,	413-18
James Mill	,,	1799-1800
Sir James Malcolm	,,	1404-1408
Sir Charles Grey	,,	2660
Charles Grant	PW/JF	1054-1071
Ram Mohan Roy	,,	1965
Alexander Ross	,,	1963
William Astell	,,	2086

Colchester Papers, at the Public Record Office, PRO. 30/9

Private correspondence of Lord Ellenborough with Lord William Bentinck (1828-34), Boxes 4, 10 and 12.

Elphinstone Papers, I.O. Library MSS Eur. F. 89, Box 2.

Correspondence between Earl of Moira (later Lord Hastings) and W. R. Elphinstone, 1814-18.

Hastings Papers, I.O. Library, Microfilm reel No. 782.

Private correspondence of Francis Rawdon Hastings pertaining to the period of his Governor-Generalship, 1813-22.

Melville Papers, National Library of Scotland, Edinburgh, MS 12.

Memoir on the judicial system by Sir Thomas Munro, 1808-9.

Minto Papers, National Library of Scotland, Edinburgh.

First Lord Minto's private correspondence with Sir George Barlow, H. T. Colebrooke and John Lumsden.

MS Nos. 47, 65, 155, 156, 160-66, 176, 372 and 377

Persian Correspondence of Lord Minto as Governor-General MS Nos. 214-35

II OFFICIAL UNPUBLISHED SOURCES (INDIAN OFFICE LIBRARY)

Appendix to Minutes of Court of Directors, and containing "Minutes of Dissent", vols. 4, 5 and 6.

Bengal Civil Judicial Consultations, 1795-1831.

Bengal Criminal Judicial Consultations, 1800-31 (only relevant volumes seen).

Bengal Revenue Judicial Consultations, 1791-93.

Committee of Circuit Proceedings, 1772-73.

Correspondence between the Court of Directors and Board of Control, vols. 3 & 4.

Home Miscellaneous Series, vols, 530, 775, 776, 824-26.

Judicial Despatches to Bengal, 1804-38 (Board's copies)

Judicial Despatch to Madras, 14th April 1814.

Judicial Letters Received from Bengal, 1803-38 (Board's copies)

Sadar Dewani Adalut Proceedings, 1793-1801.

III OFFICIAL PUBLISHED MATERIALS

A. *Imperial Gazeteer of India,* Provincial Series, Bengal, 1909, 2 vols.

B. *Parliamentary Papers of House of Lord and House of Commons* :

1810 Vol. 5, Second report of the Select Committee of House of Commons: portions relating to revenue and judicial establishments in Bengal.

1830 Vol. 6, Report of Select Committee of House of Lord, concerning administration of justice in India.

1831 Vol. 5 (Paper No. 65), Minutes of Evidence of Select Committee of House of Commons, containing papers relating to the Supreme Court of Calcutta.

1831-32 Vol. 12, Minutes of Evidence of House of Commons on Courts of justice.

1837-38 Vol. 41, Minutes of Government of India on jurisdiction of Mofussil Courts over Europeans, printed by House of Commons.

C. *India Office Library, Parliamentary Branch Collections :*

1772-73 Vol. 7, Sixth and seventh reports of Committee of Secrecy of House of Commons, relating to the state of judiciary under the Moghul administration.

1782 Vol. 14, Seventh report of Select Committee of House of Commons (Burke's Committee), on judicial reforms of Warren Hastings's Administration.

1812 Vol. 56, Fifth report of Select Committee of House of Commons, concerning existing judicial system.

1832 Vol. 77, Minutes of Evidence of House of Commons—Judicial. This volume contains very valuable statistical information on the judicial administration, and Minutes of officials on that subject.

D. *Parliamentary Debates (Hansard).* Series III, vol. XIX, 2nd to 25th July, 1833.

E. *Reports, etc., published by the Government of India* : *Papers regarding Judicial System in Bengal Presidency*, India Office Register (71) 197, Calcutta, 1815.

Historical Account of Judicial Systems of Bengal, Madras, and Bombay, by Law Commission, I. O. Register (71) 171, Calcutta, 1843.

Law Commission Report on Native Judicatories in all Presidencies, I. O. Register (71) 153, Calcutta, 1843.

History of the changes in the Civil and Criminal Jurisdiction exercised by the Courts in India over British European Subjects, Simla, 1883.

[Royal] Charters Granted to the East India Company, Madras, 1887.

Acts, Public and General, relating to India, of the reigns of George III, George IV, and William IV.

East India Register, 1800-31.

IV UNOFFICIAL PUBLISHED MATERIALS

A Collection of Treaties, Engagements and Sanads Relating to India and Neighbouring Countries, (ed.) C.U. Aitchinson, (II vols.), Vol. I, Calcutta, 1892-3.

The Regulations of the Government of Fort William (1793-1834), (ed.) R. Clarke, London, 1854.

Correspondence of Marquis Cornwallis, (ed.) Charles Ross, 3 vols., London, 1859.

The Despatches, Minutes and Correspondence of the Marquis of Wellesly, (ed.) M. Martin, 5 vols., London, 1836-7.

Memoirs of the Life of Rt. Hon. Warren Hastings First Governor-General of Bengal, (ed.) G.R. Gleig, (3 vols.), Vol. I, London, 1841.

Ain-I-Akbari, (translated) H.S. Jarret, Calcutta, 1873.

V SECONDARY SOURCES

A. *Books :*

Adams, G. B., *Constitutional History of England.* London, 1935.

Acharya, B. K., *Codification in British India.* Calcutta, 1914.

Aspinal I, A. *Cornwallis in Bengal.* Manchester, 1931.

Auber, P., *Rise and Progress of British Power in India.* Calcutta, 1914.

Baden-Powell, B. H., *The Origin and Growth of Village Communities in India.* London, 1899.

Bannerjee, D. N., *Early Administrative System of the East India Company in Bengal.* London, 1943.

Beaglehole, T. H., *Thomas Munro and the Development of Administrative Policy in Madras, 1792-1818 : the Origin of the Munro System.* Cambridge, 1966.

Bolts, W., *Considerations on India Affairs.* London, 1762.

Bryce, J., *Studies in History and Jurisprudence.* Oxford, 1901.

Cowell, H., *The History and Constitution of the Courts and Legislative Authorities in India,* (Tagore Law Lectures, 1872). Calcutta, 1872.

Dodwell, E., and Miles, J. S., *Alphabetical list of the Honourable East India Company's Bengal Civil Servants, from the year 1780, to the year 1838*. London, 1839.

Fawcett, C. G. H., *The First Century of British Justice in India*. Oxford, 1934.

Galloway, A., *Observations on the Law and Constitution of India...with an Enquiry into the Revenue and Judicial Administration, and Regulations of Police at Present Existing in Bengal*. London, 1825.

Cooch, G. P., *Political Thought in England from Bacon to Halifax*, London, 1933.

Hand, J. R., *The Early English Administration of Bihar, 1781-85*. Calcutta, 1894.

Harington, J. H., *An Elementary Analysis of Laws and Regulations Enacted by the Governor-General-in-Council, at Fort William in Bengal...*, (3 vols.), Vol. I. Calcutta, 1805-17.

Holwell, J, Z., *India Tracts*, London, 1764.

Kaye, J. W., *The Administration of the East India Company : A History of Indian Progress*. London, 1853.

Keith, A. B., *Speeches and Documents on Indian Policy*, 1750-1921 (2 vols.), Vol. I. Oxford, 1922.

—*A Constitutional History of India, 1600-1935*. London, 1936.

Macaulay, T. B., *Historical Essays (contributed to Edinburgh Review)*. London, 1913.

Maine, H. S., *Village Communities in the East and West*. London, 1876.

—*Ancient Law*. London, 1905.

Mill, J. and H. H., Wilson, *The History of British in India* (8 vols.), vols. 5, 7 and 8. London, 1820.

Miller, J., *On the Administration of Justice in the East Indies*. London, 1828.

Misra, B. B., *The Central Administration of the East India Company, 1773-1834*. Manchester, 1959.

—*The Judicial Administration of the East India Company*, 1765-1782. Delhi, 1961.

Morley, W. H., *The Administration of Justice in British India : containing an account of the Laws peculiar to India*. London, 1858.

Pandey, B. N., *The Introduction of English into India, The Career of Sir Elijah Impey in Bengal*. Bombay, 1967.

Patra, A. C., *The Administration of Justice under the East India Company in Bengal, Bihar and Orissa*. Bombay, 1962.

Philips, C. H., *The East India Company, 1784-1834*. Manchester, 1961.

Shore, F. J., *Notes on Indian Affairs,* 2 vols. London, 1837. Stokes, E., *The English Utilitarians and India*. Oxford, 1959. Thornton, E., *The History of the British Empire in India*, (6 vols.), Vol. II. London, 1841-45.

Verelst, H., *A View of the Rise, Progress and Present state of English Government in Bengal*. London, 1772.

Wilson, H. H., *Glossary of Judicial and Revenue Terms*, Delhi, 1969.

B. *Articles :*

Cohn, B. S., "From Indian Status to British Contract", *Journal of Economic History,* pp. 613-21, December, 1961.

C. *Thesis :*

Baliga, B. S., *Influence of Home Government on Land Revenue and Judicial Administration in Bengal, 1807-22,* Unpublished Ph.D. thesis, London, 1933.

INDEX